PREACHING GOSPEL

LLOYD JOHN OGILVIE INSTITUTE
OF PREACHING SERIES

SERIES EDITORS:

Michael Pasquarello III
Clayton J. Schmit

The vision of the Lloyd John Ogilvie Institute of Preaching is to proclaim Jesus Christ and to catalyze a movement of empowered, wise preachers who seek justice, love mercy, and walk humbly with God, leading others to join in God's mission in the world. The books in this series are selected to contribute to the development of such wise and humble preachers. The authors represent both scholars of preaching as well as pastors and preachers whose experiences and insights can contribute to passionate and excellent preaching.

OTHER VOLUMES IN THIS SERIES:

The Eloquence of Grace: Joseph Sittler and the Preaching Life edited by James M. Childs Jr. and Richard Lischer

The Preacher as Liturgical Artist: Metaphor, Idenity, and the Vicarious Humanity of Christ by Trygve David Johnson

Ordinary Preacher, Extraordinary Gospel: A Daily Guide for Wise, Empowered Preachers by Chris Neufeld-Erdman

Blessed and Beautiful: Multiethnic Churches and the Preaching that Sustains Them by Lisa Washington Lamb

Bringing Home the Message: How Community Can Multiply the Power of the Preached Word by Robert K. Perkins

Decolonizing Preaching: The Pulpit as Postcolonial Space by Sarah A. N. Travis

Youthful Preaching: Strengthening the Relationship between Youth, Adults, and Preaching by Richard Voelz

Stumbling over the Cross: Preaching the Cross and Resurrection Today by Joni S. Sancken

PREACHING GOSPEL

ESSAYS IN HONOR OF RICHARD LISCHER

edited by
Charles L. Campbell
Clayton J. Schmit
Mary Hinkle Shore
Jennifer E. Copeland

foreword by
Peter J. Story

CASCADE *Books* · Eugene, Oregon

PREACHING GOSPEL
Essays in Honor of Richard Lischer

Lloyd John Ogilvie Institute of Preaching Series 9

Cascade Books
An Imprint of Wipf and Stock Publishers
199 W. 8th Ave., Suite 3
Eugene, OR 97401

www.wipfandstock.com

PAPERBACK ISBN: 978-1-4982-0789-8
HARDCOVER ISBN: 978-1-4982-0791-1
EBOOK ISBN: 978-1-4982-0790-4

Cataloging-in-Publication data:

Names: Campbell, Charles L., editor. | Schmit, Clayton J. , editor. | Shore, Mary Hinkle, editor. | Copeland, Jennifer E., editor.

Title: Preaching gospel : essays in honor of Richard Lischer / edited by Charles L. Campbell, Clayton J. Schmit, Mary Hinkle Shore, and Jennifer E. Copeland.

Description: Eugene, OR : Cascade, 2016 | Lloyd John Ogilvie Institute of Preaching Series 9 | Includes bibliographical references.

Identifiers: ISBN 978-1-4982-0789-8 (paperback) | ISBN 978-1-4982-0791-1 (hardcover) | ISBN 978-1-4982-0790-4 (ebook)

Subjects: LCSH: Lischer, Richard. | Preaching.

Classification: LCC BV4222 P7 2016 (print) | LCC BV4222 (ebook)

Manufactured in the U.S.A.   AUGUST 24, 2016

For all those who have been taught by
Richard Lischer to preach gospel

For I am not ashamed of the gospel;
it is the power of God for salvation to everyone
who has faith, to the Jew first and also to the Greek.
ROMANS 1:16

Richard Lischer's confirmation verse

Contents

Acknowledgments

As TEACHER, MENTOR, COLLEAGUE, and friend, Richard Lischer has profoundly influenced all of us editors. This book is our attempt to say "thank you" by gathering together a few other scholars, colleagues, and students who share our appreciation for Lischer's life and work. We are grateful to all the authors who have given their time and energy to write for this volume. We are thankful for the people at Cascade Books, particularly Brian Palmer and Chris Spinks, who supported this project from beginning to end. We are also grateful to the Lloyd John Ogilvie Institute of Preaching at Fuller Seminary for including this volume in its Ogilvie Institute of Preaching Series.

Although widely known for his acclaimed writing, Lischer has also influenced countless students in the classroom during his thirty-seven years of teaching. His students are scattered across the globe in denominations too numerous to list and in churches too diverse to name. These students are Richard Lischer's gift to the church. We dedicate this book to all whom he has taught to preach gospel. We are grateful to be numbered among that host.

List of Contributors

Charles L. Aaron, Pastor of First United Methodist Church, Terrell, TX

Charles L. Bartow, Carl and Helen Egner Professor of Speech Communication in Ministry Emeritus, Princeton Theological Seminary, Princeton, NJ

Rein Bos, Senior Pastor of the Protestant Church in the Netherlands and coordinator of the curriculum and professor of the training program for ordained pastoral workers in the Protestant Church of the Netherlands

Charles L. Campbell, Professor of Homiletics, Duke Divinity School, Durham, NC

Jennifer E. Copeland, Executive Director of the North Carolina Council of Churches, Raleigh, NC, and Adjunct Instructor, Duke Divinity School, Durham, NC

Ellen F. Davis, Amos Ragan Kearns Distinguished Professor of Bible and Practical Theology, Duke Divinity School, Durham, NC

Gail Godwin, Woodstock, NY

Stanley Hauerwas, Gilbert T. Rowe Professor Emeritus of Divinity and Law, Duke University, Durham, NC

Richard B. Hays, George Washington Ivey Professor of New Testament, Duke Divinity School, Durham, NC

Willie James Jennings, Associate Professor of Systematic Theology and Africana Studies, Yale Divinity School, New Haven, CT

Thomas G. Long, Bandy Professor Emeritus, Candler School of Theology, Emory University, Atlanta, GA

Heidi Neumark, Pastor, Trinity Lutheran Church of Manhattan, New York, NY

Michael Pasquarello III, Lloyd John Ogilvie Professor of Preaching, Fuller Theological Seminary, Pasadena, CA·

Luke A. Powery, Dean of Duke University Chapel, Associate Professor of Homiletics, Duke University/Duke Divinity School, Durham, NC

Clayton J. Schmit, Provost, Lutheran Theological Southern Seminary and School of Theology, Lenoir-Rhyne University, Columbia, SC

Mary Hinkle Shore, Pastor, The Lutheran Church of the Good Shepherd, Brevard, NC

Peter J. Storey, W. Ruth and A. Morris Williams Distinguished Professor Emeritus of the Practice of Christian Ministry, Duke Divinity School, Durham, NC and Former bishop in the Methodist Church of Southern Africa, Simon's Town, South Africa

William C. Turner, Jr., Professor of the Practice of Homiletics, Duke Divinity School, Durham, NC

Will Willimon, United Methodist bishop, retired, and Professor of the Practice of Christian Ministry, Duke Divinity School, Durham, NC

Foreword

RICHARD LISCHER, RICK TO his friends, is a bearer of Good News. He proved that in our first meeting. I was new to Duke Divinity School when he knocked on the door of my tiny basement office, said he was going on sabbatical, and asked whether I would like the use of his parking permit while he was away. My rookie status at the time banished me to a parking lot near Siberia while Rick's seniority put him right at the school's back door. What better news could a preaching professor bring than that? The friendship begun that day continues, and I dare say the authors you will read in these pages have similar stories to tell, because they too call him "friend."

When it comes to his work, however, Lischer is serious about the word "Gospel." He is serious about the demanding task of preachers to be gospel-bearers and to carve Jesus-shaped good news into the unyielding contours of a broken world. He claims, "The most important question a preacher can ask is, 'Who is Jesus Christ for us today?'"[1] Following the lead of his beloved Martin Luther, Lischer knows that all the content in the Bible means nothing unless it is for us and for today. He has lifted up this question to the light and underscored its urgency through four decades of preaching, teaching, and writing. The fact that he has done so faithfully and with great effect is evidenced by this book of essays honoring him with the readiness of colleagues and former students to carry that same question forward in different ways through its pages. Even more so, wherever and whenever the myriad of students who have passed through his classrooms stand up to preach, his work bears fruit.

Powerful, effective preaching is more than knowledge and technique; it is word made flesh—the marriage of the unchanging and eternal gospel with a unique, complex, and susceptible human personality. It is within this unlikely blend that God gracefully wills to incarnate God's word in our words. Amid the cacophony of a world drenched in so many other words, the people who listen to sermons strain to hear an authentic voice. Richard

---

1. Quotes attributed to Richard Lischer occurred during a "long interview" in April 2015 while I was a guest in the Lischer's home, a place of hospitality I have been fortunate to enjoy over many years.

Lischer has such a voice. In obedience to the gospel, he has spent his life preaching, teaching, and—yes—quietly healing, too. Known preeminently as a teacher of preaching, he is both professor and practitioner. Along with forming hundreds of aspirant preachers at Duke Divinity School, he has demonstrated the preaching art with consummate skill and grace from many of the nation's prominent pulpits, often being called upon to articulate the gospel at a critical moment in the life of the nation or at a special hour in the life of the university.

Lischer is a Lutheran. What he says and how he says it are rooted in grace. He calls it "serious grace" because it brings with it a "freedom to serve others in ways the world does not always value." This serving finds its birth in God's redemptive action in Jesus. "Without that," he declares, "all we have is the old, stale, 'let's try to be better' moralism, dooming us to the busyness that mocks real ministry." He is suspicious of our trust in human progress: "We've lived through some of the worst human rapaciousness ever. We need gospel in the widest sense of meaning. Each of us stands under condemnation for failing to be gospel. Gospel means both suffering and joy. Gospel has both social and communal, both personal and interpersonal dimensions."

However, Lischer the Lutheran has spent his teaching life in a United Methodist divinity school. He enjoys the confluence this offers: "Luther got some things right, Wesley got other things right. They need each other," he says. Duke Divinity graduates all over the world readily acknowledge this amalgam embodied in Richard Lischer has been a particularly rich gift from God.

Lischer's doctoral work is in theology, not homiletics. For him, preaching is first a deeply serious theological exercise. This rigorous, densely theological approach has garnered massive respect for the discipline of homiletics and under his tutelage made possible the first Duke PhD in homiletics. But he is also an artist: listening to him, one is conscious of the deeply responsible way he places words in service of the Word. If words are a preacher's primary tools, this wordsmith stands tall among those of us who struggle with them week by week.

When Richard Lischer tells a story, he weaves a spell; his mind darts ahead, choosing the brightest, most illuminating words out of his vast store, positioning them with maximum artistry and effect. He has an ear for the euphonic rhythm of a sentence and alights on just the right phrases with an accuracy musicians would call "perfect pitch." The result is always elegant, never florid—oratorical art without bombast. Great preachers do not require overstatement; they respect the Holy Spirit's role in connecting the dots and penetrating the deep places in mind and heart.

This does not mean Lischer is unmindful of the role of performance in preaching or unwilling to help the Spirit along with a telling punchline. One of his more notorious sermon endings in Duke Chapel was on a Maundy Thursday evening where his sermon prepared us for the sacrament of communion we were about to share. To show that the table around which we would gather was in truth an altar of immense self-sacrifice, he took us to Bethany and the table of Jesus' last supper with his disciples. There, according to Lischer:

> Jesus said, "This meal will not be free. All the forgiveness and love that is in this little room is going to cost somebody something terrible." Then with his typical generosity, Jesus snapped his finger and said, "Check."[2]

With that seemingly inappropriate and irreverent quip, punctuated by snapping his own finger, Rick Lischer exposed the heart of Christ's sacrifice, left it hanging in the silence of Duke Chapel, and stepped out of the pulpit. Since then, he and I seldom finish a restaurant meal together without the query, "Who's going to be Jesus this time?" It can never be forgotten.

Preachers like Lischer also respect their listeners' need and capacity to wrestle with the big themes: "Too many sermons are filled with 'small–t truths,'" he says. "We need to dig into the Truth with a capital T." In his published works, beyond the expected—and deeply respected—tomes on homiletics (*The Company of Preachers*), he has tried to interact with the larger social currents such as violence and nonviolence (*The End of Words*), racism, justice, and radical hospitality (*The Preacher King*), and the pain that pours into the more vulnerable cracks in our lives—death, dying and grief (*Stations of the Heart*), as well as the clumsy stumbles and life-giving discoveries of early ministry (*Open Secrets*). In these publications, we find the reason Lischer's students experience him as healer as well as preacher/teacher. He is a pastor par excellence because he has been there. He is gifted with an ability to share out of his own journeying and the journeys of those he has loved—sometimes in pain and loss—without sentimentality, but instead with a profoundly insightful intimacy. Effective pastoring requires a deep and forgiving self-knowledge as well as confidence in grace. With typical understatement, Lischer says it is about "how we sometimes get saved in spite of ourselves." Thus, he can address the pain of both persons and society. Few authors can bridge the gulf between prophetic preaching amidst the complexities of a society broken by racism and poverty while also baring his soul with terrifying honesty and wrestling with the death of a son. The secret enabling him to do this may lie partly in that Lutheran/Wesleyan

---

2. Lischer, "We Have An Altar."

balance already mentioned. But it is also because Lischer is a disciple always on two pilgrimages—the inward and outward journeys of prayer and action—and central to both those journeys is Jesus. Whether teaching, preaching, or publishing, for Lischer, Jesus Christ remains the healing word for this person, this congregation, these students, this moment in history. Such Christocentric grounding is to be expected, since preaching, according to Lischer's other great guide, Dietrich Bonhoeffer, is nothing other than "Jesus walking through a congregation,"[3] as Jesus promised to do wherever two or three—or two or three hundred—gather together. It is among these gathered saints, whether in a classroom or sanctuary, that Lischer is at his best and most at home. He loves the faltering, failing church with the love of an old friend who harbors no false illusions, but nevertheless knows God's secret: the church will last forever, not because it is perfect, but because it belongs to Christ. Lischer's joy is to help ensure that the church will never be without witnesses to the good news of the gospel.

Finally, no tribute to Rick Lischer can be complete without acknowledging the role of his spouse Tracy, his toughest critic, fiercest supporter, and loyal soulmate. To read *Open Secrets* and *Stations of the Heart* is to discover her pivotal role in his life. To actually know her is to understand why she is pivotal. This former English professor, then top law school student, formidable trial lawyer, and protector of the weak, brings a rapier-like mind to matters of faith and truth, ensuring that nothing shallow will pass her scrutiny. In all other matters, those who take her on over the dinner table need to have their case prepared lest they be slain with consummate ease—and then rescued with a gracious smile. Above all, it has been as family fortress and sanctuary in times of great joy and of deep pain that her strength and spirit have shone. "Rick and Tracy" are names that belong together always.

When his long tenure at Duke Divinity School draws to a close, Richard Lischer will doubtless be assured in glowing terms that the James T. & Alice Mead Cleland Distinguished Chair of Preaching has been worthily adorned by his faithfulness, expertise, and scholarship. I have a feeling however, that his greatest joy will come from knowing that, in the words of one of his former students and protégé, Jennifer Copeland, "Every time one of us stands to offer a word from the Lord, we are Dr. Lischer's gift to the Church."

—Peter J. Storey
W. Ruth and A. Morris Williams Distinguished Professor Emeritus of the Practice of Christian Ministry, Duke Divinity School
Simon's Town, South Africa
July 2015

3. Lischer, "Dietrich Bonhoeffer," 34.

Bibliography

Lischer, Richard. "Dietrich Bonhoeffer, The Proclaimed Word." In *The Company of Preachers: Wisdom on Preaching, Augustine to the Present*, edited by Richard Lischer, 31–37. Grand Rapids: Eerdmans, 2002.

———. "We Have An Altar." Duke University Chapel. March 24, 2005. Online: http://chapel-archives.oit.duke.edu/documents/sermons/2005/050324.pdf.

Preaching Gospel

FOUR THEOLOGICAL TONES

Charles L. Campbell

RICHARD LISCHER'S BODY OF work is characterized by extraordinary breadth and depth. He has published important books on the theology of preaching,[1] a widely-used volume of primary documents from the history of preaching,[2] the definitive study of Martin Luther King, Jr. as a preacher,[3] two award-winning memoirs,[4] ground-breaking essays,[5] and, most recently, an impressive commentary on the parables.[6] Weaving through all of these diverse works, however, a dominant thread can be discerned: gospel. For Lischer, this gospel is not simplistic or one dimensional; it is not limited to one genre or a single theological tradition. Rather, the gospel is layered and multidimensional. I was at a dinner-party of homileticians and our spouses one evening, and I remember passing by a small group and overhearing a comment by Lischer: "The gospel has *so* many facets." While this comment may not make anyone long to attend a homiletical dinner party, it does reveal the character of both Lischer's work and this volume.

While many people know Richard Lischer primarily through his written works, thousands of former students know him more personally as a teacher and a mentor. Between 1988 and 1991, I myself served several semesters as a teaching assistant in Lischer's Introduction to Christian

1. Lischer, *A Theology of Preaching*; Lischer, *The End of Words* (the Lyman Beecher Lectures).

2. Lischer, *The Company of Preachers*.

3. Lischer, *The Preacher King*.

4. Lischer, *Open Secrets*; Lischer, *Stations of the Heart*.

5. For example, Lischer, "The Limits of Story," "The Interrupted Sermon," "Why I am Not Persuasive."

6. Lischer, *Reading the Parables*.

1

Preaching course. During those classes I not only learned about preaching, but about teaching preaching, and the insights and practices from that course have continued to inform my own reflection and practice over the years. One lecture, in particular, has remained with me: Lischer's lecture on the three theological tones of preaching. In fact, I stole that lecture and used it later in my own classes—always giving a nod to Lischer, even as the lecture morphed to reflect my own particular theology. In fact, all of the editors of this volume served as Lischer's teaching assistants, and we all remember that lecture—and I'm not the only one who stole it.

Lischer's primary concern in the lecture, in good Lutheran fashion, was to steer students away from moralistic and judgmental sermons and to focus on what God has done in Jesus Christ. But Lischer was equally concerned about "cheap grace," which also distorts gospel.[7] Drawing on a musical analogy, Lischer emphasized the interrelated dynamic of three theological tones in preaching: judgment, grace, and new imperative. Greatly oversimplifying Lischer's insights, one may say judgment denotes the problem of sin, grace the divine initiative in response, and new imperative the transformed life that grows out of grace. When any one tone becomes the entirety of preaching, problems emerge: if grace alone, then one ends up with cheap grace; if judgment alone, the consequence is despair; if new imperative alone, then one is left with moralism and a message without any divine empowerment.[8]

Over the past quarter century, I have continued to wrestle with these tones. They provide a helpful guide for preachers as we think about theology *in* preaching (in contrast to a theology *of* preaching). As I have reflected on these tones I have become increasingly interested in their complex dynamic, initially signaled by Lischer. And, as is evident from the title of this essay, I have also added a fourth tone to the mix. As an expression of gratitude from the students and teaching assistants Lischer has taught for over thirty-seven years, I offer my current "riff" on Lischer's lecture. It's not the lecture Lischer would probably give today, and he might even disagree with portions of it. But this is what students do with the insights of their teachers—and what Lischer has always encouraged his students to do: learn from these insights, and then develop them and make them one's own.

---

7. The phrase, "cheap grace" comes from Dietrich Bonhoeffer, *Cost of Discipleship*, 35–47.

8. For Lischer's extended discussion of these tones, see *Theology of Preaching*, 46–65.

Four Tones

My image is a jazz quartet. All of the musicians play together—and play in response to and off of each other. There is a dynamic interaction among all the instruments—piano, drums, saxophone (or, for those who prefer, trumpet), and bass. At various times, however, one musician will step to the fore with a solo, while all the others continue to play in ways that support and enrich the solo. All four musicians are playing, but different "voices" emerge and recede as the music proceeds. So it is with the four theological tones that characterize "preaching gospel." All of the tones work together in a dynamic, interrelated way; none can be omitted without losing something essential and distorting the proclamation of the gospel. However, at various times in an individual sermon or in the course of a preaching ministry, different tones will emerge and sound forth more fully than the others. This is not to say that every sermon moves through the four tones. Rather, the tones provide a theological dynamic for thinking about one's ongoing preaching ministry. Over time, preachers attend to these tones, noting the ways in which they are present—or absent!—in sermons, as well as the interrelationship among them.

My description of the four tones is as generic as possible, allowing for a wide range of theological convictions to flesh out each tone. Here too the image is that of a jazz musician. The four tones provide the scales and chords and rhythms that a preacher needs to master in order to preach faithfully. However, the scales and chords and rhythms will be expressed in distinctive ways by different preachers as they improvise on the tones according to their own theological traditions and convictions. Just as I am improvising on Lischer's initial lecture.

Yes

The first—and primary—tone is "Yes."[9] This tone proclaims the central affirmation that God is *for* the world, from the original creation all the way to the fulfillment of the new creation. God acts for the good of the world—in creation, redemption, and fulfillment. This tone takes the indicative form; it affirms God's initiative, not human efforts. Like human words and the divine Word itself, God's Yes is always an offer, an invitation; it is never coerced, but respects human freedom and relationship. From the perspective

9. The first two tones draw on the work of Karl Barth, who emphasizes the dynamic relationship between Yes and No in the gospel. For an excellent homiletical example, see "All," in *Deliverance to the Captives*.

of the cross, the Yes affirms that Christ died *for* the world—"for God so loved the world. . . ." (John 3:16)

The Yes tone may take many different theological forms. The "many facets of the gospel" become obvious when one begins to flesh out the character of God's Yes. Indeed, it is a good exercise for preachers to consider their immediate response to the question, "How do you understand God's Yes?" Different preachers will respond in different ways: grace, love, forgiveness, reconciliation, healing. Others may speak of redemption from the powers and principalities that hold us captive. Still others may prefer the language of God's liberating work from systems of oppression, including God's solidarity with those who suffer. In still another theological framework, preachers may proclaim God's victory over the powers of sin and death. In some African-American traditions, this tone generates celebration as the climax of the sermon. With a view to the future, this Yes may find further theological expression as promise and hope. The future is not closed because God continues to say Yes to God's creation. Through these and many other theological frameworks, preachers proclaim God's Yes to the world in a variety of ways. But all of these affirmations bring the Yes tone to the fore.

As I mentioned earlier, Yes is the primary tone of the gospel. It is the source of divine empowerment, apart from which the other tones become empty or even oppressive. This tone generates genuine hope in the face of the powers of death. It is, in short, "good news" at the very heart of gospel.

This tone, however, can never stand alone. It can never become a soloist without the rest of the quartet. For alone the Yes becomes "cheap grace" that ignores the evil and suffering in the world and does not lead to the new life of discipleship. Alone, the Yes can lead to passivity and complacency. As the Apostle Paul discovered after preaching gospel, people could come to an odd conclusion: "We should continue in sin in order that grace may abound." Paul, of course, replied, "By no means!" (Rom 6:1). Standing alone the Yes can also produce Christian triumphalism, which looks for God's triumph without any corresponding human response. As many are currently perceiving with regard to climate change, that kind of cheap triumphalism may lead to death, not just for individuals, but for the entire human race. Dietrich Bonhoeffer has stated sharply the problem when the Yes stands alone: "The word of cheap grace has been the ruin of more Christians than any commandment of works."[10] So, Yes is the primary tone, but it can never be the only tone of preaching gospel.

10. Bonhoeffer, *Cost of Discipleship*, 46.

No

The "No" is God's word against sin and evil in the world. It is the tone that addresses the gap between the way things are and the way God would have them to be. It is the tone that unmasks the rebelliousness of the world arrayed against God's purposes. The No at the foot of the cross proclaims that Christ died not just *for* the world, but *because of* the world. Again, the particular theological form of the No—the character of the sin and evil addressed by God—will vary depending on the preacher's theological convictions. The No, for example, may be a word addressed to disordered human loves that are oriented not to God but to lesser goods that become idols.[11] Or the No may speak to unjust systems and powers that hold people captive and oppress populations. Or it may be expressed in the form of lament, when God's No is experienced as God's apparent silence in the face of the world's suffering.

The No tends to take two distinctive forms. On the one hand there is the No of judgment. The Word accuses, bringing us to our knees and calling us to look deeply into human sin. The Word unmasks the powers of death, forcing us to face our captivity to systems we don't even notice because they have become the very air we breathe. In this sense the No may be likened to the second use of the law (Luther's primary use), which is to convict us of our sin. This No is liturgically enacted in the reading of the Ten Commandments immediately before the confession of sin in traditional Lutheran worship.

But there is another dynamic to the No tone. It also takes the form of discipline. "No, don't do that." "No, that will harm you." "No, that will have dire consequences." This dimension of the No calls us to repent, to turn around, to return to the ways of God against whom we have rebelled. Indeed, the disciplinary character of the No usually provides the deeper motivation behind the No of judgment. Judgment is not an end in itself for God, but a means of interrupting our rebellion and calling us to return. In this sense there is "good news" even in the No. The No reminds us that God takes humans seriously. God actually has a high opinion of us and expects something from us. God does not treat us as if our actions don't matter: "No big deal, don't worry about it." God does not sit passively by as the world suffers from injustice and oppression, singing in heaven, "I love you just the way you are." No. God has high expectations of the creation, and God judges our rebellion and calls us to return. God wants us to live into the image of God we were created to be.

11. This understanding of sin runs throughout the work of Augustine.

Though this tone is often either omitted through the proclamation of cheap grace or abused in stereotypical hellfire and damnation sermons, the No tone is important for preaching. This tone challenges the church to pay attention to the evil and suffering in the world. This tone seeks to move the church toward repentance and change and renewal. But, despite its importance, the No tone can never function by itself; it is only one tone in the dynamic of the whole. On the one hand, by itself, this tone simply leads to despair. By itself, the No creates guilt, without any empowerment for response. Indeed, even with the best of intentions, preachers often leave congregations burdened by this tone at the end of sermons. Preachers may spend much of the sermon delineating in great detail and specificity the evils in the world; that is easy to do. But then, at the end of the sermon the preacher fails to be as specific and concrete in preaching God's Yes of divine empowerment. Congregations are left with a heavy and even hopeless burden, rather than being inspired and enabled to move in new directions.[12]

On the other hand, preached in a certain way this tone can result in self-righteousness. If the preacher only speaks judgment against the sins of others—sins that do not even tempt the preacher or members of the congregation—a self-satisfied complacency can result. *They* are the sinners; *they* are judged. *We* are the righteous. This consequence is just as bad as, if not worse than, despair and guilt. As essential as it is, the No can never stand alone or be the primary tone in preaching.

Yes-No Dynamics

The relationship between the Yes and the No is complicated, and preachers often oversimplify this dynamic in their sermons. Indeed, in a deep sense God's No is an expression of God's Yes; the fact that God says No to the sin and evil in the world is an affirmation that God is for the world. So it is important to explore some of the dynamics between the Yes and the No.

Traditionally, the movement in preaching has been from the No to the Yes. The preacher convicts people of their sin, then speaks "good news" that addresses the sin. This movement is clearly evident in problem-solution sermons; in the "homiletical plot" of Eugene Lowery,[13] which moves from "disequilibrium" to an "experience of the gospel"; in many traditional sermons that move theologically from sin to grace. This movement is important in preaching; it protects the preacher against moralizing and keeps the activity of God front and center.

12. Bartlett, "Showing Mercy."
13. Lowery, *Homiletical Plot.*

But this dynamic does not encompass the fullness of the relationship between the Yes and the No. For example, God's Yes can itself reveal sin in a deep and profound way, thus serving the function of a No. Seeing the depths of God's love for the world can convict us of our rebellion and call us to repent. Often the words, "I love you," spoken by someone we have hurt, can convict us more powerfully than any word of judgment or condemnation. Just as God's No can express God's activity *for* the world, so God's Yes can unmask the depths of human sin.

Indeed, Karl Barth argues that preaching always begins with God's Yes; only in the context of that encompassing Yes can we hear the No.[14] The two tones are inextricably related, but the Yes must be spoken first. Many churches enact this reality in their liturgies. In the invitation to confession, the liturgist offers a promise—a Yes: "If we say that we have no sin, we deceive ourselves, and the truth is not in us. If we confess our sins, [God] who is faithful and just will forgive us our sins and cleanse us from all unrighteousness" (1 John 1: 8–9). There is profound wisdom in this liturgical practice. Confronting God's No, confessing our sin, is simply too threatening apart from the prior assurance of God's Yes. God's prior Yes enables genuine, honest confession.

The duet of Yes and No is rich and complex. Preachers, however, are not dealing simply with a duet, but a quartet. The theological tones of preaching become even richer and more complex.

Do/Go

The third tone is "Do" or "Go." This tone expresses God's desire for faithfulness or holiness. It is the imperative tone: "You shall be holy, for I am holy" (Lev 11:45). "I give you a new commandment, that you love one another. Just as I have loved you, you also should love one another" (John 13:34). This tone gives voice to the demands of the gospel, the call to discipleship. It is the tone that emphasizes sanctification and growth in the Christian life. This tone too is informed by the cross: "If any want to become my followers, let them deny themselves and take up their cross daily and follow me" (Luke 9:23). This tone could be interpreted as the third use of the law, the primary use in the Reformed tradition. According to the third use, the law serves as a guide that nurtures holiness. Not surprisingly, in Reformed liturgies—in contrast to Lutheran worship—the reading of the Ten Commandments traditionally *follows* the prayer of confession and assurance of pardon. The emphasis is on sanctification with the law as a guide.

14. Barth, "All."

This tone is essential to the preaching of gospel. Without it, one is left with cheap grace, which demands nothing in response. Without this third tone, discipleship is devalued and passivity encouraged.

But if this tone is the only tone, there are serious negative consequences. This tone too requires the other players in the quartet. By itself, the Do/Go tone can lead to moralism—the sense that if we obey, we will be rewarded, that our human works accomplish our salvation. Similarly, by itself this tone, like the No, can lead to despair and guilt. The demands become a heavy burden to bear, if not an impossible one, for there is no empowerment in a list of exacting demands; people are left to their own efforts, which they know are inadequate. "Don't simply tell me to go and be like Jesus. That's not helpful. The standards are too high; I can never achieve them. I give up." Finally, however, the Do/Go tone alone can also lead to a very different problem: a false sense of security. If the demands of the gospel are narrowly defined and easily achievable, believers can become self-satisfied and comfortable. "I don't drink, I don't smoke, I'm a faithful Christian." Like the other tones, the Go/Do tone cannot stand alone, but requires the dynamic support of the others.

The Dynamic Among Do/Go, Yes, and No

Traditionally, sermons have moved from the No to the Yes to the Do/Go. That is, the preacher convicts of sin, speaks a word of grace or forgiveness, then delineates the demands of the gospel as the people's response to the good news. This movement is important because it seeks to prevent moralism. The call to discipleship is a *response* to the initiative of God; human effort is not placed at the center of the equation. Rather, the empowering action of God enables the response of discipleship. Even when the Yes precedes the No, as was discussed earlier, the Yes also precedes the Do/Go in order to avoid the pitfalls of legalistic preaching. This simple theo-logic—"Because God, therefore we"—has appropriately shaped sermons for centuries; this logic prevents the Do/Go from becoming grounded in human efforts alone.

But as preachers know all too well, many biblical texts don't simplistically follow this logic. The relationship among the Yes, the No, and the Do/Go is more complex. For example, Jesus' first words to the disciples in the synoptic gospels are not simply a word of grace or forgiveness or love (Yes). Nor are they a word of judgment (No). Rather, Jesus' first words to the disciples are Do/Go: "follow me" (e.g., Matt 4:19). In these stories the Do/Go can certainly be interpreted as a mode of the Yes; Jesus' call to the disciples is in part a profound Yes to them. God calls those whom God is *for*. Likewise, the Go/Do may express God's No. To some degree, the call to "follow me" implies the need to move in a new direction, to take a different path. In still another sense, however, the Do/Go *precedes* both the Yes and the No. Only as the disciples seek to follow Jesus do they come to know the deep reality of their sin and the good news of God's Yes that sets them free. This is the case in the Gospel of John. Following his question, "What are you seeking?" Jesus' first words to the disciples are, "Come and see" (John 1:38–39). The order is important. First, the disciples "come," then along the way they will see—they will discern the reality of Jesus and believe. Following Jesus actually precedes the perception of God's Yes and No.

I discovered this truth myself when I began ministering with homeless people in Atlanta. I thought I was being a faithful disciple, getting up early in the morning to serve breakfast to hungry people living on the streets. Surely, I thought, I'm showing kindness and loving justice! But standing at the door greeting long lines of homeless people, I was convicted of my own captivity to sinful systems of privilege, and I was reminded of my need for redemption more profoundly than if I had stayed in bed. My attempt to Go and Do led me more profoundly into God's No and Yes. I learned that the order of Micah's famous words is important. If you try to do justice and love kindness, you will inevitably walk humbly with God (Mic 6:8).

The same experience happens to the disciples on the road to Emmaus (Luke 24:13–35). When do the disciples recognize Jesus? When do they experience redemption (Yes), recognize their own failure (No), and become empowered to return to Jerusalem to bear witness (Do/Go)? Only *after* they have shown hospitality to the stranger by inviting him inside for a meal. The practice of hospitality *precedes* faithful recognition of the crucified and risen Christ. We know and claim God's grace—including our own need for that grace—only as we are seeking to live the way of discipleship.

The dynamic relationship among the Yes, the No, and the Do/Go is complex indeed. There is no single starting point, no single rigid logic. Rather, as long as all the tones are interacting richly, and as long as the Yes steps forward for its essential solo, sermons that "preach gospel" may move in a variety of ways that are faithful to various kinds of texts.

Ha!

The final tone is "Ha!" Imagine fingernails being scraped across a chalkboard. Imagine that one person in the congregation who sings the loudest and the most off key. That's the Ha! tone. Ha! is the tone that disrupts all of our nice little harmonies and theological systems—including even something as generic as Yes, No, Do/Go. The Ha! gives voice to the gospel that is untamed and uncontrollable, indecent and disorderly. It is the tone that unsettles us and creates dissonance and dislocation. It is the tone through which God repeatedly throws everything off balance and out of sync. Indeed, the Ha! cuts across all the other tones, reminding us that the gospel is scandalous and unmanageable: "You're saying 'Yes' to *them*?!" "You're saying 'No' to *us*!?" "You're asking me to go *where*!? You're asking me to do *what*!?"

Laughter is a good metaphor for this tone. We say we "break up" laughing. Or we exclaim that a joke really "cracked me up." Or we report that the crowd *erupted* with laughter. Laughter shatters. It breaks up; it cracks up. It interrupts the neat totalities by which we often seek to control and make sense of our lives.[15] Laughter disrupts, even if just for a moment, the myths and rationalities—and theologies—by which the world is neatly ordered and managed.[16] Like the fool or jester, laughter tends to "melt the solidity of the world"; it interrupts the conventions and assumptions that are supposedly written in stone; it keeps reality fluid.[17] Indeed, we are often unable physically to control laughter; it seems to take over even our bodies. It often feels as if something is "laughing us."[18] Laughter invites humility, the ability to laugh at ourselves and our pretentions.

This is the character of the fourth tone: Ha! It gives voice to a gospel that is extreme, scandalous, and unmanageable. As with the other tones, this tone has been expressed in various ways throughout the Christian tradition. It has been spoken of as mystery, a recognition that God is not someone we can ever fully grasp or understand. This gospel mystery has a distinctive character as proclaimed by the Apostle Paul; the mystery is not some general amorphous reality that is beyond us. Rather, the understanding of mystery itself becomes odd and unmanageable. This mystery is enacted, enfleshed in Jesus Christ on the cross. The mystery is embodied in a scandalously particular action of God. Yet, precisely in its particularity, this act of God remains a mystery, not "solvable" by human wisdom (1 Cor 2:7). Indeed, Paul here undercuts all confidence in human wisdom to rise to the divine. The Ha! tone finds its center in the mysterious folly of the cross.

The Ha! tone may also be affirmed as the freedom of God. Moses discovers this Ha! at the burning bush. Moses' life is interrupted by his

15. Davis, *Breaking Up [at] Totality*.

16. In this sense, laughter can play a role similar to lament, which also interrupts the status quo; not surprisingly, laughter and tears often belong together. On the relationship between laughter and lament, see Campbell and Cilliers, *Preaching Fools*, 127–51.

17. Welsford, *Fool*, 223. On laughter and fluidity, see also Davis, *Breaking Up [at] Totality*.

18. Davis, *Breaking Up [at] Totality*, 23.

encounter with the living God. Possibly uneasy with this interruption, Moses tries to get control of God by asking God's name. In response, God plays a trick on Moses. God *literally* gives Moses the divine name. But, *ironically*, God's name preserves God's freedom: "I am who I am." "I will be who I will be." "I will be with you as I will be with you" (Exod 3:13–15). We should probably pronounce YHWH as YH-HA!-WH.

The Ha! tone also witnesses to the apocalyptic character of the gospel. Like laughter, the apocalyptic gospel *fractures*; it *interrupts*; it *breaks* in. These images have been highlighted in recent biblical scholarship. New Testament scholar, Roy Harrisville, for example, argues that the cross "fractures" all of the paradigms that seek to contain it, including the systems and narratives the biblical writers brought to it. The gospel creates an unmanageable anomaly that requires a revolution in thinking and living.[19] Of the Apostle Paul, Harrisville writes: "The apostle could not master his theology in any ultimate way because it never existed as a system; in fact, it could not, since the event at its core spelled the death of system."[20] Another New Testament scholar, Alexandra Brown, speaks of the gospel "disrupting" and "dissolving" the structures and conventions of the old order.[21] As a result, she writes, the Apostle Paul engages in an extreme, unsettling rhetoric that employs "unconventional and destabilizing pairings of opposites"—crucified Messiah, wise folly, weak power—in order to disrupt the assumptions of the old age.[22] From this apocalyptic perspective, the in-*breaking* of the new creation cracks up the myths and rationalities of the old age that lead to death and sets believers in an unsettled threshold space between the ages. The apocalyptic Ha!

This tone has been enacted through Christian history by the holy fools, including such remarkable figures as St. Francis of Assisi and Margery Kempe in the West and Symeon the Holy Fool and St. Basil the Blessed in the East. Holy fools sought to embody Paul's words in 1 Cor 4:10: "We are fools for the sake of Christ." Enacting this text, holy fools engaged in bizarre, even obscene, activities, appearing to be lunatics, idiots, or buffoons.[23] Some lived out their folly in monasteries, while others wandered the streets like madmen or madwomen. Others have appeared as anti-social eccentrics or as simpleminded; still others as jesters, both pleasant and very unpleasant.[24] Many of them went around unclean, even unclothed. Some wore chains or

19. Harrisville, *Fracture*, 4–6.

20. Ibid., 108.

21. Brown, *Cross and Human Transformation*, xxi, 13.

22. Ibid., 30.

23. Wright, "Fools for Christ," 25.

24. Ibid.

iron collars. And they engaged in all kinds of bizarre and offensive behavior. Often appearing on the scene when the church had become complacent or complicit with the status quo, these figures, through their strange behavior, disrupted both religious and social conventions; they embodied the divine Ha!

This tone is depicted in Fyodor Dostoevsky's short story, "The Dream of a Ridiculous Man," a rich homiletical text.[25] The story opens with these words of the first-person narrator, which bring to mind the holy fools: "I am a ridiculous man. They call me a madman now."[26] From the beginning we know the narrator is a madman, but we don't yet know if it's a holy madness or not. He tells his story.

The ridiculous man (who is never named) had despaired of the world and given up on it. He had cut himself off completely from other human beings, even cruelly dismissing a poor, desperate young girl of the streets who cries out for his help. In the midst of his cynicism and despair, on the verge of committing suicide, he falls asleep and has a dream. In the dream he has a vision of salvation, a vision of the universal harmony of shalom. But in the dream, this salvation becomes corrupted. The corruption cannot be overcome because there is no Christ; there is no crucifixion or resurrection. As a result there is no hope. The vision cannot become reality in the dream.

When the ridiculous man awakes, however, he realizes that his vision of salvation can come to fulfillment on earth because Christ has come here. In this sense, the earth—human history with all of its anguish and suffering and corruption—is a place of more hope than the dream.[27]

When the ridiculous man awakes to this realization, he longs for life. But that is not all. He also desires something more. In rather typical melodramatic Dostoevskian fashion, the ridiculous man exclaims,

> Oh, how I longed for life, life! I lifted up my hands and called upon eternal Truth—no, not called upon it, but wept. Rapture, infinite boundless rapture intoxicated me. Yes, life and . . . [and here's the something more] . . . life and—preaching. I made up my mind to preach from that very moment and, of course, to go on preaching all my life. I am going to preach, I want to preach. What? Why, truth. For I have beheld truth, I have beheld it with my own eyes, I have beheld it in all its glory.[28]

25. Dostoevsky, "Dream of a Ridiculous Man."
26. Ibid., 263.
27. Thompson, "Problems of the Biblical Word," 86.
28. Dostoevsky, "Dream of a Ridiculous Man," 283–84.

Life and preaching become one for the ridiculous man; he has learned to look, he has seen the truth, and now he must preach.

But there's only one problem. He cannot find the words. He simply cannot categorize or master what he has seen. And everyone ridicules him and laughs at him. As he states at the beginning, "They call me a madman now"—now that he is preaching. And he draws us into the anguish of preaching—the anguish of trying to proclaim a word in which holiness and madness are essentially and inseparably related. "I do not know how to put it into words," he says. "After my dream I lost the knack of putting things into words. At least, into the most necessary and important words. But never mind. I shall go on and I shall keep on talking, for I have indeed beheld it with my own eyes, though I cannot describe what I saw."[29] Exasperated, he finally exclaims, "The main thing is to love your neighbor as yourself—that is the main thing, and that is everything, for nothing else matters."[30] But even that exclamation sounds rather ridiculous in the context.

The Ha! tone thus takes preachers deep into the anguish of "preaching gospel." We are trying to bring to speech the scandal, the folly, the Ha! of the good news. We are seeking to proclaim a Word that fractures and interrupts, a Word we can never fully get into words. We are seeking to preach a gospel that is so odd and unruly that it always confounds and claims us both at the same time. It may even drive us crazy as we struggle and ache to bring it to speech. But this struggle lies at the heart of preaching gospel. Because in the midst of that struggle we are preaching in the fullest sense; we are going deep and getting real. We are not keeping a safe distance from God's good news, but engaging up close in the unsettling space of encounter with the living God.

A student of mine summed this up several years ago:

> It works out really well, this distancing, until you ask me to preach. Preaching is becoming the bane of my existence. I can get through all my other classes, the rest of my life, without having to really face the claims of the text. But you ask me to preach and I just can't avoid them. I can distance myself from the texts in my life, but I can't get up and preach *distance*. . . . So I am slammed in the face with these texts—with the implausible promises [Yes/Ha!] and the injunctions to do the insane [Go/ Do/Ha!].

In this comment about preaching gospel, the Ha! tone punctuates the other theological tones. Almost all of us who preach know the experience

29. Ibid., 285.

30. Ibid.

this student describes. We know that preaching often seems foolish or ridiculous. We know the struggle of trying to find the words to proclaim the Word. And at times we may even feel like we're losing our minds. But we are moved to keep preaching by the dynamic music of the gospel quartet: Yes, No, Do/Go, Ha! In our unsettled wrestling, we sometimes feel more deeply and profoundly alive than at any other time in our ministry.

Bibliography

Barth, Karl. "All." In *Deliverance to the Captives*, translated by Marguerite Wieser, 85–92. New York: Harper and Row, 1961.

Bartlett, David. "Showing Mercy." In *What's the Matter with Preaching Today?* edited by Mike Graves, 23–36. Louisville: Westminster John Knox, 2004.

Bonhoeffer, Dietrich. *The Cost of Discipleship*. Translated by R. H. Fuller. 2nd ed. New York: MacMillan, 1960.

Brown, Alexandra R. *The Cross and Human Transformation: Paul's Apocalpytic Word in 1 Corinthians*. Minneapolis: Fortress, 1995.

Campbell, Charles L., and Johan H. Cilliers. *Preaching Fools: The Gospel as a Rhetoric of Folly*. Waco, TX: Baylor University Press, 2012.

Davis, D. Diane. *Breaking Up [at] Totality: A Rhetoric of Laughter*. Carbondale: Southern Illinois University Press, 2000.

Dostoevsky, Fyodor. "The Dream of a Ridiculous Man." In *The Best Short Stories of Fyodor Dostoevsky*, translated by David Magarshack, 263–85. New York: Modern Library, 2001.

Harrisville, Roy A. *Fracture: The Cross as Irreconcilable in the Language and Thought of the Biblical Writers*. Grand Rapids: Eerdmans, 2006.

Lischer, Richard. *The End of Words: The Language of Reconciliation in a Culture of Violence*. Grand Rapids: Eerdmans, 2005.

———. "The Interrupted Sermon." *Interpretation* 50 (April 1996) 169–81.

———. "The Limits of Story." *Interpretation* 38 (January 1984) 26–38.

———. *Open Secrets: A Memoir of Faith and Discovery*. New York: Doubleday, 2001.

———. *The Preacher King: Martin Luther King, Jr. and the Word that Moved America*. New York: Oxford University Press, 1995.

———. *Reading the Parables. Interpretation Resources for the Use of Scripture in the Church*. Louisville: Westminster John Knox, 2014.

———. *Stations of the Heart: Parting with a Son*. New York: Alfred A. Knopf, 2013.

———. *A Theology of Preaching: The Dynamics of the Gospel*. Nashville: Abingdon, 1981.

———. "Why I Am Not Persuasive." *Homiletic* 24.2 (Winter 1999) 13–16.

Lischer, Richard, editor. *The Company of Preachers: Wisdom on Preaching, Augustine to the Present*. Grand Rapids: Eerdmans, 2002.

Lowry, Eugene. *The Homiletical Plot: The Sermon as Narrative Art Form*. Exp. ed. Louisville: Westminster John Knox, 2000.

Thompson, Diane Oenning. "Problems of the Biblical Word in Dostoevsky's Poetics." In *Dostoevsky and the Christian Tradition*, edited by George Pattison and

Diane Oenning Thompson, 69–100. Cambridge Studies in Russian Literature. Cambridge: Cambridge University Press, 2001.

Welsford, Enid. *The Fool: His Social and Literary History*. Gloucester, MA: Peter Smith, 1966.

Wright, Wendy. "Fools for Christ." In *Weavings: A Journal of the Christian Spiritual Life* 9 (1994) 23–31.

Reading the Text with Richard Lischer

Will Willimon

A GROUP OF SEMINARIANS once asked Richard Lischer to outline, as simply as possible, each of the steps he takes toward the production of a sermon. His fateful first step was almost laughably obvious to the students, yet every experienced preacher knows it to be perilously difficult: *take a biblical text*. Early on Lischer offered a definition of preaching as primarily a matter of wrestling with the text, paying strict attention to the text: "Preachers are charged with *proclaiming the gospel in texts, by means of texts, and in faithfulness to texts*."[1] Generations of students have profited from Lischer's homiletics classes. In this essay I will share with my fellow preachers the main gifts that Lischer models for us and offers for us in our fateful, scary move from text to sermon.

Much is at stake in any preacher's submission to the biblical text. In the fine article on "Exegesis" by Richard Hays for the *Concise Encyclopedia of Preaching*, Hays asserts that, "If the sermon is not informed by careful study of scripture, the preacher is likely to offer the congregation recycled common sense . . . It is the primary task of preaching to unfold the message of scripture, not to explain it away or to trim it to fit the patterns of conventional wisdom; . . . The preacher's imaginative task of bringing scripture and congregation into dialogue can occur only through direct wrestling with the text."[2]

Lischer is certainly an imaginative preacher, but his imagination is not only stoked, funded, and fueled by Scripture; it is also disciplined by the text. As everyone knows, Lischer is an inveterate, creative lover of words, widely read in contemporary literature, conversant in recent philosophical

1. Lischer, *Theology of Preaching*, 5.
2. Hays, "Exegesis," 122–28.

16

and literary critical thought. *Open Secrets* and *Stations of the Heart* display some of the most luminous and masterfully creative writing in the contemporary church.

But in his sermons his literary art and fertile imagination are governed by an unashamedly partisan, advocatory, and accountable reading of the biblical text. In every sermon Lischer places the text in a privileged place in the conversation between the ancient text and whatever contemporary congregation he has before him.[3] While he obviously crafts his sermons to fit the differing contexts in which he speaks, contextual factors like culture, audience, race, age, and gender do not figure as prominently in his preaching as his own binding theological commitments.[4] In all of his writing, whether he writes about the loss of a son, his forlorn first parish, or the genius of Martin Luther King, Jr., Lischer reflects upon all these phenomena as theological events. In his biblical interpretation, Lischer's theological commitments are even more apparently decisive.

Faced with the daunting task of preaching in Duke Chapel on the University Founders Sunday—a sort of quasi-civic occasion where the university smugly gives thanks to God for our success—Lischer displays his skill in enticing his university congregation into theology whether they want it or not.[5] I have preached this service in Duke Chapel before and I am telling you that any preacher who manages to preach the gospel in this context is better than good.

The first half of the sermon is a rather conventional, though eloquent testimonial to the goodness of higher education, admitting that the faith which once gave birth to Duke is now marginalized at the grand institution that faith created. Up to this point in the sermon, Lischer has made no mention of the biblical text for Advent 2. Then, in the closing moments of the sermon, Lischer slyly introduces the biblical text in a more topical than strictly exegetical way. Yet he finds in the figure of John the Baptist a trenchant critique that the university needs to hear:

> There is another consequence of Duke's Christian origins, and
> that is critical for today, the second Sunday in Advent. Even if

3. Lischer prefaces his *Reading the Parables* by quoting with approval Kierkegaard's question, "What is the difference between criticism of a text and radical accountability to it?"

4. In an otherwise laudatory review of Lischer's *The End of Words*, Susan K. Hedahl says her, "only critique of its contents is that there is much from the traditional male homiletical point of view that could profit with the inclusion of input from female and black homiletical scholars and even more on what it means to preach in a wildly pluralistic world." "Book Corner," in *The Ridge*, Lutheran Theological Seminary, March, 2006.

5. Founders' Day, Advent II, Duke University Chapel, December 10, 1995.

you tried, you could not find a less appetizing reading for an institution's celebration of its own history than the appointed words of John the Baptist, beginning with his festive greeting, "You brood of vipers" and ending with "I tell you God is able from these stones to raise up children to Abraham." What a pity we can't read these verses in July when the place is sleepily half-empty!

I remember some eight or nine years ago when Chrysler Chairman Lee Iaccoca came to town to give the commencement address. . . . He eyed the graduating class and said, "You know, the only thing standing between you and your degree is me!" I feel that way every Advent: the only thing standing between us and an old-fashioned Christmas is John the Baptist. The only thing standing between us and an uncritical celebration of ourselves is this eternally-recurring critic named John. But that's the way it is: when you put Jesus' name on the plaque [reference to the plaque with the university motto], you get his socially-maladaptive cousin, John, in the package.

He is our own critical theorist, and what he is most critical of is us. His cry of "Repent" falls not only on individuals, but institutions, schools, and nations. He is most critical of wealth, power, and organized religion and the ways in which these have ridden roughshod over the demands of God. He is our most persistent critic.

John is also our own anti-revisionist historian. He will not let us read Jesus out of our history or apologize for his presence. Jesus once said of John, "I tell you, he is more than a prophet," that is, more than a critic, because he always points to salvation . . . to the crucified one. To any who would reduce the Savior to some principle of good cheer or prosperity, that boney finger seems to say, Worship him.

Few preachers turn aside from their sermons to make explicit how they move from text to sermon. Lischer is an exception. In his *Reading the Parables*, Lischer gives his "methodological premise" for his complex hermeneutics of parables. He says that his method "is both medieval and postmodern in nature: no parable can be limited to the one exclusive meaning or to a meaning that is unrelated to the milieu in which it has originated or the situation of those who read it. Reading begins with listening carefully to the text and allowing oneself to be perplexed by it. Reading comes in a flood of perceptions, including mixed and simultaneous messages, as well as echoes from other literature and from one's own experience. A community reads together . . . for the sake of its common life and mission."[6]

Even though he is offering rules for reading parables, it is fair to take this statement as containing all the major elements of the way Lischer moves from text to sermon. While he almost never takes a congregation step-by-step through a biblical text, and while his use of a biblical text in his sermons in more often distilled and topical than anything close to expository, all of his sermons are definitely guided by a biblical text. He is a creative rather than a fastidious reader of the text. Even in his *Reading the Parables,* Lischer seems more interested in the overall literary clout of a parable, or its revelation of God, or the perplexity that it elicits in us than in the details of the text itself. Yet it is clear that he wants not simply to put a text under critical scrutiny but rather to let the text speak.

If you listen to much contemporary Christian preaching, particularly in North American mainline Protestantism, you know that in his assumptions that scripture is more interesting than either himself or us, that we are answerable to the text rather than the text being answerable to us, Lischer is a *rara avis.* I have been listening to Lischer sermons for thirty-eight years; I therefore pronounce with authority that *Richard Lischer reads the text like a Christian,* allowing his congregations to be perplexed, addressed, and commissioned by the biblical text in the following ways.

Lischer Reads the Biblical Text Like a Theologian

Lischer's first book at Duke was *A Theology of Preaching,* in which he makes much of Gerhard Ebeling's statement that "theology is necessary in order to make preaching as hard for the preacher as it needs to be."[7] His primary academic preparation was in Systematic Theology. When he was invited from his parish in Virginia Beach to join the Duke Divinity School faculty in the mid-1970s I recall one faculty member expressing misgivings about hiring a homiletician who had no graduate training in homiletics. David Steinmetz, professor of Church History, countered, "At least now we might enjoy the possibility of having our students base their sermons on God." Steinmetz was right.

In *The Preacher King,* after noting the distance between Martin Luther King's introduction to "higher" and "historical/critical" biblical study, Lischer notes that "the African-American tradition of interpretation, however, did not pass through the Enlightenment, never enjoyed the leisure of

6. Lischer, *Reading the Parables,* 2.

7. Lischer, *Theology of Preaching,* 5.

disinterested analysis, and therefore did not distance itself from the Bible or settle for moral applications. The cruelties of slavery made it imperative that African Americans not step *back* but step *into* the Book and its storied world of God's personal relations with those in trouble."[8]

Lischer praises King's use of typology and figural interpretation, his recognition of the political, public implications of the gospel that permitted King "a richness of expression not obtainable from historical literalism."[9] At the same time Lischer noted King's flirtations with the psychologizing of biblical texts that plagued liberal preaching. When King "strayed from typology . . . the more he underwrote the Enlightenment's 'step back' from the text—and the more susceptible he became to the banality of religious lessons."[10]

King unleashed Scripture with an "interpretive master code" that enabled King to "escape the moralizing of liberal homiletics. King let the *church* guide his interpretation of scripture," working "within the boundaries of the church's convictions about God."[11] I am bold to believe that Lischer has consistently moved from text to sermon to congregation with the same theological determination that he praises as the best of the Preacher King.

When I asked a recent student of Richard Lischer's what she had learned in his introductory preaching course, she replied, "If it's not about God, it's not worth saying in the pulpit." And yet, Lischer's interpretation is more challenging even than being theological. He invariably moves in his preaching toward an unashamedly Christological interpretation of all texts. As he says at the end of his *Reading Parables*, Christology judges all of our biblical reading: "For all our readings . . . fall under some provision of God's intervention in human affairs through the ministry, death, and resurrection of the Son."[12]

He opens his Beecher Lectures with an announcement inspired by Bonhoeffer, "If there is to be preaching, all it can do is conform itself to the life of Christ in the community. . . . conform to Jesus. The sermon, in fact, *is* Jesus trying to speak once again in his own community."[13]

---

8. Lischer, *Preacher King*, 200.

9. Ibid., 205–6.

10. Ibid., 208.

11. Ibid., 210.

12. Lischer, *Reading Parables*, 166.

13. Lischer, *End of Words*, 7–8. Lischer follows this statement, with self-evident sadness, "Christianity in America has followed a different course than the one Bonhoeffer predicted."

His *Reading the Parables* is a dazzling display of the fruitfulness of rhetorical and literary analysis of the parables.[14] But in every case, Lischer is unwilling to let the literary mastery of the parables have the last say. For instance, after a lucid discussion of the Pharisee and the Tax Collector (Luke 18:9–14), Lischer says that this parable is not simply a story of two kinds of faith, it is "ultimately about God." "The Teller of the tale makes all the difference. Without the ministry and impending death of Jesus, we have a stale vignette of two kinds of people and two sorts of religious behavior. But reading with Luke yields much more. For in the context of Jesus' love for the poor, the outcast, and sinners, this little story glows with insight and hope."[15]

After showing the fruitfulness of a sociological reading of the parables in his chapter, "Reading the Parables with the Poor," drawing upon the work of Werner Herzog, Lischer says, "I find myself sympathetic to Herzog's concern for social realism but unable to follow his atheological conclusions."[16] Lischer notes the irony that if Herzog's exclusively, self-avowed "materialist" reading is permitted, it makes the evangelists themselves into "theopoetic conspirators" who perverted Jesus' revolutionary agenda in his parabolic tracts for the times into a tame, economically determined "kingdom of heaven" spiritualization. Lischer also dismisses the existentialized readings of Via and the linguistic theories of Funk and Crossan for the same reason—they all interpret the parables of Jesus as if the gospel writers have unfairly interposed false ethical and theological meanings into the parables. Herzog's reduction of some great stories about God into a "codification" of unjust situations in Judea is exposed by Lischer as, finally, rather preposterous. Lischer suggests that these interpreters ought "not begin from a social theory. . . but with a rereading of the Jesus stories themselves," and not attempt to bracket out Jesus or the Kingdom of God from our readings as if these are later pious accretions.[17]

I find ironic that Lischer prefaces his *Reading the Parables* by challenging the title of the series in which his volume appears, *Interpretation*. "I prefer *Reading* because that is actually what we do with the parables. The word 'reading' is a reminder that any piece of literature, including a parable, is not defined by its source, transmission, or this history of its interpretation, but by a text on the surface of a smooth page that lies across the lap. 'Interpretation' ties the average person into knots. The very word implies

14. Lischer, *Reading Parables*, 12.

15. Ibid., 110.

16. Ibid., 135.

17. Ibid., 138–39.

expertise, finality, and a critical position that has been staked out and must be defended."[18]

I appreciate Lischer's modesty in wanting to replace active "interpretation," with more receptive "reading." However, part of the power of his preaching is that he is a well-formed (Lutheran schools began training him for the pastorate well before puberty), biased, convinced reader of the text who expects to hear a commanding, demanding (if often perplexing) word from Christ in every biblical text.

I wonder if much of contemporary preaching (including my own) is uninteresting to the world because it offers the world no news the world could not hear in some other less demanding, non-Jewish way. When we preachers attempt to assume a bogus position with the text of the disinterested reader, the best we can hope for is a sermon on some contemporary version of Stoic fate or virtue or else that homiletic evil that Lischer has spent a lifetime attempting to defeat, that Methodist bane, *moralism*.[19]

Lischer Reads Scripture Like a Lutheran

Lischer is a product of an ecclesial tradition that had a clear sense of what it wanted from its preachers. The Lutheran sense of the radicality of grace, the silliness of human presumption, salvation that comes only from a crucified God, the sense that all sermons must finally be Good News, the earthy, incarnational way that God comes to us in Jesus, are evident in nearly every Lischer sermon. He really believes and practices his dictum that, "The church has one doctrine, the *doctrina evangelii*, the gospel, to which other

---

18. Ibid., 1–2. Lischer quotes with approval Gerhard von Rad's "exceptional" statement on hermeneutics in the move from text to sermon in which von Rad links both exegesis and preaching as inherently interpretive acts:

> Both scientific exegesis and preaching are interpretation. Interpretation is always appropriation of an intellectual content that is being transmitted to us . . . no understanding is possible unless what is to be interpreted is applied to ourselves, unless it touches us existentially. Therefore there is also no fundamental distinction between exegesis and preaching. Preaching too, is interpretation only in a different form of speech, in a different confrontation. (Quoted in *A Theology of Preaching*, 2)

19. If I were declared King of Methodism, which may happen any day now, I would require all my fellow Methodist preachers to read Lischer's wonderfully Lutheran, scathingly unwesleyan early essay, "How Law and Gospel Work in Preaching." Lischer, *A Theology of Preaching*, chapter 3. How very Lutheran is his claim "Christian life is not a simple matter of exchanging an external law for an internal one . . . but of exchanging the extrinsic demand for the indwelling Christ."

articles are organically joined. This gospel always speaks in the indicative mood and offers all that God has done."[20]

Lischer moves from text to sermon utilizing the same Christological hermeneutic with which Luther defended Christian preaching of the Old Testament as gospel:

> There are some who have little regard for the Old Testament. They think of it as a book that was given to the Jewish people only and is now out of date, containing only stories of past times. But Christ says in John 5, "Search the scriptures for it is they that bear witness to me." The scriptures of the Old Testament are not to be despised but diligently read. Here you will find the swaddling cloths and the manger in which Christ lies. . . . Simple and lowly are the swaddling cloths, but dear is the treasure of the Christ who lies within them. Scripture is not Christ but rather "the manger in which Christ lies."[21]

In typical Lutheran fashion, Lischer asserts that the Incarnate One who lies in the manger is also the Crucified One. Around our Divinity School I hear some loose talk about the Incarnation (and not only among Anglicans), as if by God's enfleshment we mean some sort of vague divine affirmation that the world is basically good and so are we. How our various forms of what Luther dismissed as "ladder theology" need a strong dose of cruciform truth.

In a somber Good Friday sermon on, "My God, my God, why have you forsaken me," after speaking about the ways in which we can find comfort in our suffering by knowing that Jesus also suffered, after rejecting any attempt to soften these awe-filled words, Lischer concludes his sermon by taking us deep into the heart of the Trinity:

> Jesus was forsaken by God. There, I've said it (even though I don't understand it). The one who promised Israel, "I will never leave you or forsake you," forsook his own son. And like the aggrieved child he was, he cried out in protest—against his own Father. That's a start for you and me. When we are plunged into a deep place and feel abandoned by God, we too will cry out— but to God! So I say, Go ahead, *"Rage, rage against the dying of the light,"* always in the name of him who for your sake cried out, "My God, my God . . ."[22]

20 Lischer, *Theology of Preaching*, 5

21. Luther, "Preface to the Old Testament," 235–36.

22. Lischer, "He Was Forsaken," Duke University Chapel, Good Friday sermon on Matt 27:45–50, March 25, 2005.

In a sermon at the ordination of a student, Lischer preaches on the text chosen by the young ordinand, Jacob's wrestling on the banks of the Jabbok. Lischer admits that "this is not an ordination text," but an unexpected word with which to begin a ministry. He shows an implicit *theologia crucis* in telling the young pastor that when we are called "that's when the battle begins." He moves the sermon from consideration of "What do I need to do to be a successful pastor?" to the deeper, "Who is the God who has called me to this venture?"

> You must have sensed something of the darker side of minis-try when you chose the Old Testament reading for tonight, the story Jacob's wrestling with mysterious stranger at the Jabbok Ford. This is not an ordination text. It is not an ordinary text. This is not a list of duties you must perform to please God or a congregation. It goes deeper than that. It cuts to the basic ques-tions. They are the "pre-seminary," "pre-professional" questions that we all must ask and come to terms with: Who is God? How does God name me into the world? How can I serve God in this dangerous world?
>
> You remember the story. Twenty years earlier Jacob . . .
>
> When God calls a person to ministry, peace does not de-scend upon the soul. No, that's when the battle begins. Jacob becomes a symbol of Israel, the people of God, who will always contend with God but will bear God's blessing to the world.
>
> Tonight, only you know the contours of your battlefield. Everyone's lines are drawn in different places.[23]

As he began in *The End of Words*, "God (and the preacher) can relate to the world only via the great symbol of marginalization, the cross. . . . Bonhoeffer understood better than any of his generation the incongruity of standing on a soapbox, puffing out your chest, and making a speech about the crucified God."[24] Lischer's subject, message, and even style of preaching tend to be a performance of *theologia crucis*.

Lischer Reads Scripture as an Imaginative Literary Critic

I have first noted Lischer's theological reading of the biblical text because no matter where he begins a sermon, that's where he always ends. Yet, nearly every Lischer sermon contains some literary reference (his masterful

23. Ordination of Andrew Jacob Tucker, September 5, 2014, St. Paul's Lutheran Church, Durham, NC.

24. Lischer, *End of Words*, 8.

reading of Flannery O'Connor cannot be due to his Missouri upbringing). He cannot speak of the parables of Jesus without speaking of Aristotle's *Poetics*, Kafka's stories, or Eliot's poems. (Some of this may be the result of a long marriage to a PhD in English Lit.)

Yet I am trying to point to more than Lischer's love for and practice of the literary arts. Though he is a wonderfully theological reader of Scripture, his preaching and biblical interpretation also show the fruitfulness of the literary criticism of Scripture, a movement that took shape soon after Lischer arrived at Duke and to which he made major contributions. A text is a literary artifact, and yet that text is also scripture. Its intention is to make strong claims upon us. The primary way biblical literature engages us is through a wide array of literary devices and stratagems. Lischer's fruitful move from text to sermon, therefore, ought to be characterized as theological/literary.

In his section, "Biblical Interpretation," contained in his rich collection of the best thought on preaching through the ages, *The Company of Preachers,* Lischer opened with Augustine's thought on literal and figurative interpretation.[25] He returned to Augustine's *On Christian Doctrine* many times during his career, particularly Augustine's guidance for how to handle the metaphorical, figurative aspects of many texts.

David Steinmetz published his "The Superiority of Pre-Critical Exegesis" during Lischer's early years at Duke, enabling him fully and unashamedly to embrace Augustine's figural interpretation.[26] "All Scripture unfolds the essence of God's love," is the way Lischer characterizes Augustine's chief hermeneutical principle.[27] When confronted with a confusing passage, Augustine advises "refer it to the rule of faith," that is, submit to the theological wisdom of the church rather than attempt historical reconstruction and contextualization. "The letter kills, but the spirit gives life," (2 Cor 3:6), cites Augustine, a verse dearly beloved by another Augustinian, Martin Luther. Indeed, I would argue Lischer is wonderfully "Lutheran" (and therefore Augustinian) in his move from text to sermon.

While Augustine warns "to beware of wanting to treat literal, proper statements as though they were figurative," he encourages us to read a broad range of texts in an imaginative, creative, and poetic way so that "their secret meanings have to be winkled out for the nourishment of charity" in ourselves and our listeners.[28] In regard to the Old Testament, Augustine advises

25. Lischer, *Company of Preachers,* 169–274.

26. Steinmetz, "Superiority of Pre-Critical Exegesis," 26–38. Lischer was a key figure in making Duke Divinity School an early and leading center for the theological interpretation of Scripture.

27. Lischer, *Company of Preachers,* 169.

28. Ibid., 174.

Old Testament texts "are to be taken not only in their literal sense, but also in their figurative sense." If we limit our reading of Scripture to the literal meaning, the ironic passages or tropes seem "absurd."[29]

Lischer states that the purpose of his Beecher Lectures is to consider preaching through a process he describes as tracing "a path from some of the frustrations and dead ends of language through the nurturing tasks of reading the scripture and re-narrating the story, to the true and eternal end of language itself: the message of reconciliation."[30] To define "the true and eternal end of language" as "reconciliation," reveals much about the way Lischer reads all texts, including the text that qualifies for the church as scripture.

Lischer Reads Scripture with Humor and Humility.

Though I would not say Lischer takes pride in his humility, his work with a text shows the virtue of practicing hermeneutical humility. In discussing the tragic sense of the parable of the seed (Mark 4:13–20), Lischer humbly admits to the precariousness of preaching: "Preaching the word *is* like sowing seeds in harsh and uncertain conditions. . . . The preacher puts it out there, unsure of whom is listening and who is not, unable to calibrate the sermon to its 'target audience,' and *never* able to predict its outcome. Sadly, the word does *not* take root in many cases and is choked by the cares of the world and the lure of wealth."[31]

Humility before the biblical text is atypical for preachers who are steeped in Western modernity. Arrogance—the assumption that we are privileged to live at the summit of human development (Durham, NC in 2015)—is endemic among us. Lischer never takes a superior attitude toward the text, perhaps as a result of his deep Lutheran conviction that both text and sermon are not for the aggrandizement of the preacher but *soli Deo Gloria*.

In an excellent article on "Hermeneutics" in *Encyclopedia of Preaching*,[32] James A. Sanders urges preachers, in encounters with the biblical texts, to "keep in mind three hermeneutic H's, honesty, humility, and humor." Honesty requires that we "theologize any passage before moralizing on it." Humility entails that we read "dynamically rather than statically," identifying "not only with the so-called good folk in it but also with those we do not

29. Ibid., 181.

30. Lischer, *End of Words*, ix.

31. Lischer, *Reading the Parables*, 49.

32. Lischer, *Concise Encyclopedia*, 175–82.

like." Humor means "to take God a little more seriously and ourselves a little less so than we normally do." Though Lischer demonstrates a mastery of all three of Sanders' "hermeneutic H's," I prize especially his gentle, ironic, Midwestern, usually self-deprecating humor.

While I have never heard Lischer tell a joke in a sermon, and I doubt that many think of his preaching as "funny," I find humor (linguistic corre- late to "humility") to be a key to his biblical interpretation. Perhaps Lischer's type of humor is what one receives as a byproduct of a deeply ingrained Lutheran theology of the cross, taking "God a little more seriously and our- selves a little less so." Some of his best humor occurs as he stands before the biblical text, particularly as he notes the incongruity between the text and us. A preacher could bemoan the distance between the witness of the sacred text and our puny attempts to live out the faith, or the preacher could simply dismiss the text as irrelevant to sinners such as us. Lischer chooses instead to invite us to smile.

His humor is the sort that arises when he holds aloft the chalice before his rather pitiful, misconstruing, inept first congregation in *Open Secrets* and sees them all reflected and subsumed in the cup that holds the Blood of Christ. His humor shows through the irony of a university that thinks it appropriate to celebrate itself by inviting a person like Lee Iaccoca to speak at commencement: "There he stood behind his personal podium flown in for the occasion, a bank of white Chryslers shimmering in the distance."

Lischer begins an ordination sermon by noting the gap between what the world is doing that evening and what is going on in the church: "It's Fri- day night, and we are approaching the shank of the evening. A band named Barley Corn & Rye is setting up for a big evening of Irish music in Brightleaf Square. Over at Durham County stadium they're testing the Friday night lights for another great high school football game. Both the quarterback and the drum major are practicing their Johnny Manziel moves. And here we are, in what we call the House of the Lord. We have lit our own Friday night lights and rounded up our own musicians to celebrate the launching of a new minister and a new ministry."

On All Saints, Lisher takes as his text Revelation's church descending from heaven and recalls his first congregation: "It does *not* appear to be descending from heaven but its worn red bricks seem to grow up out of the soil. There are no tour busses in its parking lot, and it definitely does *not* shimmer in the morning mist. It is capped off not by a majestic tower but a peeling steeple with a cross from which one arm is sadly missing."[33] This

---

33. Lischer, "God's Faculty," Duke University Chapel, All Saints Day, November 1, 2009.

notation of the incongruity between the church as Christ sees it and the empirical reality of the church as it is, this inharmonious gap, is not only the standard stuff of good humor but also typical of Lischer's references to the church in his sermons. The church may be the Body of Christ, but it is crucified, full of holes, and for all of that, the Bride of Christ. It is much better for us to smile than to weep.

Lischer reads every text expecting to find preached therein good news so that he can proclaim gospel. All of his literary skill, his delight in Scripture, his affection for and realism about the church as it is and as Christ intends it to be, his humility and humor, all this is in service to the good news of Jesus Christ. What he says of Jesus' purpose in telling parables, Lischer applies to every biblical text he apprehends, defining that purpose as, "*Gospel* . . . God's move *toward* Israel and, through Israel, to the church and all humanity."[34]

Bibliography

Hays, Richard B. "Exegesis." In *Concise Encyclopedia of Preaching*, edited by Richard Lischer and William H. Willimon, 122–28. Louisville, KY: Westminster John Knox, 1995.

Hedahl, Susan K. Review of *The End of Words* by Richard Lischer. *Ridge* (March 2006). Online: http://www.gettysburgseminary.org/studies/re-views/endofwords.htm.

Lischer, Richard. *The Company of Preachers: Wisdom on Preaching Augustine to the Present*. Grand Rapids: Eerdmans, 2002.

———. *The Preacher King: Martin Luther King Jr. and the Word that Moved America*. Oxford: Oxford University Press, 1995.

———. *Reading the Parables*. Louisville: Westminster John Knox, 2014.

———. *A Theology of Preaching: The Dynamics of the Gospel*. Durham, NC: Labyrinth, 1992.

Luther, Martin. "Preface to the Old Testament." In *Luther's Works*, vol. 35, edited by E. Theodore Bachmann, 235–36. Philadelphia: Muhlenberg, 1960.

Steinmetz, David C. "The Superiority of Pre-Critical Exegesis." Republished in *The Theological Interpretation of Scripture*, edited by Stephen E. Fowl. Oxford: Blackwell, 1997.

---

34. Lischer, *Reading the Parables*, 166.

Preaching Gospel from the Old Testament

Rein Bos

AFTER A PILGRIMAGE TO Jerusalem, an Ethiopian eunuch returns home (Acts 8:26–40). The apostle Philip joins the eunuch in his chariot and hears him reading what appears to be verses from Isaiah 53 about the suffering of the Servant of the Lord. Next, the Ethiopian court official asks the question that intrigues every theologian until this very day: "About whom does the prophet say this, about himself or about someone else?"

The question of the Ethiopian court official is paradigmatic for the issues involved in the Christian interpretation of the Old Testament. In fact, we can say that the preparation of a sermon on an Old Testament text confronts preachers time and again with the eunuch's question: "About whom does Moses or David or the prophets say this?" When Christians open a book in the pulpit, containing both Old and New Testaments, these hermeneutical questions are unavoidable and inescapable.

This essay aims to answer the question: How does the preacher proclaim the gospel, the "good tidings" of the crucified and risen Christ, "starting with Moses and the prophets" (Luke 24:27; Acts 8:35)? I will answer this question from a homiletical point of view, being well aware that there are other possible and necessary angles, such as (philosophical) hermeneutical or biblical-theological approaches.

In this essay I will first provide a brief general description of the process of sermon preparation as it can be found in some of the major textbooks and as it is taught and practiced in the introductory preaching courses at many seminaries and divinity schools. After that I will present an alternative model for preparing a sermon on the books of Moses and the prophets.

A Typical Process of Sermon Preparation

Scripture is considered to be both the source and standard for preaching. Therefore every major textbook that deals with sermon preparation pays attention to the study of the biblical text. These models have a few ingredients in common. Summarizing, we can discern the following steps.[1]

In the process of preparation preachers start by selecting the text (a pericope) for the sermon, either following a lectionary or by free choice. Preachers try to get a basic understanding of the wording and the context. Next follows a spontaneous, even naïve, engagement with the text, an encounter to feel, taste, smell, imagine, and question. In a third step, preachers employ the technical tools and methods of exegesis as provided by biblical scholarship. This step provides new, broader, or deeper insights, as well as some control over the first impressions. In a more or less concluding step, preachers try to summarize their preparation so far. Several expressions are used for this moment in the homiletical literature: big idea, theme sentence, focus and function, concern of the text. Preachers seek to name the claim of this text, for this sermon, on this Sunday, for this congregation. After that, preachers bring together the solid material and the "bits and pieces" they have found to design a whole sermon.

Four Fields of Tension

The concentration on a pericope from the Old Testament—with its thoughts, social context, concern, history, grammar, and vocabulary—confronts the preacher with several fields of tension. We can think of ellipses, each with two juxtaposed foci. While the two foci are opposed, they are nevertheless always interrelated and interdependent. One focal point needs to be understood in the interplay with its antiphonal focal point. This dialectical relation of opposites provides meaning in the field of tension. Four of these fields are especially important in preaching gospel from the Old Testament: Old and New Testaments; Bible and Gospel; *theologia prima* and *theologia secunda*; and *explicatio* and *applicatio*.

Old and New Testament

In its dispute with Marcion, the early Church affirmed that the God who revealed himself to Abraham, Moses, and the prophets was the same God who

---

1. See for instance Long, *Witness of Preaching*; Wilson, *Four Pages*; Engemann, *Einführung*; DeRuijter, *Horen Naar de Stem van God*.

revealed himself in Jesus Christ. The church also made the bold statement that the books of Moses and the prophets were indeed the Word of God and would never cease to be that. Successive synods and councils affirmed that statement in the early centuries. The church was convinced that it would be a fatal mistake to preach the gospel of Jesus Christ independent of the Old Testament and disconnected from its Jewish roots.

The young church also accepted certain writings of apostles and evangelists as authoritative. The collection of those books came to be called the "New Testament." As a result, the writings of Moses and the prophets were called "Old Testament." Consequently, the church generated important interpretative questions. What is the relation between the books of the already-existing "old" scripture and the "new" writings? Every contemporary preacher discovers sooner or later that this "old" question is not just one of the problems of interpretation, but a problem that touches the kernel of every sermon that comes from an Old Testament text.

Bible and Gospel

Preparing a sermon using the typical process assumes that authentic preaching (in the tradition of the Reformation) is necessarily biblical preaching; it is preaching "on" a particular biblical text or pericope.[2] However, while Jesus, the apostles, the early evangelists, and the early church used and quoted the words of Moses and the prophets, they did not preach "on" discrete portions of these books in our present sense of the word. What they proclaimed was not a specific text, but the gospel: the "Gospel of the Kingdom" (Mark 1:14–15; Matt 4:2; 9:35; 24:14; Acts 8:12) or the "Gospel of Jesus Christ" (Mark 1:1; Rom 1:16; 15:29; 1 Cor 9:18; 2 Cor 2:12).

It is evident that not every text or pericope has enough kerygmatic capacity to proclaim the gospel in its fullness. And that is not only true for Old Testament texts! There is as such a tension between the content of a discrete pericope and the gospel. According to Edward Farley these two can even be in tension with each other, as he argues in his seminal article, "Preaching the Bible and Preaching the Gospel."[3] The gospel is more encompassing than an individual text. As Farley writes,

> Gospel is not simply a clear and given content. It is the mystery
> of God's salvific working. Thus, we never master it, exhaust it, or

2. As Barth paradigmatically summarizes, "Preaching is exposition of Scripture." *Homiletics*, 75.

3. Farley, "Preaching the Bible and Preaching the Gospel" and "Toward a New Paradigm for Preaching," in *Practicing Gospel*.

directly or literally comprehend it. Rather, we continue to struggle to fathom its reality. Gospel is not simply given all at once
like a gift-wrapped package. It is something to be proclaimed,
but the summons to proclaim it is a summons to struggle with
the mystery of God's salvific action and how that transforms
the world. To proclaim Gospel is to enter the world of Gospel,
struggling with questions of suffering, evil, idolatry, hope, and
freedom.[4]

And Farley concludes, "I have argued that we preach not the Bible
but the Gospel. And I have argued that to make the what of preaching the
materials . . . of a passage is to substitute something else for the Gospel."[5] In
a challenging way, Farley highlights the field of tension between preaching
the gospel and preaching the biblical text.

Theologia Prima and Theologia Secunda

The preparation of a sermon on a text from the Old Testament requires
the use of several theological tools: grammars, dictionaries, commentaries,
books on the theology of the Old Testament and on systematic theology. The
language used to refer to these tools is *theologia secunda* or second-order
theology. "This is the disciplined reflection on those practices by which the
church articulates the norms, or grammar, by which it seeks to understand
and articulate its commitments."[6] This kind of reflection is, by nature, the
lingua franca of the education and training of preachers in divinity schools
and seminaries.

The language of preaching is, by contrast, that of *theologia prima* or
first-order theology. This language is first-to-second person, evocative, and
direct. It is the unconditional proclamation of the "things concerning Jesus
of Nazareth" (Luke 24:19) in the present-tense: "I baptize you." "You are a
child of God." "You are a city on a hill."

In the process of sermon preparation preachers have not only to translate Hebrew into English or Dutch, but must also translate *theologia secunda*
into *theologia prima* because preaching is, by nature, primary discourse.[7]

---

4. Farley, "Preaching the Bible," 81.

5. Ibid., 82. While "Bible and Gospel" stand peacefully next to each other in Farley's
title, there is distance, even conflict, between the two in his article, as his conclusion
indicates.

6. Lose, "Systematic, Constructive Theology," 487.

7. Forde, *Theology Is For Proclamation*, 93; Idem, *Preached God*, 45.

Explicatio and Applicatio

Preaching also has to address both the "what" question, dealing with the contents and meaning of a passage from Scripture, and the "so what" question, focusing on the relevance of the word for the listeners. It is therefore crucial for preachers to hold scripture in one hand and the newspaper in the other.[8] Simply explaining or repeating what the text says is not enough to make a "good" sermon because such preaching omits the "so what" of the gospel.

The "so what" question cannot wait until the end of the preparation process. Every step in this process must be done in relation to or with an eye on the actual life-situation of the listeners. All homiletical labor, exegetical craftsmanship, and creative art is in vain if the sermon has no relevance for the existence of the listeners. Sermons that simply talk about grace and the Kingdom of God—however theologically correct they may be—run the risk of not proclaiming actual grace or the Kingdom for the listeners. Such sermons leave the listeners in the role of spectators of an event from the past instead of inviting them to become participants in the dynamic movement of the gospel here and now.

The Rule of Faith

In each of the above-mentioned ellipses there are two ingredients that do not form a natural unity; they sometimes even compete with each other. What is the preacher to do when she has two things that do not easily or naturally mix to form a homogeneous fusion? In cooking, this often occurs when one tries to combine oil and vinegar. Even if one puts them in a container together and stirs them up, eventually, like cats and dogs, they will separate and stick with their own kind. To make tasty vinaigrettes one needs an emulsifying agent, like mustard or an egg yolk, which will act as a bond between the two ingredients. Unless one emulsifies the vinaigrette, a salad will end up with a pile of leaves dressed in oil and a pool of vinegar at the bottom of the salad bowl, destroying the flavor of the dressing. The emulsifier helps both oil and vinegar cling tightly to the leaves.

In the practice of preaching the two elements of each ellipse do not mix easily into a homogeneous process of sermon preparation; neither do they mix easily or naturally in homiletical reflection. This is true in general,

8. This expression is ascribed to Karl Barth. The Center for Barth Studies at Princeton Theological Seminary has not been able to pin down exactly from whence that quote emanated. However, it is widely known that Barth made the Bible/newspaper connection frequently throughout his career.

but especially for preaching the Old Testament. In the process of sermon preparation there is the risk that Old and New Testament, Bible and Gospel, *Theologia prima* and *theologia secunda*, and *explicatio* and *applicatio* will remain separate ingredients. Sermons will then end up with a pile of words dressed in exegesis or abstract theology, with a pool of applicative sermon-wisdom or psychological pep-talk at the bottom, destroying the flavor of the gospel.

In the course of the church's history, the Rule of Faith has functioned as an "emulsifying agent" to combine and unite the two foci of each of the ellipses discussed above. This Rule of Faith was a kind of outline of the basic Christian *kerygma* that served through history as the chief guide for inter-pretation and proclamation.[9] The *Regula Fidei* was flexible in wording but authoritative in content. It provided an "overarching story" in which the quest for interpretation and proclamation could take place.[10]

This emphasis on the Rule of Faith does not involve making a text say things that it does not say; nor does this approach extract things from an Old Testament text that are not actually there. Rather, through the Rule of Faith one listens to Moses and the prophets in the context of the canon as a whole, in which one can hear a multi-voiced choir singing, one of the voices being a witness to the cross and resurrection of Jesus Christ.[11] "The Rule of Faith thus functions hermeneutically to hold together theologically the confessions of God the Creator and Jesus Christ the Son, and thus also to bring together in a dialectical relation the two testaments."[12]

The structure of the Heidelberg Catechism, I want to suggest, offers such an "emulsifying agent" that brings together the different ingredients of the theological ellipses in the preparation of sermons on the Old Testament.

A Heidelberg Experiment

The first question posed by Zacharias Ursinus and Caspar Olevianus, the authors of the Catechism, concerns one's "only comfort in life and death." The answer declares "that I am not my own, but that I belong with body and soul, both in life and death to my faithful Savior Jesus Christ" (Q&A 1). This comforting knowledge has three "ingredients." The answering "I" has to know, first, the greatness of "my" sin and misery; second, how "I"

9. Kelly, *Early Christian Doctrines*, 87–90.

10. Young, "Alexandrian and Antiochene Exegesis."

11. I elaborated the (four) voices of this choir in my book, *We Have Heard That God is With You*.

12. Greene-McCreight, *Ad Litteram*, 704.

am redeemed from all "my" sins and misery; and third, how "I" am to be thankful to God for such redemption (Q&A 2).

The Catechism as Rule of Faith

The threefold structure "misery, redemption, and thankfulness" or "guilt, grace, and gratitude" is as famous as it is infamous.[13] This threefold division has had a great impact not only on Reformed church life in general, but also on the spirituality and devotional life of the individual believer. Not only sermons dealing with the Catechism, but sermons in general were structured—both in content and form—according to this threefold division. Sermons started with a dark sketch of the human condition and the situation in the world of the listeners. Preachers proclaimed the redemption in Jesus Christ in a second step, and they concluded with an admonition and exhortation to live a life of thankfulness.[14] Both the first and the third step suffered heavily from the risk of moralistic derailment. And at times, a rigorous and purely formal employment of this division led to rigidity and predictability.

Calvin meets Luther

Despite these caveats, this structure does provide three ingredients or facets that are part of the dynamics of our faith. In Chapter 3 of his *A Theology of Preaching*, Richard Lischer (being a good Lutheran!) examines "How Law and Gospel Work in Preaching."[15] Lischer discerns three theological movements "which continue to appear in sermons of every shape and design."[16] The first movement is *analysis*: "what it means to be dead in sin and by nature a child of wrath"—"a near-ontological misery in humankind."[17] The second movement discerned by Lischer is *transition*: the proclamation that our "destiny has been linked with Christ's, that new life in the risen Lord meant a new kind of life on earth and the promise of greater fulfillment 'in the coming ages.'"[18] This was not "an offer of something God might do, nor

13. The threefold division is no invention of Heidelberg. It was taken from "the common stock of Protestant theology." Bierma, *Introduction*, 81–86.

14. This is the origin of the Dutch version of the famous "three points and a poem" sermon model.

15. Lischer, *Theology*, 30–47.

16. Ibid., 33.

17. Ibid., 31.

18. Ibid., 32.

was it an exhortation to 'get saved,' but was indicative perfect: 'By grace you have been saved.' God has already done it. Not only that, God has done it for you."[19] The third movement is *integration*. This is not a conditional exhortation in the sense of, "If you want to get right with the Almighty, then this is what you ought to do." Rather, it is the liberating "because of God's grace . . . this is what you can do. Become what you are!"[20] When one compares Lischer's three movements with the threefold division of the Catechism of Heidelberg, it is as if Calvin meets Luther![21]

As an experiment, I propose to organize the process of sermon preparation by means of the structure of the Catechism of Heidelberg. In this proposal, there are three successive engagements with the biblical text, each with its own set of questions and interests. The benefit of this method is that from the start, in all three engagements, both foci of all the ellipses are in full play. The process can be organized as follows. First, we ask which elements of our broken existence are named and interpreted by the text. Second, in what way can we proclaim the gospel of grace and redemption for this congregation, starting with this text? Third, which impulses can be offered to the listeners for a liberated life in joyful gratitude according to the scriptures?

It is important to stress that this experiment follows the steps of the process of sermon *preparation*. The threefold division does not necessarily provide the structure for a particular sermon. In sermon construction these three ingredients may be "reshuffled," "varied," and "played with" in a multitude of forms.[22]

Our Damaged and Disfigured Existence

The first division of the Catechism invites preachers to describe and interpret the "misery" of the listeners. The biblical proclamation of human misery digs deeper than merely talking about moral failure or giving a summary of wrongdoings. The appalling reality of sin refers to the incomprehensible fact that humans have cut themselves off from God the Creator and God's economy of grace and blessing, and instead try to construct blessing

19. Ibid.

20. Ibid., 33.

21. Comparable threefold divisions—in various wordings—with a comparable theological paradigm can be found in other publications. See, for example, Buechner, *Telling the Truth*.

22. See Wilson, *Four Pages*. See also Wilson's collection of sermons, *Broken Words*, where he shows how his *Pages* can be employed in a creative way.

and provide peace on their own. Genesis 3–11 unveils and proclaims from the beginning that this enterprise is as dangerous as it is fruitless. These chapters frankly acknowledge the catastrophic power of misery, sin, and evil on the one hand and the corresponding need for God's salvation and deliverance on the other.

This dimension of human misery names the perplexing and bewildering reality that we deny both our origin and destiny in words and deeds.[23] This fundamental refusal expresses itself in concrete words and actions, in a blamable vandalism of the *Shalom* of the Lord.[24] The refusal extends so far that in the end we do not accept and tolerate the Lord in our midst. We are willing to remove, excommunicate, and even crucify him when he comes too near.[25]

In the process of sermon preparation preachers can ask which words, theology, images, or metaphors the particular pericope offers to name, unveil, or unmask the character of our human existence. The Old Testament provides preachers with an abundance of metaphors, stories, confessions, and diagnoses to describe and interpret our human "misery."

Grace and Redemption

The Old Testament likewise bears witness to the one-sided faithfulness of the Lord. God's loyalty to the covenant triumphs time and again over the unfaithfulness of God's partner. Stories tell, psalms sing, and prophets dream about the Lord's capacity and readiness to intervene effectively against powers and principalities that enslave and belittle us and prevent a life that is "good, behold, very good." Gerhard Forde is correct when he says that in "proclaiming the Word, our goal is absolution, the doing of the deed that ends the old and begins the new. . . . The proclaimer should attempt to do once again in the living present what the text once did and authorizes doing again."[26]

The faithfulness of God gives us the permission and the freedom to look up to the Lord for grace, comfort, forgiveness, and liberation (Ps 34:5). We have the freedom to know of, believe in, and hope for the grace and mercy of the Lord (Ps 103:8–13). Scripture knows about this deep joy because of God's gracious intervention and God's saving and redemptive

---

23. Berkhof, *Christian Faith*, 194.
24. Plantinga, *Not the Way*, 7–27.
25. Fretheim, *Suffering of God*.
26. Forde, *Theology Is For Proclamation*, 150, 155.

word. Moses and the prophets proclaim that we can and may be joyful and breathe freely the air of the Lord's grace. In the words of the Heidelberg Catechism, "Even though my conscience accuses me . . . nevertheless . . . God grants and credits to me the perfect satisfaction, righteousness, and holiness of Christ" (Q&A 60). How do "I" know that? Because there is someone more trustworthy than my conscience: the loyal covenant-partner, the God of Israel, and God's son, the crucified and risen Christ! God sees me "as if I had been as perfectly obedient as Christ was obedient for me" (Q&A 60). This is language of "eucatastrophic" proportion![27]

In this second engagement with the text, preachers can ask in what way the pericope provides them with words, images, metaphors, or theology to proclaim the gospel of God's Kingdom, God's liberation and freedom for contemporary listeners.

Life in Liberated Gratitude for Head, Hearts, and Hands

In a third engagement with the pericope, gospel, and life situation of the listeners, we come with another set of questions and interests. This time we want to know how the text inspires and challenges contemporary listeners to a life of liberty and gratitude.

The third section of the Catechism challenges the readers to run away from sin (Q&A 89) to a wholehearted joy in God through Christ, loving and delighting to live according to the will of God by doing every kind of good work (Q&A 90). This section deals with the Decalogue and the Lord's Prayer—with both our contemporary life in society and our personal devotional life.

In the process of sermon preparation we can ask what the liberating effect of the gospel might be for everyday life and spirituality. We scan or survey the words, images, metaphors, and theology of a particular pericope to sharpen our eyes and ears to find both the realities and possibilities of the Kingdom of God and God's righteousness.

The effect of the proclamation of the Lord's grace is not "a matter of 'should,' 'must,' 'have to,' and 'called to,' but is a matter of excitement and a sense of empowerment in joining God in a great endeavor."[28] It is not about

---

27. In his essay "On Fairy Stories" J. R. R. Tolkien speaks of the "eucatastrophe" of the gospel, the joyous opposite of a catastrophe, the surprising and delightful turn of events for the good. Tolkien, *Monsters and the Critics*, 109–61. Tolkien calls the incarnation the "eucatastrophe" of human history and the resurrection the "eucatastrophe" of the incarnation. Idem, 156.

28. Wilson, *Four Pages*, 226.

conditional exhortations like, "If you want to get right with the Almighty, then this is what you ought to do." Rather, it is the liberating "because of God's grace, this is what you can do. Become what you are!"[29]

And What about Christ?

In each of these three engagements with a text, we scan or examine the wording, theology, and imagery of a particular Old Testament pericope. We do so in the context of the Rule of Faith. That means that while scanning and examining the text from the Old Testament, we not only hear the voice of this particular pericope. In addition, the context of the Rule of Faith triggers resonances or echoes of the multi-voiced choir of scripture as a whole. That is not a kind of *eisegesis*—making a text say what is not there and what it actually does not want to say. Rather, we are invited to take this perspective by the context of the canon and the guidance of the Rule of Faith.

A recently discovered phenomenon in Hebrew poetic texts opens the door for this approach.[30] Two Dutch specialists in Semitic languages, Johannes C. de Moor and Marjo C. A. Korpel, discovered what they have called the "Law of Expansion and Contraction" in Hebrew poetry. They mean that "the length of every structural unit of a North-West Semitic poem was flexible and could be expanded or contracted according to the mood and skill of the singers. It was parallelism that allowed them to express the same basic thought in a much more elaborated form or to reduce it to a smaller unit if they wanted." Korpel and de Moor have deduced this law from controllable evidence "like added or omitted feet, cola, strophes and even canticles in duplicate manuscripts and parallel passages."[31]

The Old Testament texts thus have in themselves the "potency" to expand or contract. This potency invites and challenges interpreters over time to use the same technique in their (re)interpretation, not only with poems but also with narratives and prophetic oracles. The books of Moses and the prophets are, so to speak, inclined and ready to be expanded by a skilled preacher in the context of the Christian community of faith. Within both

---

29. Lischer, *Theology*, 33.

30. The poetic character of Hebrew texts is not limited to the literary genre "poetry." This characteristic can also be found in what we consider to be narratives and prophetic oracles.

31. DeMoor and Korpel, *Structure of Classical Hebrew Poetry*, 638; DeMoor and Korpel, "Fundamentals of Ugaritic," 1–61. This "law" also helps to explain the differences between the several versions of the *Gilgamesh Epic*. This "law" could also help to explain the different versions of the *Spirituals* (e.g., "Go Down, Moses").

the limits and the space given by the Rule of Faith, we can expand an Old Testament text so that it becomes a witness to Jesus Christ.[32]

Advantages of the Heidelberg Model

This model for sermon preparation has at least two advantages in Western, twenty-first century culture. The first is that in this model the life and world of the listeners are dealt with under the aegis of a *theological* diagnosis, rather than through social-cultural statistics or psychological analysis. The "what" and the "so what" questions are dealt with theologically in their mutual relation from the start as part of the process of preparation. The Heidelberg Catechism thus functions as a "theological emulsifying agent" for explication and application in the practice of preaching.

The questions of the Heidelberg Catechism are relevant for lived human experience: What is your (only) comfort? What is the aim? What does it mean? What good does it do to you? How do you come to know? How does it benefit you? What is the profit? Questions like these invite and challenge preachers to translate the secondary discourse of theological reference books into the primary discourse of preaching. Seen from this perspective, the Catechism can be viewed as the "language-school" for preaching because preaching, in its very nature, has to use "primary discourse."[33]

This approach also invites and challenges *listeners* to respond in the appropriate way to the primary discourse of the sermon. The listeners' response will likewise be in primary discourse: a confession, a prayer, an act of trust. Proclamation in this mode evokes and expects an answer, either positive ("I believe." "I trust." "I know.") or negative ("I don't." "I won't." "I can't."). A "good" sermon makes it impossible for listeners to stay neutral. We say either yes or no, and in both cases something happens in the relationship between our heart and God that touches the heart of our existence. The "primary discourse" character of preaching prevents sermons from devolving into a mere visit to a museum.

The second advantage of this model is that it enables preachers from the start to confront the Grand Narratives of our secularized and/or secularizing culture(s). In 1979, Jean-François Lyotard published *La Condition Postmoderne*, an essay about the "end of the grand narratives."[34] Since then, more and more scholars hesitate to agree with his conclusions. Walter

32. For this "technique," see also Hays, *Reading Backwards*.

33. Forde, *Theology Is For Proclamation*, 93; Forde, *Preached God*, 45.

34. Lyotard, *La Condition Postmoderne*.

Brueggemann is one of his critics in the area of theology. Brueggemann thinks that we experience more a competition between narratives than the end of meta-narratives.[35] Richard Lischer points in the same direction when he writes, "Christians are living waist-deep in competing narratives—stories of empire, nation, progress, and self-actualization, each of which whispers in our ear, 'This is who you really are. You belong to us.'"[36]

The books of Moses and the prophets are well aware of the human attempt to construct blessing and provide peace on our own. Throughout the Old Testament there are ongoing risks, threats, dangers, and temptations toward becoming enslaved, belittled, dehumanized, oppressed, and occupied by contemporary "powers and principalities" and "elements of this world." In ancient times the powers had names like Egypt, Pharaoh, Golden Calf, Baal, Leviathan, Philistines, and Babel. Over time their faces and presentations change, but their "spirits," or "nature," or "grand narratives" remain the same. Their verdict is also always the same: woe to you if you are disabled or a slacker or a coward or a failure or someone who dances out of rhythm! The powers and principalities have sanctions ready in order to drive us on. In modern times the powers are even more merciless, be it the authority of one's social group, one's super-ego, societal convention, or one's conscience.

The influential contemporary value systems consider humans to be mere playthings of anonymous and blind forces in a grace-less universe, be it the financial markets, the social media, or the latest electronic gadgets. There are still tribunals, principalities and powers we have to please or whose affirmation of us we have to safeguard. These powers require and demand obedience, promising us the consciousness that our life matters and is worth something. The proposed model that includes three engagements with the biblical text enables us to confront these secular grand narratives that (attempt to) dominate the discourse in culture and society.

Paul labels these systems with the expression, the "elementary principles of the world" (Gal 4:3, 9; Col 2:8,20). Preaching sues, so to speak, these gods and powers, calling witnesses to the stand to speak against the case of these "elementary principles." Preaching proclaims that the forces are disarmed and dismantled in Christ's cross and resurrection (Col 2:15) so that we can breathe freely again *coram Deo*.[37]

The principalities and powers prevent God's salvific intentions and disqualify the life the Lord would have Israel live. The metaphorical and symbolic power of these names and labels goes beyond what can be established

---

35. Brueggemann, *Theology of the Old Testament*, 712.

36. Lischer, *End of Words*, 101.

37. Wink, *Unmasking the Powers*, 139–56.

historically, opening the doors for employing this imagery in contemporary preaching to designate what the Catechism names "our sworn enemies" (i.e., the devil, the world, and our own flesh, the forces that never stop attacking us; Q&A 127). The proclamation of the gospel can empower the congregation with the strength of the Holy Spirit, "so that we may not go down to defeat in this spiritual struggle, but may firmly resist our enemies until we finally win the complete victory" (Q&A 127).

Preachers as Counter-Narrativists

In each of the three sections of the Catechism, preachers can ask where and how the specific answers of the proclamation of scripture differ from the answers given by the "proclamation" of contemporary idols, utopias, illusions, myths, ideologies, powers and principalities.

Christian preaching can confront what the dominant "principalities of this world" consider to be our "misery," what these powers offer as "salvation" or "grace," and what they ask or demand as "gratitude" and "thankfulness." The books of Moses and the prophets are full of confrontations with the "gods," be it in narratives (like the struggle of Elijah and the priests of Baal in 1 Kgs 18), in poetry (like Ps 115), or in prophetic utterances (like Jer 10, Is 44 and 46). Storytellers, prophets, and poets ridicule the ultimate powerlessness, weakness, and idleness of the false gods—at times sounding as if the biblical authors were stand-up comedians![38]

The church of Christ proclaims the liberating and comforting news that we belong—body and soul, in life and in death—not to ourselves but to our faithful Savior, Jesus Christ. Because we belong to him, Christ, by his Holy Spirit, assures us of eternal life and makes us wholeheartedly willing and ready from now on to live for him (Q&A 1). The proclamation of God's Kingdom, according to the scriptures, offers a liberating and salvific alternative for a world in need. As Lischer has written, "In the wake of modernity, it is faithful disciples and ordinary preachers who have become the counter-narrativists, the rebels, who now dare to tell another, more excellent story."[39]

38. Webb, *Comedy and Preaching*, 111–25.
39. Lischer, *End of Words*, 104.

Bibliography

Barth, Karl. *Homiletics*. Louisville, KY: Westminster John Knox, 1991.

Berkhof, Hendrikus. *Christian Faith: An Introduction to the Study of the Faith*. Grand Rapids: Eerdmans, 1979.

Bierma, Lyle D., et al. *An Introduction to the Heidelberg Catechism: Sources, History, and Theology: With a Translation of the Smaller and Larger Catechisms of Zacharias Ursinus*. Grand Rapids: Baker, 2005.

Bos, Rein. *We Have Heard that God is With You: Preaching the Old Testament*. Grand Rapids: Eerdmans, 2008.

Brueggemann, Walter. *Theology of the Old Testament: Testimony, Dispute, Advocacy*. Minneapolis: Fortress, 1997.

Buechner, Frederick. *Telling the Ttruth: the Gospel as Tragedy, Comedy, and Fairy Tale*. San Francisco: Harper & Row, 1977.

Engemann, Wilfried. *Einführung in die Homiletik*. Tübingen [u.a.]: Francke, 2002.

Farley, Edward. *Practicing Gospel: Unconventional Thoughts on the Church's Ministry*. Louisville, KY: Westminster John Knox, 2003.

Forde, Gerhard O. *Theology is For Proclamation*. Minneapolis: Fortress, 1990.

Forde, Gerhard O., Mark C. Mattes, and Steven D. Paulson. *The Preached God: Proclamation in Word and Sacrament*. Grand Rapids: Eerdmans, 2007.

Fretheim, Terence E. *The Suffering of God: An Old Testament Perspective*. Minneapolis, MN: Augsburg Fortress, 1984.

Greene-McCreight, Kathryn. *Ad Litteram: How Augustine, Calvin, and Barth Read the "Plain Sense" of Genesis 1–3*. New York: Peter Lang, 1999.

Hays, Richard B. *Reading Backwards: Figural Christology and the Fourfold Gospel Witness*. Waco, TX: Baylor University Press, 2014.

Kelly, J. N. D. *Early Christian Doctrines*, 3rd ed. London: Adam & Charles Black, 1965.

Korpel, Marjo C. A., and Johannes C. de Moor. "Fundamentals of Ugaritic and Hebrew Poetry." In *The Structural Analysis of Biblical and Canaanite Poetry*, edited by Willem van der Meer and Johannes C. de Moor, 1–61. Sheffield, England: JSOT, 1988.

———. *The Structure of Classical Hebrew Poetry: Isaiah 40–55*. Leiden: Brill, 1998.

Long, Thomas G. *The Witness of Preaching*. Louisville, KY: Westminster John Knox, 1989.

Lose, David J. "Systematic, Constructive Theolog." In *The New Interpreter's Handbook of Preaching*, edited by Paul Scott Wilson, 486–89. Nashville, TN: Abingdon, 2008.

Lyotard, Jean-François. *La Condition Postmoderne: Rapport sur le Savoir*. Paris: Éditions de Minuit, 1979.

Plantinga, Cornelius. *Not the Way it's Supposed to Be: A Breviary of Sin*. Grand Rapids: Eerdmans, 1995.

Ruijter, C. J. de. *Horen Naar de Stem van God: Theologie en Methode van de Preek*. Zoetermeer: Boekencentrum, 2013.

Tolkien, J. R. R., and Christopher Tolkien. *The Monsters and the Critics, and Other Essays*. Boston: Houghton Mifflin, 1984.

Webb, Joseph M. *Comedy and Preaching*. St. Louis, MO: Chalice, 1998.

Wilson, Paul Scott. *The Four Pages of the Sermon: A Guide to Biblical Preaching*. Nashville, TN: Abingdon, 1999.

Wilson, Paul Scott. *Broken Words: Reflections on the Craft of Preaching.* Nashville: Abingdon, 2004.

Wink, Walter. *Unmasking the Powers: The Invisible Forces that Determine Human Existence.* Philadelphia: Fortress, 1986.

Young, Frances. "Alexandrian and Antiochene Exegesis." In *The Ancient Period*, edited by Alan J. Hauser, 334–54. Grand Rapids: Eerdmans, 2003.

Preaching Paul's Gospel

Mary Hinkle Shore

MY SEMINARY HEBREW PROFESSOR said one day in class, "Any Semitic language is easier after you know them all." A collective groan went up from the students. Even so, he had a point. It is also true that any particular Pauline text is easier to preach when one is familiar with all the letters and therefore better able to step inside Paul's thought world at a single point. Paul's thought world was forever reshaped by what he calls a revelation of Jesus Christ (cf. Gal 1). In this essay, I will explore how preachers can recognize the revelation of Jesus Christ in Paul's letters and proclaim it. I have organized my work around the three questions I commend to students who are beginning to preach Paul's gospel:

- **What time is it?** In other words, where in the text is Paul orienting his readers to the ends of the ages that he speaks of explicitly in 1 Cor 10:11?

- **Who is Lord?** That is, how is the lordship of Christ manifest in the text, bearing in mind that the lordship of Christ is almost always described with references to Christ crucified?

- **What now?** Given where we are in time, and who our Lord is, what now? How do we embody the new creation even as we wait for it to be fully revealed?

What Time Is It?

Years ago, I read some of the exercises in Ira Progoff's book, *At a Journal Workshop*. Progoff was a Jungian analyst who led workshops in which people wrote as a method of self-discovery. The question I remember from his book was this: "The part of your life that you are currently living, when did it begin?" The question directs you to imagine your life in phases. How would you split it up? A job change? The birth of a child? A death? A fire or flood? Whenever we think about our life in "before" and "after" pictures, there is some event there at the hinge of before and after.

For the letter-writer Paul, the present chapter of his life began with a revelation (an *apocalypsis* in Greek) of the risen Jesus. The content of that revelation, the "hinge" between before and after is not just a personal thing, or even just a Jewish thing. It is cosmic. The whole created order shifts as the resurrection of Jesus signals the beginning of a whole new age. Apocalyptic thought in general understands our only hope to have its source outside the current order of things. For those who read and write apocalyptic, it does not work to fight city hall. It does not work to fight city hall with letters or leaflets or occupations or ballots or bombs. Nothing in our power is powerful enough to overcome the forces arrayed against us. This is the insight of apocalyptic thought. If change is to come, it will come as God intervenes from outside the natural order of things.

In Jewish apocalyptic, a sure sign of such an intervention is the resurrection of the dead. (If you are dreaming, you might as well dream big, and life from the dead is just about as big a dream as anyone can imagine.) So here is Paul, who knows Scripture and who is familiar with the ways that hope is articulated in Jewish Scripture, and he is encountered by the risen Jesus. At the beginning of Galatians he says this: "For I want you to know, brothers and sisters, that the gospel that was proclaimed by me is not of human origin; for I did not receive it from a human source, nor was I taught it, but I received it through a revelation of Jesus Christ" (Gal 1:11–12). As a result of his revelation of Jesus Christ, Paul has inside information—good news—that he shares with his churches. He knows that Jesus is Lord, and he knows also that if anyone is in Christ, there is a new creation.

Paul understands the encounter on the road to Damascus—what he calls in Galatians the revelation of Jesus Christ—to be proof that the turn of the ages has begun. In this view, the resurrection is not just a personal favor to a personal friend. It is not just the pat on the back that the Father gives the Son after the Son takes one for the team, whether the team is the Holy Trinity or just humanity. Leander Keck describes the resurrection this way: "For Paul, Jesus' resurrection was not a miracle, an exception to the rules, but an event whose beginning is marked by Christ's accession to power 'at the right hand of God' (Rom 8:34) and whose *telos* will be reached when all enemies of God have been subdued and Christ transfers to God the dominion which he is actualizing in the meantime (1 Cor 15:24–38)."[1] The resurrection is a work in progress.

1. Keck, "Paul and Apocalyptic Theology," 236.

If the *resurrection* of Jesus and Paul's encounter with the risen Lord convinces Paul that everything he knew about the structure of the world, time, and society had changed, why is the *cross* always showing up in Paul's letters? A few texts will demonstrate Paul's emphasis on the cross in different contexts:

> "When I came to you, brothers and sisters, I did not come proclaiming the mystery of God to you in lofty words or wisdom. For I decided to know nothing among you except Jesus Christ, and him crucified" (1 Cor 2:1–2).

> "You foolish Galatians! Who has cast a spell on you? Before your eyes Jesus Christ was vividly portrayed as crucified!" (Gal 3:1, NET).

> "May I never boast of anything except the cross of our Lord Jesus Christ, by which the world has been crucified to me, and I to the world" (Gal 6:14).

> "I want to know Christ and the power of his resurrection and the sharing of his sufferings by becoming like him in his death, if somehow I may attain the resurrection from the dead" (Phil 3:10–11).

In various contexts, speaking to different situations in his churches, Paul returns to the event of Christ's cross. Why is that so central for him? How is it that the cross is a point of argument when Paul is trying to move the Corinthians from their enthrallment with all things lofty and wise, and also when he is reminding the Galatians that they did not receive the Spirit by doing works of the Law, and again when he is reflecting on his own biography and the relative worthlessness of his accomplishments before Christ appeared to him? In each of these cases, Paul displays the cross as his best argument for what he wants to say. One of the things Paul knows after his revelation of the risen Christ is that "Jesus is Lord," and the lordship of Christ cannot be rightly understood without the crucifixion to exegete it.

Who Is Lord?

Caesar?

There are at least two big pretenders to lordship in Paul's imaginative thought world. Roman emperors never met a title they didn't like, and "Lord" was as welcome as any. As a way to distinguish between the lordship of Caesar and the lordship of Christ, listen for how the Roman historian Tacitus, describes one of the two: "They plunder, they slaughter, and they steal: this they falsely name Empire, and where they make a wasteland, they call it peace."[2] This is what "Lord" means in Paul's world. It is what "dominion" implies. Wastelands are the stuff of leadership.

To the Corinthians, who probably comprise a church of about three dozen people and who have almost as many ways of lording it over one another—the spirituality of their leaders, the strength of their consciences, the extent of their freedom in Christ, the abundance of their own spiritual gifts—Paul says, "Here is what I know about lordship: 'Jesus Christ, and him crucified.'"

To the Galatians, who are probably just trying to be as sincere as possible in the faith, and who have started to worry that Paul has misled them about the equality of Jews and gentiles, Paul says, "The only thing I want to learn from you is this: Did you receive the Spirit by doing the works of the law or by believing what you heard?" (Gal 3:2).

And when he is in prison, maybe in Nero's Rome, and Nero is busy demonstrating his lordship by laying waste to his own populace, Paul says, "I want to know Christ and the power of his resurrection and the sharing of his sufferings by becoming like him in his death, if somehow I may attain the resurrection from the dead" (Phil 3:10–11). When Jesse Ventura was elected governor of Minnesota, a bumper sticker became popular that read, "Our governor can beat up your governor." Paul resists the empire and rejects the claims of anyone but Christ to lordship, and he does not do so by saying, "Our Lord can beat up Caesar." Paul says, "Crucified."

In the Gospel of Matthew, when Jesus is in the Garden of Gethsemane and someone decides to defend him with the sword, swinging wildly and slicing off the ear of a slave of the high priest, Jesus says, "Put your sword back into its place; for all who take the sword will perish by the sword." And then Jesus adds, "Do you think that I cannot appeal to my Father, and he will at once send me more than twelve legions of angels? But how then would the scriptures be fulfilled, which say it must happen in this way?" (Matt 26:52–54). It is as if he is saying, "A sword? An ear? Really? This is your idea of taking it to the man?" Twelve legions of angels equals 72,000 troops. Gethsemane would have gone differently. And Jesus says, "No."

There in prison, writing to the Philippians, Paul does not lobby for twelve legions of angels to demonstrate the lordship of Christ. He says, "This is what I want: I want to know Christ, and the power of his resurrection and the sharing of his sufferings" (Phil 3:10). To say Jesus is Lord is to say "no" to standard definitions of who rules and how.

---

2. Tacitus, "Life of Julius Agricola," ch. 30.

Sin?

Caesar is one of the big pretenders to lordship in Paul's thought world. Probably more vivid for us who live in a democracy is the other pretender to lordship in Paul's letters. Paul sees humanity and the rest of creation as caught in a cosmic battle. He does not describe it as a battle between good and evil, but as one between God and Sin.

Sin, in the singular, is a power in Paul's thought. It is the bully on the playground who enthralls everyone, gathering devotees, terrorizing would-be opponents into silence, enslaving all. Sin vies with the Creator for control of humanity and the rest of creation to such an extent that Paul can speak of our having been "enslaved to sin" (Rom 6:6).

One of the hallmarks of slavery, ancient or modern, is that slaves do not have control over their own bodies. By definition, a master may force a slave into labor, inflict corporal punishment at will, and assault slaves sexually with no fear of prosecution for a crime. To be enslaved to sin is to have one's body commandeered every bit as much as one's soul.

In Romans, Paul says that sin's mastery over humankind has been broken in the death and resurrection of Jesus Christ. The opening verses of Romans 6 are a helpful summary of the new state of things.

> What then are we to say? Should we continue in sin in order that grace may abound? By no means! How can we who died to sin go on living in it? Do you not know that all of us who have been baptized into Christ Jesus were baptized into his death? Therefore we have been buried with him by baptism into death, so that, just as Christ was raised from the dead by the glory of the Father, so we too might walk in newness of life (Rom 6:1–4).

Slaves of sin have been buried with Christ in baptism. While it is a drastic form of escape, it is an effective one: the former master has no hold on a dead slave. Paul says simply, "whoever has died is freed from sin" (Rom 6:7). For Paul, the death of Christ breaks the power of sin over the whole creation. In the cross of Christ, sin is shown to be capable only of destruction, and after Christ is destroyed, sin has no moves left to make.

Paul goes on, "But if we have died with Christ, we believe that we will also live with him. We know that Christ, being raised from the dead, will never die again; death no longer has dominion over him. The death he died, he died to sin, once for all; but the life he lives, he lives to God. So you also must consider yourselves dead to sin and alive to God in Christ Jesus" (Rom 6:8–11).

Now we see that the lordship of Christ has implications for the life together of the people reading Paul's letters. Following Jesus is embodied. It is a practice. Just as being enslaved to sin was an embodied existence, so is being alive to God. We bring our bodies to the new life, and so Paul writes in Romans 12, "I appeal to you therefore, brothers and sisters, by the mercies of God, to present your bodies as a living sacrifice, holy and acceptable to God, which is your spiritual worship" (Rom 12:1). Notice plural bodies, singular sacrifice. Christ is Lord, and members of his body offer living, holy and spiritual worship, by practicing the kind of embodied gifts-sharing in community that Paul outlines just after these verses in Romans 12.

Philippians 3, with its reference to the power of Christ's resurrection and the fellowship of his sufferings, also offers a connection between the cross and the Christian life. Paul mentions the power of Christ's resurrection before he talks about the sharing in or fellowship of Christ's sufferings. It seems backwards. Or perhaps it only seems backwards if we imagine that after the resurrection, Jesus is a different kind of Lord than he was before the resurrection. We know that suffering love is Jesus' way of being Lord in the crucifixion, but we imagine that in the resurrection, he would give that up for something better, stronger, and faster than he was before, as if the risen Jesus had said, "We can all be glad that object lesson in humiliation is done. From now on, it is legions of angels all the way."

To be alive in Christ, then—to be raised up with him through baptism—is to share in a life characterized by Christ's alternative lordship. To be alive in Christ is to know the power of Christ's resurrection; sin no longer has dominion over him or those in him. To be alive in Christ is also to share in Christ's sufferings as Christ keeps loving the world in order to embody that event of resurrection. Paul knows all this, even as he struggles with it. He wants to boast in order to prove himself superior to the Galatian teachers and the Corinthian super-apostles. But as soon as he starts down that road, he knows that it is all wrong. In Philippians 3, when he says that he wants a share in the resurrection and the sufferings of Christ, he may have figured it out more decisively than he does in some other places.

What Now?

A colleague uses a story of three fish to explain what he is trying to do in confirmation classes. A couple of small fish are swimming along. A bigger, older, fish swims toward them, and as he is passing the little ones, the big fish says, "How's the water, boys?" The little fish swim a little farther, and

then one of them turns to the other and asks, "What the hell is water?"[3]
Confirmation teachers try to help kids notice what they are swimming in,
especially the faith and faithfulness of God that surrounds them, provides
what they need for life, and is often entirely unnoticed.

It is, of course, notoriously difficult to get fish to notice water. It is difficult to notice anything that structures one's whole existence, but Paul, as a
result of that "revelation of Jesus Christ" that he speaks of in Galatians, has
noticed the structures of existence, and he testifies to their change.

In Galatians 3, Paul is trying to convince his readers that they have
been misled concerning the role of law and the nature of community in
Christ. So how are the boundaries of the community to be drawn? Is there a
group known as "those baptized into Christ" and a subgroup of that known
as "Abraham's offspring"? For hundreds of years before Paul, the world had
recognized "Abraham's offspring" as distinct from other people. Paul claims
that that way of understanding reality—that way of describing the real
world—is out of date. He writes,

> As many of you as were baptized into Christ have clothed your-
> selves with Christ. There is no longer Jew or Greek, there is no
> longer slave or free, there is no longer male and female; for all
> of you are one in Christ Jesus. And if you belong to Christ, then
> you are Abraham's offspring, heirs according to the promise
> (Gal 3:27–29).

J. Louis Martyn describes the change in the water, that is, the shift in the
fundamental structures of the universe that Paul is describing here with
these words:

> There was a world whose fundamental structures were certain
> pairs of opposites:
>
> Circumcision / Uncircumcision
> Jew / Gentile
> Slave / Freeman
> Male / Female
>
> Thales, Socrates, and Plato—not to mention the later Rabbi Ju-
> dah—finding themselves in such a world, may give thanks that
> they exist on the preferable side of the divide. Those who have

---

3. My colleague may be referencing David Foster Wallace, who tells this story in
his Kenyon College commencement address (https://web.ics.purdue.edu/~drkelly/
DFWKenyonAddress2005.pdf).

been baptized into Christ, however, know that, in Christ that world does not any longer have real existence.[4]

The world as Paul now understands it is not just a mush of undifferentiated blobs. Martyn points out that Paul is not saying there are no structures to reality, only that the ones formerly taken as bedrock are now seen to have had much less staying power than previously thought. Instead of these structures, Paul now describes the universe as organized around the cosmic categories of flesh and spirit. Galatians, we recall, is the letter where Paul goes on to draw a contrast between works of the flesh and fruit of the Spirit.

In Galatians, Paul closes the letter with the announcement that "neither circumcision nor uncircumcision is anything but a new creation is everything." Martyn points out that we might expect there that Paul would say, "Neither circumcision, nor the rules of *kashrut*, nor the keeping of the sabbath is anything," but Paul does not say that. He says, "Neither circumcision nor uncircumcision is anything but a new creation is everything."[5] Law-observance is too small a dream for the Christian community. Likewise, it turns out, is license. License is that place where freedom becomes an excuse for self-indulgence.

Instead of an exhortation to law-observance or an invitation to self indulgence, the Christian community gets the experience of having been clothed with Christ. Paul said, "It is no longer I who live but it is Christ who lives in me. And the life I now live in the flesh I live by faith in the Son of God, who loved me and gave himself for me" (2:19–20). In chapter 3, he makes it clear that this life is not his alone but belongs to all: "As many of you as were baptized into Christ have clothed yourselves with Christ" (3:27). This life is so different from the old life that it can only be described in terms of a new creation.

New creation. This is exactly the kind of language that makes Paul so hard to preach. Imagining that we might *want* to give voice to the new creation, how? Often it seems like our choices in the pulpit are either to shrink the new creation down to something like turning over a new leaf, or just to say "new creation" with a lot of excitement and not explain it at all. Either way the dream—and the good news that Paul offers—goes un-proclaimed.

Richard Lischer names this difficulty as being at the heart of the peculiarity of Christian speech:

> In a culture obsessed with improvement, preaching speaks an eschatological word. It announces God's open future that has

4. Martin, "Apocalyptic Antinomies," 415.
5. Ibid., 413.

broken into time in Jesus Christ. What a challenge! We preach
to people exactly like ourselves—who want a better job, a bigger check, a happier marriage, a slimmer tummy, a longer life,
a safer neighborhood, and a better government. But we have
been given no word for self-improvement, only this majestic
unveiling of a new age begun in Jesus Christ and awaiting consummation. . . . The sermon participates in something larger
than improvement, the reality of which is hard to put into words
and whose end cannot be seen. In Luke 10 after Jesus sends out
the Seventy, they return with glowing reports of their success.
The Lord replies in an eschatological non sequitur, "I saw Satan
fall like lightning from heaven." What we see in our parishes is
improvements and setbacks; he sees on our behalf what is the
beginning of a whole new age.[6]

Maybe it is okay to say this sort of thing to each other, to say, "I'm
seeing fits and starts here; I agree that there is a lot about the fulfillment of
this promise that we cannot see but here is a window." One might resort to
poetry: "Lo, I tell you a mystery! We shall not all sleep, but we shall all be
changed" (1 Cor 15:51, RSV) or, "the Lamb at the center of the throne will
be their shepherd, and he will guide them to springs of the water of life and
God will wipe away every tear from their eyes" (Rev 7:17). One might also
resort to prayer: "Thy kingdom come, thy will be done, on earth as it is in
heaven" (Matt 6:10, RSV). Either poetry or prayer is better than scaling back
our dreaming to what we can see.

As I preach about the hope present in this new community, I endeavor
not to say something like, "Be the change you want to see in the world,"
or "Be the new creation."[7] When preachers offer this advice, they probably
mean to be empowering rather than exhausting (and the words may have
a place as sort of conventional wisdom for people who are getting enough
sleep and so have some energy for being the change they want to see), but
exhorting one another is not the same as proclaiming a new creation. Part
of the reason eschatological language is *good* news is that it makes clear that
the hoped-for end does not depend on our own understanding or effort.
"Come, Lord Jesus!" we pray, understanding that we are not the ones to
make that happen.

6. Lischer, "Interrupted Sermon," 178–79.

7. I learned to distinguish preaching the gospel from preaching moralism chiefly
from listening to Richard Lischer's lectures in introductory preaching as a teaching
assistant in the class. I have taught it with the help of his article, "The Sermon on the
Mount as Radical Pastoral Care."

Nancy Duff offers a helpful contrast between the kind of ethics that imagines the Christian life as an imitation of Christ and the kind of ethics that imagines the power of Christ's Spirit as drawing us into the realm where everything is new. With Duff, I agree that the second alternative is the more accurate description of Paul's thought. Duff says that Paul's image of Christ's second coming gives us "a reinterpretation of the *imitatio Christi*, the imitation of Christ. This interpretation begins with the understanding that Pauline ethics is not based on a Platonic ideal by which everything else is judged. Human behavior, according to Paul, is not judged by some perfect image that stands above us, out of reach. Rather, human action is defined by a power that draws us into its realm."[8]

Drawn into The Life of Christ

Imagine we are presently being formed into community across established boundaries; we are boldly hopeful for a new creation, while at the same time clear that it is God rather than we who will bring it to fulfillment. What now? What would human action defined by the power of the Spirit drawing us into God's realm look like? I offer two notes.

First, my Luther Seminary colleague, David Fredrickson, describes this experience of being drawn into Christ as combining action and imagination. Paul says in Rom 12:1–2 that it involves both body (Rom 12:1) and mind (Rom 12:2). As the sacrifice (a singular noun) had been shared in Romans 12:1, so the mind is shared and singular in Rom 12:2.

Imagine working with someone to move one of those large racks of folding chairs that populate church basements and school gymnasiums. It takes a theory ("I think this will work if you're on one side and I'm on the other"); you have to share at least elements of a vision, to be of "one mind" on the nature of the task and its execution. Even so, as vital as it is, imagination does not move the chairs. Action—walking, pushing, pulling, steadying—is required, too, as are mid-course communication and correction. The whole thing is common work in which people with different functions share, if only for a few moments, the same mind.

Such shared imagination-in-action does not ignore the difficulties of living with others. Chairs fall off of racks and tempers flare. Paul knows the difficulties of living in community, and yet he refuses to try to solve them by ranking some in the church basement as more important than others, or by imagining that "gifted" in such a context means the same thing for

8. Duff, "The Significance of Pauline Apocalyptic," 291.

everyone. In fact, it does not; by design, the body includes members with different gifts.

Second, being drawn into the action of Christ means also that primary questions of congregations (and their preachers) are different from those that so often occupy us. The primary questions are not: How can we grow? How can we get more?

While it is not a Pauline text, the parable of the unforgiving servant is instructive here. The text is Matt 18:23–35. Peter and Jesus have just had a conversation about how many times one might be expected to forgive the same member of the community. Peter suggests seven. Jesus suggests more: seventy-seven times, he says. An answer like that makes it sound as if Jesus expects repentance and forgiveness to be one of the rhythms of life in community instead of a commodity to be measured out more or less generously.

Then Jesus tells the story of the unforgiving servant. Here we have a guy who actually lives in a world characterized by forgiveness. The tragedy, both for himself and his neighbor, is that nothing about his behavior gives evidence that he knows it. He cannot pay, will probably never be able to pay, the debt he owes, and in response to his plea for mercy, his master forgives his debt. The slate is wiped clean. The kingdom is at hand, and it's good news! He is forgiven an astronomical debt, and he acts as if nothing at all has changed. He walks away from having a huge debt forgiven as if nothing had happened. Could that happen to us? Could we or our congregations receive what amounts to a whole new life and miss it?

In the story of the unforgiving servant, the slave walks out of the meeting where Jubilee has been enacted, after which the appropriate response is to say is something like, "Bartender, drinks for everyone!" and instead, he pounces on a fellow slave who owes him what amounts to a few months' wages, and shakes him down for the money. When the man begs for mercy, just as he himself had begged moments before, the first slave shows no mercy. Technically, of course, he is within his rights to ask for what is owed him. That is a perfectly natural way of understanding how the present will plod forward into the future. The ink in the ledger never fades. It's the way the world works, right?

But that is not the way the world is working here: here, someone just tore a page out of the ledger, but the forgiven debtor sees nothing of the implications of that missing page. Instead of recognizing his future in the world ushered in by the master's mercy, he goes right on living in the world of red ink. The tragedy of the parable is that, in its last scene, the world that the slave has acted as if he were living in becomes, in fact, his real world. What the future looks like now, at the end of the story, is one day after another of imprisonment and torture.

Also, none of it had to happen. A completely new world was opened up for the slave and he just kept living in the old one. If Paul were telling this parable, I imagine that at the end of it, he would jump up and down and wave his arms, echoing Isaiah, "See, now is the acceptable time; see, now is the day of salvation!" (2 Cor 6:2; cf. Is 49:8).

In the context of "the acceptable time, the day of salvation," in the context of a giant debt forgiven and a new life begun, the question "How can we get more?" is out of place. How can we get more members? How can we get more money? How can we get more security, status, assurance, energy? The question for a congregation is instead, "What do we have that the world needs?" Or maybe just, "Where's the party?" (as long as the party doesn't send half the crowd home drunk and the other half hungry, Paul reminds us in 1 Corinthians 11). Pretty much any question will work as long as it gets us and our congregations wondering how the Spirit is creating in us the mind of Christ and drawing us into the action of Christ so that we may share the power of his resurrection and the fellowship of his sufferings.

Bibliography

Duff, Nancy. "The Significance of Pauline Apocalyptic for Theological Ethics." In *Apocalyptic and the New Testament: Essays in Honor of J. Louis Martin*, edited by Marion L. Soards and Joel Marcus, 279–96. Sheffield: Journal for the Study of the Old Testament, 1989.

Keck, Leander E. "Paul and Apocalyptic Theology." *Interpretation* 38 (1984) 229–41.

Lischer, Richard. "The Interrupted Sermon." *Interpretation* 50 (1996) 169–81.

———. "The Sermon on the Mount as Radical Pastoral Care." *Interpretation* 41 (1987) 157–69.

Martyn, J. Louis. "Apocalyptic Antinomies in Paul's Letter to the Galatians." *New Testament Studies* 31 (1985) 410–24.

Progoff, Ira. *At a Journal Workshop.* New York: Dialogue House Library, 1975.

Tacitus. *Agricola. Germania. Dialogue on Oratory.* Translated by M. Hutton and W. Peterson. Loeb Classical Library 35. Cambridge: Harvard, 1914.

Preaching In the Ruins

REFLECTIONS ABOUT WORDS
WITH SERMONIC EXHIBITS

Stanley Hauerwas

Words Matter

"IN THE SHADOWS OF a dying Christendom, the challenge is how to recover
a strong theological voice without that voice betraying the appropriate
fragility of all speech and particularly speech about God." That is the first
sentence in my response to the papers about my work by Jennifer Herdt,
Jonathan Tran, and Sam Wells at an event in November 2013 to mark my
retirement.[1] In truth I did not discover that sentence for that event. The sentence had come to me weeks previously when I was trying to find a language
about the language we must use as Christians to speak of God.

In this paper for my longtime friend and colleague, Richard Lischer,
the sentence with which I begin is not irrelevant. Words have always been
at the center of his work. That should not be surprising. As he observes in
his book, *The End of Words: The Language of Reconciliation in a Culture of
Violence,* words are the stock and trade of a preacher.[2] Yet given the horrors
of our century, he wonders what words can be said in the face of the Ho-
locaust Museum or Dachau. The normative response to such stark realities
seems to be silence.

Yet Lischer is a preacher. He has to have *something* to say and it can
only be said with words. The preacher's task is "to do nothing less than shape
the language of the sermon to a living reality among the people of God—to

1. Collier, *Difference Christ Makes.*
2. Lischer, *End of Words,* 6.

make it conform to Jesus."[3] Even stronger, Lischer argues that the sermon is Jesus who is trying to speak to his people. This is not a new theme with Lischer. Christology has always been at the heart of his understanding of preaching.[4]

Lischer draws on Christology to make an essential point about preaching: because Jesus fully assumed our flesh—our fallibility—Lischer observes the power of his word often seems hidden. Lischer suggests this means that just as believers organize their common life around Jesus, the preacher must also model a Christ-like way of speaking. For the sermon to be Christ before a hostile world, the sermon—like Christ himself—must refuse to resort to the coercive strategies of the world to gain a hearing.[5]

To preach like this, Lischer acknowledges, is hard. It is hard not merely because we live in a world dominated by cultural and political forces that seem to make the gospel fantasies we entertain for our private enjoyment. Even if that were not the case preaching would be hard because according to Lischer, preaching bears "the impossible weight of its own message." Drawing on Bonhoeffer, Lischer explains what he means by suggesting that the sermon bears the impossible weight of its own message; that is, the God who is the subject of a Christian sermon is the God who was willing to be "pushed out of the world and onto a cross."[6]

Lischer's Christological understanding of the sermon is not unlike the challenge I tried to articulate in the sentence with which I began. Of course, Lischer is a Lutheran, which means he is identified with a form of Christianity that has had little good to say about those people who worry about how Christendom results in a severely compromised church. Yet I think Lischer's understanding of the social and political implications of "the language of reconciliation in a culture of violence" shares much with those figures such as Barth and Bonhoeffer who were intent on challenging the cultural captivity of the church.[7]

Christendom is a complex and varied phenomenon that in many ways is a faithful response to the gospel. Yet, as Lischer puts the matter, Christendom also names the attempt by Christians to seize power to insure that the crucified Lord could not be pushed out of the world. In Christendom the cross becomes a symbol of triumph rather than defeat. The words used in

---

3. Ibid., 7–8.

4. See Lischer's *Speaking of Jesus: Finding the Words for Witness*.

5. Lischer, *End of Words*, 8.

6. Ibid.

7. The phrase is the subtitle of Lischer's, *The End of Words*.

the sermons of Christendom too often confirm a world in which the worship of a crucified savior do not call into question the powers of this age.

I understand Lischer's criticism of those whose sermons "have accommodated their rhetoric to the bloodless cadences of civil discourse" to be a characterization of the sermon in Christendom.[8] Lischer challenges the Christendom presumption that if the preacher wants to communicate she must seek to find some common ground between the preacher and those to whom she preaches.[9] Accordingly the sermon too often confirms what is assumed everyone thinks without challenging that very assumption.

In contrast to this view, Lischer insists that the sermon is first and foremost an ecclesial reality. One might wonder, what else could it be? But Lischer's point is the church provides the resources that make the words of the sermon work. He insists that the sermon is a word from one church to another across time and space made possible by the common use of the Holy Scripture. Accordingly the common denominator between Christians is not human nature but the church gathered around the lectern, listening to the word of the Lord.[10]

That is what it means for the sermon not only to be about Jesus, but to *be* Jesus. Thereby, the sermon for those who preach and those who hear participates in the mysterious heart of the universe found in the ministry, death, and resurrection of Christ. The church must preach because we have the responsibility to communicate "the distinctiveness of the Christian message in a world of counter-messages and conflicting values."[11]

Lischer calls attention to Martin Luther King's presence in scenes of bombings to hold services of prayer and preaching. King would preach in the still smoldering ruins. Lischer interviewed people who heard those sermons to ask them what King had said. They often responded that they could not remember what he had said, but they would never forget where he had said it. Lischer suggests that King understood that preaching in the ruins symbolized the triumph of the word of God over every attempt to destroy it.[12] I take "preaching in the ruins" to be a good description of where Lischer thinks we now find ourselves; namely, we exist in "a sea of words" that result in a debasement of the speech we need if we are to preach truth.[13]

8. Lischer, *End of Words*, 17.

9. For my more developed critique of this way of understanding the task of preaching see my, *Without Apology*, xi–xxxii.

10. Lischer, *End of Words*, 75.

11. Ibid., 133.

12. Ibid., 33.

13. Ibid., 127.

If we are living in the shadow of a dying Christendom, the challenge is how to avoid using words that have grown tired and thus are unable to tell us the truth. Lischer's preaching has been a model for how words that have been subjected to sentimental ends can be rescued to do the work they were intended to do by helping us see "reality."[14] I hope I have learned from him how that can be done. Since examples are crucial, I offer the following sermons as examples of how I have tried, often without success, to recover in the ruins of Christendom the true end of words.

In the first sermon I try to recover the significance of "the" in order to emphasize that this was not just any young virgin but this was Mary. I do so to challenge the sentimental view of Mary that would turn her into an abstraction rather than the first born of the new creation who was more than ready to challenge the powerful and rich. The "the" is also a way to emphasize the historical reality that Jesus is not the exemplification of what it means to be in general "sacrificial" or to be "a person for other persons." Rather the "the" of Mary is the "the" that denotes that this particular human with the name of Jesus came at a very specific time to a very specific people. Accordingly, I wanted the sermon to challenge the endemic Gnosticism that shapes much of Protestant practice.

I have included the second sermon because it deals with words—and silence. I always write my sermons as a commentary on the texts assigned for the day. In this one I try to explore the philosophical question of how words are necessary to create a silence. I worry that in response to the so-called "new atheist" Christians try to say too much. When we say too much we turn our faith into a mode of explanation that cannot help but give the impression that we know more than we do when we say "God."

The Significance of a "the"

Mary: Mother of God
A Sermon for Christ Church Cathedral
Nashville, Tennessee
December 22, 2013

Isaiah 7:10–16
Psalm 80:1–7, 16–18
Romans 1:1–7
Matthew 1:16–18

14. Ibid., 126.

"Do you believe in the virgin birth?" That was *the* question people asked one another when I was a boy growing up in that Southern Baptist dominated land called Texas. It was *the* question because how you answered would indicate who you were, what you believed, as well as where you stood in the world. If you expressed any doubts about the birth of Jesus by a virgin, you were identified as one of those liberals that did not believe that the Bible was inspired. That is to put the matter in too general terms. It was not that you not only failed to believe the Bible was inspired but you refused to believe that every word of the Bible was inspired.

Refusal to believe in the virgin birth also entailed ethical and political implications. If you did not believe in the virgin birth you were probably a person of loose morals, which meant you also wanted to destroy everything we hold dear as Americans. In particular if you did not believe in the virgin birth it was assumed you did not believe in the sacredness of the family and, if you did not believe in the sacredness of the family, it meant you were an enemy of the democratic way of life. In short, a failure to believe in the virgin birth was a sure indication that you were a person not to be trusted.

One of the anomalies, at least what I take to be an anomaly, of this use of the virgin birth to determine one's standing in the world is those that used the virgin birth as the test case for moral rectitude often seemed to forget who it was that was the virgin. What was crucial for those that used the virgin birth in the manner I am describing is what seemed to matter to them was *some* woman that was a virgin had given birth. It did not seem to matter if Mary was the one that had been impregnated by the Holy Spirit.

But Isaiah does not say that "a" virgin or young woman will bear a child. Isaiah says "the" young woman will bear a child. "The" is a definite article indicating that not anyone would give birth and still be a virgin, but someone in particular would be a virgin mother. We did not know who the "the" would be until Mary was singled out to be the mother of Jesus, but we knew it would be a "the." Not just any young Jewish girl would do. The one to carry Jesus would be named "Mary."

That "the" made all the difference for how the church fathers read this text. For them what was significant was that Mary, the mother of Jesus, was the virgin. An indication of how important her singularity was regarded is that at Council of Ephesus in 431 she was given the name "Mary, the Mother of God." That title meant that Mary is not a replaceable instrument in the economy of God's salvation. Rather, she is constitutive of God's very life making it impossible to say God without also saying Mary.

Such a view of Mary, a view held throughout the Christian tradition, was not how those that used the virgin birth as a test understood matters. They had a high view of virginity, but a low view of Mary. They had a low view of Mary because the last thing they wanted was to be identified with the Roman Catholics. Roman Catholics even seemed to think you could pray to Mary. Those whose focus was primarily on the virgin birth assumed that such a prayer bordered on being idolatrous.

Those who used the virgin birth as a test to determine your character were and continue to be identified as people who are theologically and politically conservative. In general that assumption is probably true. I think, however, this way of thinking about Christianity can also be found among those who represent more liberal theological and political positions. Conservatives and liberals alike assume that any account of Christianity that can pass muster in our time will be one in which the Christian faith is understood to be a set of strongly held ideas. Conservatives have the virgin birth and satisfaction theories of the atonement. Liberals have love and justice. Conservatives and liberals understand the Christian faith as a set of ideas because so understood Christianity seems to be a set of beliefs assessable to anyone upon reflection.

But then there is Mary. She is not just another young Jewish woman. She is the betrothed to Joseph. She has known no man yet she carries a child having been impregnated by the Holy Spirit. In Luke we have her annunciation in which her "let it be" indicates her willingness to be the mother of the Son of God. In Matthew we have the annunciation of Joseph who is told to take Mary for his wife and he faithfully does so. Accordingly Joseph is given the task of naming Mary's baby. He names him Jesus, Emmanuel, because this child is the long awaited sign that "God is with us." The son of David, the King of Israel, has been conceived and born.

Mary and Joseph are not ideas. They are real people who made decisions on which our faith depends. Christianity is not a timeless set of ideas. Christianity is not some ideal toward which we ought always to strive even though the ideal is out of reach. Christianity is not a series of slogans that sum up our beliefs. Slogans such as "justification by grace through faith" can be useful if you do not forget it is a slogan. But Christianity cannot be so easily "summed up" even by the best of slogans or ideas. It cannot be summed up because our faith depends on a young Jewish mother called Mary.

Mary and Joseph are real people who had to make decisions that determined the destiny of the world. Isaiah had foretold that a Mary would come, but we had no idea what Isaiah's prophecy meant until Mary became the Mother of God. This is no myth. These are people caught up in God's care of his people through the faithfulness of the most unlikely people. They are unlikely people with names as common as Mary and Joseph, but because of their faithfulness our salvation now depends on acknowledging those names.

This is the last Sunday of Advent. Advent is a time the church has given us in the hope we can learn to wait. To learn to wait is to learn how to recognize we are creatures of time. Time is a gift and a threat. Time is a gift and a threat because we are bodily creatures. We only come into existence through the bodies of others but that very body destines us to death. We must be born and we must die. Birth and death are the brass tacks of life that make possible and necessary the storied character of our lives. It is never a question whether our lives will be storied, but the only question is which stories will determine our living in and through time.

Stories come in all shape and sizes. Some are quite short, such as the story of a young Texan trying to figure out what it means to believe or not believe in the virgin birth. Other stories are quite long beginning with "in the beginning." We are storied by many stories, which is an indication that we cannot escape nor should we want to escape being captured in and by time.

Jesus, very God, became for us time. He was conceived by the Holy Spirit and born of a virgin named Mary. Jesus, so born, is very human. He is fully God and fully human making it possible for us to be fully human. To be fully human means that through his conception and birth we have become storied by Mary. We are Mary's people.

What could it possibly mean that we are Mary's people? In his monumental book, *A Secular Age*, Charles Taylor characterizes the time that constitutes our time as "empty." By "empty" Taylor means as modern people we think of time as if it were a container that can be filled up by our indifferent likes and dislikes. As a result our sense of time has a homogeneous character in which all events can be placed in unambiguous relations of simultaneity and succession. Taylor suggests our view of time has a corresponding account of our social world as one constituted by a horizontal space, that is, a space in which each of us has direct access to time without the assistance of a mediator.

If Taylor's characterization of our time as empty is accurate, a characterization I suspect many of us will find forces a self-recognition we would prefer to avoid, we can better understand why we have trouble knowing how to acknowledge we are Mary's people. We may be ready to acknowledge that the stories that constitute our lives are ones we may not have chosen but we nevertheless believe that when all is said and done we get to make our lives up. But Mary did not choose to be Mary, the one highly favored by God. Rather she willingly accepted her role in God's salvation by becoming the mother of God—even while asking, "How can this be?"

How extraordinary it is that we know the name of our Lord's mother! The time we live in as Christians is not empty. It is a time constituted by Isaiah's prophecy that a particular young woman will bear a son whose name will be Immanuel. It is a time constituted by a young woman named Mary who was chosen by God to carry and give birth to one fully human and fully God. It is a time that is made possible by Joseph, her husband, who trusted in what he was told by the Holy Spirit. It is that time in which we exist. It is a time that gives us time in a world that thinks it has no time to worship a Lord who has Mary as a mother.

"Do you believe in the virgin birth?" was a question generated by a world that had produced people who feared they no longer knew the time they were in. That is they had no other way to tell time but to think they must force time to conform to their fantasy that they could make time be anything they wanted it to be. "Do you believe in the virgin birth?" was a desperate question asked by a desperate people. It was a question asked by good people lost in a world they feared threatened all they held dear. Yet it was a question that could only distort the gospel by failing to see that the good news is Mary is the Mother of God. I fear, however, that question, "Do you believe in the virgin birth?" remains in the hearts of many who count themselves Christians.

If you try to answer that question I fear you will only distort the gospel. Mary, the Mother of God is not an answer to that question. Mary, the Mother of God, is not an answer to a question. Mary, the Mother of God, is a declarative assertion that makes clear that it was from Mary that Jesus assumed our humanity by becoming a creature of time.

That Mary is the Mother of God means we do not begin with speculative accounts about God's existence or nature. Our God is to be found in Mary's womb. Because our God is to be found in Mary's body we believe that same God desires to be taken in by us in this miraculous gift of the holy eucharist, the body and blood of Christ. By partaking of this gift, a gift that if pondered leads us to ask with Mary, "How can this be?" But the gift makes the question possible because through this gift we become participants in a time that is filled with God's providential care of us. We are Christians. We live in Mary's time.

Such a time is anything but empty. Rather it is a time storied by people whose lives witness to the Lord of time, the Lord who encompasses all life and death. I suggested above that there was a politics often associated with the question "Do you believe in the virgin birth?" There is also a politics that is entailed by our affirmation that Mary is the Mother of God. The politics of Mary is a politics of joy characteristic of a people who have no reason to be desperate. They have no reason to be desperate because they have faith in the Lord of time.

So on this Sunday, a Sunday when Christmas seems so near, let us remember because we are Mary's people we are in no hurry. Let us wait in patience for the Christ-child whose own life depended on the lives of Mary and Joseph. The Word of God was made flesh. He came so that we might experience the fullness of time. Let us wait with Mary and Joseph for the child who will redeem all of time. Let us wait with patience and hope so that the world may discover that time is not empty; rather time remains pregnant with God's promise found in Mary, the Mother of God.

The Silence of Words

The Sound of Silence
A Sermon for The Church of the Holy Family
Chapel Hill, North Carolina
June 23, 2013

1 Kings 19:1–15
Psalm 42 and 43
Galatians 3:23–29
Luke 8:26–39

"There is no longer Jew or Greek, there is no longer slave or free, there is no longer male or female: for all of you are one in Christ Jesus. And if you belong to Christ, then you are Abraham's offspring, heirs according to the promise." Finally, like me, you have to be thinking, finally. Finally we have a Paul that does not embarrass us. We have had to struggle with Paul's seeming indifference to slavery; we have cringed at some of his judgments about the place of women in the church; we have had to put up with his judgmental attitude about sex; but now it seems we have a Paul with whom we share some fundamental convictions.

After all, what could be more precious to us than the democratic commitment to treat all people equally? We want everyone to be treated fairly. We want to be treated fairly. We want to be treated equally not only at work and home, but also in the church. The church accordingly should be inclusive, excluding no one. Of course, Christians no longer have a problem about Jews or Greeks, slaves or free, but certainly equality between males and females remains a challenge. In spite of some of Paul's judgments in some of his other letters about what women can and cannot do in the church, in this passage from Galatians Paul seems to be on the side of equal treatment. He finally got one right.

There is just one problem with our attempt to read Paul as an advocate of democratic egalitarianism. As much as we would like to think that Paul is finally on the right side of history I am afraid that reading this text as an underwriting of egalitarian practice is not going to work. Paul does not say Jew or Greek, slave or free, male or female are to be treated equally. Rather he says that all who make up the church in Galatia, and it is the church to which he refers, are one in Christ Jesus. It seems that Jew and Greek, slave and free, male and female have been given a new identity more fundamental than whether they are a Jew, free, or male. In so far as they now are in the church they are all one in Christ.

For Paul our unity in Christ seems to trump equality. Let me suggest that this is not necessarily bad news for us, because one of the problems with strong egalitarianism is how it can wash out difference. In truth most of us do not want to be treated like everyone else because we are not simply any-one. Whatever defeats and victories have constituted our lives they are our defeats and victories and they make us who we are. We do not want to be treated equally if that means the history that has made us who we are must be ignored. For example, I think being a Texan is one of the determinative ontological categories of existence. I would never say I just happen to be a Texan because being a Texan, particularly in North Carolina, is a difference I am not about to give up in the hope of being treated fairly.

But what does it mean to be "one in Christ Jesus"? Some seem to think being one in Christ means Christians must be in agreement about matters that matter. In particular we must be in agreement about the beliefs that make us Christian. The problem with that understanding of what it means to be one in Christ is there has been no time in the history of the church when Christians have been in agreement about what makes us Christians. To be sure, hard-won consensus has from time to time been achieved, but usually the consensus sets the boundaries for the ongoing arguments we need in order to discern what we do not believe.

That we often find ourselves in disagreement, moreover, is not necessarily the result of some Christians holding mistaken beliefs about the faith. Rather our differences are often the result of our being a people scattered around the world who discover different ways of being Christian given the challenges of particular contexts and times in which we find ourselves. If we were poor we might, for example, better understand the role of Mary in the piety of many that identify themselves as Roman Catholics.

If unity was a matter of agreement about all matters that matter, it clearly would be a condition that cannot be met. We certainly cannot meet the de-mand at Holy Family. For example, I happen to know some of you are fans of the New York Yankees. Clearly we have deep disagreements that will not be easily resolved. So it surely cannot be the case our unity in Christ Jesus is a unity that depends on our being in agreement about all matters that matter.

There is another way to construe what it might mean to be one in Christ Jesus that I think is as problematic as the idea our unity should be determined by our being a people who share common judgments about what makes us Christian. Some, for example, seem to think that unity is to be found in our regard for one another. We are united because we are a people who care about one another. Some even use the language of love to characterize what it means for us to be united in Christ.

That way of construing our unity is plainly false. We do not know one another well enough to know if we like, much less, love one another. Of course it is true that you do not have to like someone to love them, but I suspect like me you tend to distrust anyone who claims to love you but does not know you. If love, as Iris Murdoch suggests, is the nonviolent apprehension of the other as other, then you cannot love everyone in general. The love that matters is that which does not fear difference. Christians are, of course, obligated to love one another and such love may certainly have a role to play in our being one in Christ Jesus. But that does not seem to be what Paul means in this letter to the Galatians.

Paul seems to think that what it means for us to be one in Christ Jesus is a more determinative reality than our personal relations with one another make possible. Indeed when unity is construed in terms of our ability to put up with one another the results can be quite oppressive. For the demand that we must like or even love one another can turn out to be a formula for a church in which everyone quite literally is alike. A friendly church can be a church that fears difference. As much as we might regret it, I suspect it remains true that those we like, and perhaps even love, are those who are just like us. Whatever it means, therefore, for us to be one in Christ Jesus it surely cannot mean that we must like one another.

How then are we to understand what it means to be one in Christ Jesus? Paul says that if we belong to Christ we are Abraham's offspring and heirs according to God's promise that he would make us his people. Once we were no people but now we are a people who through baptism have been clothed anew by Christ. What it means for us to be one in Christ is to be a people who have been given a new story. We are the children of Abraham, which means the kind of struggle against idolatry Elijah faced, is now part of our history. We are one with our Jewish brothers and sisters because together we face a world that knows not the God who refuses to let Elijah accept defeat.

The very fact that the Old Testament is Christian scripture means the story of Israel's faithfulness, trials, and persecutions must illumine our life as the church of Jesus Christ. For example, I suspect there are few things we do as Christians more important than pray the Psalms. The Psalms give voice to Israel's faith in God even when the enemies of that faith, the Ahabs and Jezebels, seem to have the upper hand. Thus Israel asks,

> Why have you forgotten me?
> And why do I go so heavily while the enemy oppresses me?

While my bones are being broken,
my enemies mock me to my face;

All day long they mock me
and say to me, "Where now is your God?"

"Where now is your God?" is a question that haunts us. It haunts us not because we do not believe in God, but because we simply don't know how to answer it. We stammer for explanations. We believe God remains present in this world—in our lives. And we want desperately to believe we have been made one with Christ Jesus, but that seems like some ideal that has little bearing on reality. In fact, the evidence seems to testify to God's absence. To read the Psalms is to discover that the current challenges posed by the "new atheists" to the faith are not nearly as significant as those voiced by the Psalmist. Thus Elijah asks God to take his life because, being "no better than his ancestors," he assumes his situation is hopeless. What can it mean for this to be the history that makes us one with Christ?

I think it has everything to do with learning to hear, as Elijah does, God's silence. Better put: it means that we become for the world God's silence so that the world may know that the salvation offered by God is not just another failed ideal. Elijah stands on the mountain to be encountered by God. There is a mighty wind, but the Lord is not in the wind, God is not in the earthquake, nor is God to be found in the fire. Rather God is in what is described as "the sound of sheer silence," a silence we are told that Elijah heard. We cannot help but wonder how silence can have a sound that can be heard, but then we must remember that this is God who is passing by Elijah.

I suspect if you are like me you would prefer a God who chooses to be in the wind, earthquake, or fire. We want a God who leaves little doubt about what it means to be God. We are not at all sure we want to be a people capable of hearing the "sound of silence." To hear the sound of silence means we face a God we cannot make serve our peculiar purposes. Like Elijah we must first listen.

In truth I find listening to be a hard discipline. I am seldom silent. I am, after all, an academic. I am not supposed to be at a loss for words. I am to be the kind of person who always has something to say. To learn first to be silent, to listen, threatens loss of control. My only power is the power of the word. So I try to anticipate what you are going to say prior to what you say so I can respond before you have said anything.

I try to play the same game with God. I want God to be loquacious. I want God to be like me. But God is not like me. That God is present in silence suggests that listening to silence is as essential as listening to what God says.

This is what Elijah had learned about the God of Israel. And this is what we must learn if we are to hear the word of the Lord today. For the same Word that speaks to us today has spoken through the prophets. And God has not left us without resources for learning to be faced by silence.

What it means for us to be one in Christ, moreover, I think we discover in the silence that engulfs as we confront the most decisive moment of God's silence, that is, the crucifixion. That is when we learn to listen to the sheer silence of our God. That is the moment we discover we are one in Christ Jesus. During Holy Week we hear again how our Lord is silent before his accusers. On Maundy Thursday we kneel in silence as the body and blood of our savior is carried away, the nave is stripped, and we leave the church. That silence, the stunning silence of the crucifixion, is the silence of our God who refuses to save us by violence. The silence of Jesus is echoed by the silence of those who helplessly stood by with his holy Mother to bear witness to his silent submission to the Father's will, for our sake. It is this silence that makes us one with him in a manner more determinative than our agreements or commonalities.

This means that there are times when asked "Where now is your God?" we best remain silent. Yet it is enough. By learning to be silent we have learned to be present to one another and the world as witnesses to the God who has made us a people who once were no people. Such a people have no need to pretend we know more about our God than we do. We need not pretend that we do not face the reality of death and how that reality makes us doubt if our lives have purpose. But we believe we have been given every gift needed to remain faithful. Just as Elijah was commanded to eat so that he would have strength for the journey, so we have been given this bread and wine, which through the power of the Holy Spirit, makes us one with and in Christ Jesus.

"There is no longer Jew or Greek, there is no longer slave or free, there is no longer male or female; for all of you are one in Christ Jesus." This is indeed good news, but the new identity we have in Christ is one that cannot be attested to by words. The words we use must be surrounded by the silence of God. To belong to Christ, to belong to one another, means we must, like Christ—and like Elijah before him—trust in the sound of that silence.

A Concluding Word

Neither of these sermons makes front and center the agenda of recovering the true "end of words" but I hope they nonetheless suggest how trying to preach after Christendom demands we resist trying to make the sermon "useful." We must try, or at least I tried in these sermons, to refresh our words by calling attention to their scriptural grammar. We must try to help our listeners and readers rediscover how what we have to say about God draws at once on our everyday talk as well as the rediscovery of how odd our everyday talk is. That is not easily done but we have the advantage of having Richard Lischer's insistence that we must never stop seeking "the true end of words, which is the ultimate purpose of the act of preaching."[15]

Bibliography

Collier, Charlie M., editor. *The Difference Christ Makes: Celebrating the Life, Work, and Friendship of Stanley Hauerwas.* Eugene, OR: Cascade, 2015.

Hauerwas, Stanley. *Without Apology: Sermons for Christ's Church.* New York: Seabury, 2013.

Lischer, Richard. *The End of Words: The Language of Reconciliation in a Culture of Violence.* Grand Rapids: Eerdmans, 2005.

———. *Speaking of Jesus: Finding the Words for Witness.* Philadelphia: Fortress, 1982.

15. Lischer, *End of Words*, 132–33.

Preaching the Gospel of Resurrection

Thomas G. Long

Whatever happened to Jesus in the darkness of Easter morning
happens to all who associate their lives and language with him.
—RICHARD LISCHER[1]

IN HIS 1993 BOOK, *Unleashing the Scripture: Freeing the Bible from Captivity to America,* Stanley Hauerwas hyperbolically (or perhaps not!) suggested that all copies of the Bible be wrested from the soiled clutches of North American Christians. He wrote,

> Most North American Christians assume they have a right, if not an obligation, to read the Bible. I challenge that assumption. No task is more important than for the Church to take the Bible out of the hands of individual Christians in North America. Let us no longer give the Bible to all children when they enter the third grade or whenever their assumed rise to Christian maturity is marked. . . . Let us rather tell them and their parents that they are possessed by habits far too corrupt for them to be encouraged to read the Bible on their own.[2]

Of course, taken at face value Hauerwas's proposal is wildly improbable. The odds of separating North American Christians from their red-letter, black-clad editions of the KJV or their paperbound copies of *The Message* are roughly the same as banning kielbasa and beer in Milwaukee

---

1. Lischer, "Why I Am Not Persuasive," 15.

2. Hauerwas, *Unleashing the Scripture,* 15. Hauerwas was prompted by a similar suggestion from Kierkegaard, who wrote in his *Journals,* "Christendom has long been in need of a hero who, in fear and trembling, had the courage to forbid people to read the Bible."

or outlawing football in Alabama. Hauerwas nevertheless makes a serious point: what is potentially toxic about the Bible are the ways it can be read in cultural context. Along with Stanley Fish, Hauerwas argues that "strategies of interpretation are . . . those of an interpretive community of which the reader is but a member." The same holds for Scripture. In short, what people understand from the Bible depends very much on with whom it is read and the implicit processes for reading they employ.

For Hauerwas, the proper community for reading Scripture is the church, construed as an authoritative and "truthful" community, a community that puts into play norms for reading Scripture guided by "spiritual and moral transformation." He says, "Scripture can be rightly interpreted only within the practices of a people constituted by the unity found in the Eucharist."[3]

But that is mostly not where the Bible gets read. Most North American readers, he claims, "read the Bible not as Christians, not as a people set apart, but as democratic citizens who think their 'common sense' is sufficient for 'understanding' the scripture."[4] Consequently, the Bible becomes captive to norms of rationality, standards of truth, and protocols for interpretation alien to the Christian faith, and what comes from the Bible read this way "inherently becomes the ideology for a politics quite different from the politics of the Church."[5] The Bible speaks of the radical kingdom of God, but what gets "read" are helps and hints for finding personal fulfillment as contented consumers, reinforcements for conceptions of "the Christian family," and the like.

I wish to make a similar observation regarding what is arguably the central claim of the New Testament, that God raised the crucified Jesus of Nazareth from the dead. Indeed, as Paul wrote to the Corinthians, "If Christ has not been raised, then our proclamation has been in vain and your faith has been in vain" (1 Cor 15:14). "Every [New Testament] document," observes New Testament scholar Steven Kraftchick, "refers to the raising of Jesus from the dead, at least implicitly, and the belief is considered foundational."[6] Another New Testament authority, Pheme Perkins, adds, "The early Christian kerygma stands or falls with resurrection since exaltation forms the foundation of the confession that Jesus is Lord."[7]

---

3. Ibid., 23.

4. Ibid., 15.

5. Ibid.

6. Kraftchick, "Resurrection."

7. Perkins, *Resurrection*, 17.

What Paul saw as crucial and essential, the resurrection of Christ, many contemporary Christians view as an impediment to belief and finally a claim that is quite incredible and, thus, dispensable. Much of what makes the resurrection a stumbling block for contemporary readers of the New Testament—and, thus, a challenge for preachers—is once again the way that the Bible is read and the protocols for reading employed. Hauerwas is right; contemporary people read the stories and claims of the Bible, including the stories of Easter, confident that their "common sense" is sufficient for understanding. But this time, what is in play is not mainly what Hauerwas decries, the political and economic "common sense" employed by the democratic citizenry of North America, but rather the broader "common sense" of the scientific age.[8]

The Tangent and the Circle

In the Upper Hall of the Scuola Grande di San Rocco in Venice hangs Tintorello's striking painting, "The Resurrection of Christ." The scene is set at the rock tomb at dawn on Easter morning. Christ rises in a blaze of light as angels swirl around the mouth of the tomb. In the early morning darkness, the guards lie on the ground, either asleep or paralyzed with fear, and in the background, the two Marys can be seen making their way to the place of burial.

A remarkable feature of this painting is that, while all of the characters obviously are represented on the same canvas, the risen Christ seems to occupy a separate plane of reality than do the others. Charles Taylor, commenting on this painting in his magisterial book *A Secular Age,* says, "The figure of Christ emerging from the tomb is in a zone of sharp discontinuity from the rest of the picture where the guards are."[9] It is almost as if the canvas has a hole ripped in it just above the area depicting the tomb and that light streams through this hole from another realm, indeed from another time. The risen Christ is embedded in that light. "[S]ome break in the painting," says Taylor, "allows us to see the irruption of higher time. . . ."[10]

Taylor describes how Renaissance Italian painting, and later Dutch religious art, gradually moved away from this attempt to depict Christ and

8. By using the term "scientific age" I mean to describe ways of understanding reality, employing rationality, and adjudicating truth popularly held among educated people at this point in history. There are, of course, more nuanced approaches to science and more complex results of scientific inquiry.

9. Taylor, *A Secular Age,* 97.

10. Ibid., 145.

other iconic figures as lodged in higher time, in favor of portraying them as people fully immersed in the everyday world, as people we might encounter in the ordinary round of life. While some art critics describe this shift in art as itself an early expression and stimulant of the process of secularization inaugurated by the Renaissance, Taylor believes that at this early stage, it was more an expression of a devotional impulse, a desire to affirm the incarnational Christian faith by bringing it closer to the embodiments of everyday life. Ironically, though, this desire to affirm the faith more fully, by tending to collapse the distinction between immanence and transcendence, between temporality and eternity, paved the way, Taylor claims, "for an escape from faith, into a purely immanent world."[11]

What Tintorello sought to portray with paint—the juxtaposition of immanence and transcendence in the resurrection—the New Testament writers tried to capture in words. The resurrection was an event that happened in time and space and yet it violated the normal constraints of time and space. The only way ordinary language could gather this up was in a series of dialectics so sharp they lean toward paradox and outright contradiction. So, the risen Christ is recognized by his followers as Jesus (e.g., Matt 28:9), and he is not recognized (e.g., Luke 24:16; John 20:14); he has flesh and bones and an appetite (e.g., Luke 24:39–43), and yet he passes through locked doors and appears and disappears abruptly (e.g., John 20:19; Luke 24:31); he invites his followers to touch him (e.g., Luke 24:39; John 20:27), and he forbids them to hold onto him (John 20:17). Like Tintorello, the writers of the New Testament viewed the resurrection within a double frame. Though the evangelists would not have used these terms, of course, the resurrection happened *in* history, but it was not *of* history. Since language is a product of history, human words can describe the resurrection only by being broken, and ultimately broken open—into poetry, symbol, and paradox. The result, as Rowan Williams states, is that the "very confusion and historical uncertainty" of the biblical resurrection accounts, the very nature of them that refuses to yield closure to the critical mind, "may be of theological import."[12] He goes on to say,

> The stories themselves are about difficulty, unexpected outcomes, silences, errors, about what is not readily accessible or readily understood. We have a variety of stories, not easily reconcilable as regards location or timing or *dramatis personae,* stories which . . . are in fact about laborious recognition, as often as not, the gradual convergence of experience and pre-existing

11. Ibid.

12. Williams, "Between the Cherubim," 91.

language in a way that inexorably changes the language; but this seems to have something to do with the fact that the Christian communities of the last quarter of the first Christian century didn't find it all that straightforward either.[13]

Karl Barth famously employed the image of the circle and the tangent to depict the double frame, the relationship between the resurrection and history as ordinarily understood:

> The Resurrection is the revelation: the disclosing of Jesus as the Christ, the appearing of God and the apprehending of God in Jesus. The Resurrection is the emergence of the necessity of giving glory to God: the reckoning with what is unknown and unobservable in Jesus, the recognition of Him as Paradox, Victor, and Primal History. In the Resurrection the new world of the Holy Spirit touches the old world of the flesh, but touches it as a tangent touches a circle, that is, without touching it. And precisely because it does not touch it, it touches it as its frontier—as the new world. The Resurrection is, therefore, an occurrence in history, which took place outside the gates of Jerusalem in the year AD 30. . . . But inasmuch as the occurrence was conditioned by the Resurrection . . . the Resurrection is not an event in history at all.[14]

If both Williams and Barth seem to stammer here, with all this talk of unexpected outcomes, all this pointing toward stories of an event not readily accessible, and this image of a tangent that touches a circle without touching it but touches it nonetheless as its frontier, then welcome to the world of Easter proclamation. Williams and Barth are simply tracing their fingers along the contours of the New Testament itself, whose witnesses also stammer, not with duplicity or contrivance, but with perplexed awe, with the broken prose of those who are testifying to an event that has happened in their experience but that cannot be contained by it. What is certain is that the resurrection cannot be described without viewing it in two frames of reference: the historical, immanent, and material, on the one hand, and the eschatological and transcendent, on the other. To lose the first renders the resurrection a spiritualized abstraction and to lose the second renders it absurd.

But this loss of a double frame is precisely the condition in which the message of the resurrection is largely received in our time, and the collapse

13. Ibid.

14. Barth, *Epistle to the Romans,* 30.

of the double frame into a single viewpoint constitutes the major challenge faced by Easter preachers.

The Resurrection Becomes Existential

In his 1941 essay "Kerygma and Myth," Rudolf Bultmann set forth his now well-known program of demythologizing the New Testament. Bultmann's starting point was what he called the "essentially mythical" cosmology of the New Testament, by which he meant that the New Testament writers lived and wrote in an assumptive three-storied cosmos, with heaven above and the underworld below, in a dualistic realm filled with good and evil spirits, angels, miracles, and other forms of supernatural activity. Any contemporary preaching of the kerygma that continues embedded in this mythological view, argued Bultmann, runs the risk of irrelevance, because the mythologized "kerygma is incredible to modern man, for he is convinced that the mythical view of the world is obsolete."[15]

For Bultmann, convinced that modern people, imbued in a scientific worldview, could no longer hear a proclamation of the gospel wrapped in a three-story universe, the only possible solution was the thorough demythologizing of the kerygma, the transformation of the proclamation of the gospel by producing "an existentialist interpretation of the dualistic mythology of the New Testament . . . ,"[16] an enormous task, thought Bultmann, that would "tax the time and strength of a whole theological generation."[17]

Even though Bultmann envisioned the process of demythologizing as a long-term project, the essential content of the demythologized kerygma was already visible. The proclamation of the gospel precipitated in hearers a personal crisis of self-understanding, a crisis that called for a decision between what Bultmann, following Heidigger, termed "authentic" and "inauthentic" existence. Properly proclaimed, "The event of Jesus Christ is . . . the revelation of the love of God," which summons a person away from inauthenticity—the false security found in objectifying the world of the flesh—and toward an existential freedom:

> It makes a man free from himself and free to be himself, free to live a life of self-commitment in faith and love. . . . Yet such faith is only a subtle form of self-assertion so long as the love of God is merely a piece of wishful thinking. It is only an abstract idea

15. Bultmann, *Kerygma and Myth* 1, 3.

16. Ibid., 16.

17. Ibid., 15.

so long as God has not revealed his love. That is why faith for the Christian means faith in Christ, for it is faith for the love of God revealed in Christ.[18]

But, to return to our main interest, how does the resurrection fit into this program of demythologizing? First, the resurrection for Bultmann was not history but was a part of the mythological machinery of the pre-scientific world and, as such, was a target for demythologizing. "A historical fact," he wrote, "which involves a resurrection from the dead is utterly inconceivable!" The only place where the event of Easter is gathered into history is in the fact that the disciples came to faith: "If the event of Easter day is in any sense an historical event . . . ," he wrote, "it is nothing else than the rise of faith in the risen Lord. . . . The resurrection itself is not an event of past history."[19]

Second, and this follows from the first, the resurrection for Bultmann was cut free from any particular moment in history and absorbed into the constantly repeated event of preaching. The difference between Barth and Bultmann on this point is significant. Both agree that the resurrection is not an historical event in the ordinary sense of the word. For Barth, however, it nevertheless occurred, as we have noted, *in* history, "outside the gates of Jerusalem in the year AD 30," but it cannot be encompassed by or described in only historical terms. It touches history like a tangent touches a circle. For Bultmann, though, Easter is historical only in the sense of something happening existentially to the disciples, and that what happened then happens over and again whenever the kerygma is preached. In other words, Jesus is raised, but not outside a tomb in first-century Jerusalem, but raised, instead, in preaching every time the kerygma is proclaimed.

Bultmann was aware that his program still left a non-demythologized residue. If he had stayed with the personal, the historical, and the existential, if he had merely described the human internal responses to preaching, if he had remarked only that, whenever the kerygma is preached, people feel personally addressed and spoken to in the moment, he would have stayed safely within the confines of demythologized language. But Bultmann wanted to say more; he needed to say more; he wanted to affirm that preaching is an eschatological event involving divine agency, that "God acts on me, speaks to me, here and now."[20] This is, of course, the language of myth. As many of Bultmann's critics have pointed out, to engage in a thorough-going demythologizing of the whole cosmos except for a tiny place of divine action

18. Ibid., 32.
19. Ibid., 42.
20. Bultmann, *Jesus Christ and Mythology*, 64.

inside the self is only to play poker with the house. Paul Ricoeur names the inconsistency when he observes that the non-mythological core of Bultmann's kerygma is essentially the notion of "justification by faith," so well-known to Paul, so congenial to Barth, so treasured by Lutherans. But, as Ricoeur goes on to say, when Bultmann talks of this "justification of faith," as well as other notions of God's action and word, the realization that this is actually talk of the "wholly other, transcendent, and beyond . . . is avoided. It is striking that Bultmann makes hardly any demands on this language of faith, whereas he was so suspicious about the language of myth."[21] Or as Kevin J. Vanhoozer puts it, "Bultmann is critical of the mythos . . . employed by the biblical authors for speaking of God's acts, but uncritical of his own."[22]

Bultmann realized that the preaching of the kerygma and the community of faith it provoked could, in a radically demythologized world, both be viewed as entirely historical and sociological phenomena. But for Bultmann, an angel with a flaming sword barred that path, and blocked the way to any demythologization so radical and thoroughgoing as to lead to only immanent conclusions. Instead, the preaching of the gospel and the life of the faithful church, he insisted, are paradoxical realities, both historical and eschatological at one and the same time, "the paradox of a transcendent God present and active in history."[23]

The Collapsing of the Frames

For Bultmann, then, the word "myth" operates in two distinct ways. There is what could be called "obsolete myth," a relic of the pre-scientific world. As Bultmann observed, the defect of this kind of myth is that—as is the case with the Roman and Greek myths of gods and goddesses—transcendence is translated into immanence, resulting in confused, outmoded, and implausible talk of *this* world as inhabited by spirits, demons, miracles, and divinities, all occurring within the architecture of a three-storied cosmos. Even if the New Testament customarily talks this way, we can talk this way no longer. But there is also for Bultmann "good myth," namely the affirmation that certain historical events, such as the preaching of the gospel and the decisive response of faith in some who hear, cannot be exhausted by mere historical description but must also be described as eschatological actions of the transcendent God.

21. Ricoeur, *Conflict of Interpretations*, 390.

22. Vanhoozer, *Remythologizing Theology*, 17.

23. Bultmann, *Kerygma and Myth*, 44.

Some readers of Bultmann have been astonished—or scandalized—that he could hold together these two views of myth. On one occasion Bultmann visited Heidelberg to deliver an academic lecture. While he was there, he also preached a sermon at Peterskirche. Philosopher Karl Jaspers, who heard both the lecture and the sermon, was unsettled by the difference between the two performances. "I was amazed," Jaspers wrote to Bultmann, "by the orthodox, conventional content of your sermon, which did not accord with the spirit of your lecture." Because Bultmann stopped short of doing to his preaching and his theology what he was eager to do with his scientific worldview, purging it of all myth, Jaspers assessed his program of demythologizing to be "evil, all the more because it has affected a man and scientist of your caliber."[24]

Jaspers later got his wish, not in Bultmann, but in the triumph of a common-sense naturalistic materialism that prevails in the outlook of most educated people today, both in and out of the church, a worldview resulting from an allegiance to certain understandings of science and scientific "truth." As Charles Taylor has said,

> But today, when a naturalistic materialism is not only an offer, but presents itself as the only view compatible with the most prestigious institution of the modern world, viz., science; it is quite conceivable that one's doubts about one's own faith, about one's ability to be transformed, or one's sense of how one's own faith is childish and inadequate, could mesh with this powerful ideology, and send one off along the path of unbelief, even though with regret and nostalgia.[25]

If Taylor is right, then Easter preachers are proclaiming the resurrection not simply to a disbelieving world but to what Taylor (and Weber before him) would call a "disenchanted world." For Taylor, this is a world in which marked by "the fading of God's presence," is a world in which people look afresh at alternatives to God for moral and spiritual "fullness."[26] The practical expression of this, it seems to me, is not that Easter congregations are filled by people self-consciously searching out alternatives to the Christian gospel for truth and fulfillment (although some surely are), but instead congregations in which many present are oblivious to what we earlier called the "double frame" necessary for hearing the proclamation of the resurrection. As self-understood "scientific people," they pass all truth claims through the single frame of empiricism, which is the product of a home-brewed process

24. Jaspers, "Issues Clarified," 105.
25. Taylor, *A Secular Age*, 28.
26. Ibid., 27.

of demythologizing. Science and history, narrowly defined, become the ar-
biters of what is possible, and all claims are submitted to the arbitration of
"common sense." Consequently, statements such as, "This Jesus God raised
up, and of that all of us are witnesses" (Acts 2:32) is placed in the same class
as "water boils at 100 degrees centigrade under one atmosphere of pressure,"
and the truthfulness of these statements is assessed on the same naturalistic,
materialistic grounds.

Now, the truth is that for many Easter worshippers, claims of the resurrection go essentially unchallenged. The resurrection of Jesus is received
at face value as a divinely initiated disruption of the so-called laws of nature,
and, as such, the resurrection becomes not the eschatological in-breaking
of the reign of God, but an exception to the closed and regulated world of
science, which remains otherwise intact. The Bible and the Easter preacher
are, in other words, making truth claims of the usual historical and scientific
nature, just extraordinary ones—the tomb was empty, Jesus was raised from
the dead, and he appeared in embodied form to his followers.

For others, though, the resurrection finally presses credulity to the
breaking point, forcing a redefinition in which the resurrection is spiritualized and translated into completely immanent terms. Some popular theologians, who themselves have but a single frame of vision, are only too happy
to assist in this reductionism. John Shelby Spong, for example, describes the
"Easter event" as a noetic event, a visionary experience, a moment of illumination, a light "that went on in Simon's head" after a good day of fishing with
the disciples by which he suddenly "saw Jesus as part of God's being and
God's meaning." Peter then "opened the eyes of the others to what he saw.
Each of them grasped this vision, experienced Jesus alive, and were themselves resurrected. That was Easter. It was both objective and subjective, but
above all it was real."[27] It is difficult to know precisely what Spong means
by "objective," "subjective," and "real," but he probably means to assure his
readers that Peter was not simply hallucinating or "making believe" but that
he was sensing something like the spirit of Jesus still with him.

Robin Meyers, in *Saving Jesus from the Church: How to Stop Worshiping
Christ and Start Following Jesus,* warms up some Bultmann by saying, "We
don't live in a three-story universe anymore," and then he defines the traditional understanding of the resurrection as claims about "the disappearance
and reappearance of corpses." Of course, theologically the resurrection of
Christ is not, and has never been, a claim about a resuscitated corpse, but
if one reads the Easter narratives with the same protocols that one employs
to read a high school physics textbook, what else could it be? Resting one's

27. Spong, "Easter Moment."

faith and life on tales about a revivified corpse is not only backward and obsolete, according to Meyers, it also flirts with downright evil and "should be left behind with the ideas of demon possession, slavery, and the subordination of women."[28] Thus the Easter message, as traditionally proclaimed, is a hindrance:

> Today we stumble over the claim [of the resurrection] because we find it incredible, missing the real scandal of saying about Jesus, "He is risen!" The church has failed generations of would-be followers of Jesus by confusing the transrational with the irrational. They come to Easter service believing that they must believe the impossible in order to feel the implausible. Before they can sing the "Hallelujah Chorus," they must check their brain at the door. God's "yes" to Jesus is assumed to be a "no" to the laws of the physical universe. Tears of joy are then, by definition, the counterfeit symbols of sentimentality. Why not say it as plainly as the renowned biblical scholar John Dominic Crossan: "I do not think that anyone, anywhere, at any time brings dead people back to life."[29]

In Meyers, Spong, and others the double-framed vision necessary to receive the Easter gospel has begun to collapse into monism; there are "laws of the physical universe," and because these laws set out the limits of plausibility, however the resurrection is explained and whatever it may mean must fall within these constraints. When some New Testament scholars see the various gospel accounts of the resurrection as essentially political tracts aimed at elevating particular figures or parties to power, when British biblical scholar Michael Goulder compares the early church's experience of the resurrection to the collective delusions around sightings of Bigfoot,[30] or when novelist Phillip Pullmann buys into the old theory that Jesus had a twin brother who stimulated the so-called post resurrection sightings,[31] the collapse of frames is complete. So, too, on the other side of the theological ledger with philosopher Stephen Davis's claim, "A camera could have taken a snapshot of the risen Jesus."[32] We are now a long way from Paul's, "But in fact Christ has been raised from the dead" (1 Cor 15:20), from Tintorello's paradoxical "The Resurrection of Christ," from Barth's tangent and circle.

28. Meyers, *Saving Jesus from the Church*, 89

29. Ibid., 77.

30. Goulder, "Baseless Fabric of a Vision," 53.

31. Pullman, *Good Man Jesus*.

32. Davis, "Seeing the Risen Jesus," 128.

Preaching the Resurrection

In one sense, the disenchanted world in which we preach today simply heightens our awareness of an aspect of Easter preaching that has been present since the beginning of the Christian movement. Proclaiming the resurrection is far more than announcing an event that took place in a cemetery outside Jerusalem; it is the announcing of the breaking in of an eschatological kingdom that brings the present world to an end—to an end both in the sense of destroying its corruptions and pretensions and in bringing the divine intentions in creation to completion. Theologian Arthur McGill, attacking overly optimistic approaches to Christian ethics, once said,

> [A] merely ethical approach to the condition of selfishness is completely futile. . . . whether people serve themselves or serve others is not in their power to choose. This is decided wholly in terms of the kind of world they think they live in, in terms of the kind of power they see ruling the roost. The issue lies at the level of the god they worship and not in the kind of person they may want to be. In New Testament terms, they live or die according to the king who holds them and to the kingdom to which they belong.[33]

If it is true that we "live or die according to the king who holds us and the kingdom to which we belong," Easter preachers need to recognize that the task at hand is not simply to announce an event but to proclaim a collision of kingdoms. Hauerwas is concerned that the Bible read in the context of North American culture by people using their "common sense" results inevitably in disfigurement of the politics of Scripture. Just so, it does no good to preach in ways that simply allow the resurrection to become another piece of data absorbed into the single frame of naturalistic materialism. Easter is not a one-off violation of nature, not the idea of Jesus preserved in the memory of his followers, not the wistful vision of mourners longing for their departed beloved teacher. If our hearers are police officers enforcing rigid "laws of the physical universe," then Easter preaching must take the form of civil disobedience. It must raise the limited single-frame of our culture to audibility and imaginative visibility and then proclaim it as a failure of nerve and a lack of faith. Easter sermons should proclaim that the risen Christ has broken in and broken through from another realm to bring life where there is only death. "In Jesus," McGill states, "[people] are saved, not primarily from themselves, but from a whole realm of existence."[34]

33. McGill, *Suffering*, 92.
34. Ibid., 98.

This Easter collision of worldviews and clashing of kingdoms is precisely why many recent scholars, reclaiming the apocalyptic imagery in the Easter accounts, have increasingly spoken of Easter as an invasion. "What God does is invade, not rescue," writes Brian K. Blount, commenting on the Gospel of Mark. He continues,

> In a rescue, the primary objective is the securing of the prisoner/hostage and the subsequent retreat to the closest-held safe zone. . . . Invasion has a different strategic objective: to meet and engage all opposing forces with the aim of creating a safe zone *of the entire occupied region.* The goal is not to snatch and leave; the goal is to crush, conquer, and claim.[35]

The canonical Easter stories have, of course, been through the usual editorial migrations of all other Jesus narratives, but what was never effaced in all their tellings, retellings, and redactions is the underlying sense of astonishment, fear, perplexity, and disbelief that encounters with the risen Christ provoked. Bultmann was right; in a truly mythological world transcendence is translated into immanence. In a mythological world, one hears of the goddess Diana walking through the enchanted Cyprus grove speaking to the deer or of her stilling the winds to keep the Greek fleet from sailing to Troy in the same way as one hears of the adventures of sailors on the sea. One expects enchantment woven into the fabric of ordinary life.

But the resurrection accounts are no such tales. In the risen Christ, something had jutted through the immanent frame, something that summoned amazement, disbelief, and fearful silence. When Paul preached on Mars Hill, the city beneath him was spangled with monuments to the mythological deities. Indeed, Paul's Athenian audience, having heard rumors of his resurrection message, assumed that he was here to propose adding a few more shrines to "foreign divinities" (Acts 17:18), a perfectly reasonable prospect in religiously eclectic Athens. But when they heard of the resurrection, even divinity-saturated Athens could not assimilate the kerygma, and the only available choices were scoffing, a cautious willingness to hear the message again, or conversion (Acts 17:32–34).

Just as Tintarello's painting portrayed the resurrection as the jutting through of a "higher time" into historical time, so Jürgen Moltmann discerns in the "christophanies" of the biblical Easter narratives that this inbreaking of the eternal radiates into the three dimensions of historical time, specifically into all historical tenses: future, past, and present. Easter, says Moltmann, is "prospective" in that Jesus' followers encounter "the crucified Christ as the Living One in the splendor cast ahead by the coming glory of

35. Blount, *Invasion of the Dead*, 90 (emphasis added).

God." It is also "retrospective" in that "they recognized him from the marks of the nails and in the breaking of bread: the One who will come is the One crucified on Golgotha." And it is also "reflexive" in that "they perceived (in the present) their own call to the Apostolate: 'As the father has sent me even so I send you.'"[36]

It is here that we see the import of the claim that Easter involves a bodily resurrection. Critics may scoff at the naïve and literal view of many Christians that the corpse of the dead Jesus was revivified on Easter, that he walked around the earth for forty days, and that he then ascended "up" into heaven, but this naiveté does not stem from the New Testament. There the risen Christ is embodied, but not in the sense of a resuscitated corpse. The risen Christ, like those who will be raised in his power, have what Paul will later describe as a "spiritual body" (1 Cor 15:44), or, perhaps clearer, a "glorified body." This theological notion of embodiment deserves, and has received elsewhere,[37] detailed treatment. For our purposes it is sufficient to point out that a "glorified body" is an expression of the double frame we have been describing. The risen Christ is embodied, but in a way unlike any other body we have experienced. At one and the same time, he is the same Jesus, and not.

The glorified body of the risen Christ is not bound by time, but comes as a gift to those of us in time. It touches our world as a tangent touches a circle, and it shines light, as Moltmann indicated, in every temporal direction. In the resurrection, the past and all earthly history are not escaped in some Gnostic fantasy, but creation, incarnation, and long unfolding of history are brought to completion. The wounds and scars of suffering are still visible, preserved and remembered in the glorified body. The embodied life of Jesus, who healed and taught and prayed and broke bread among us, is validated and gathered into glory. The risen Christ confronts us, confronts all our idolatries and false desires, and calls us to live out the hope of God's coming reign here and now, in the present, and with our own bodies. A Jesus who is raised only in our minds, who is merely some inner illumination, would have no right to ask us to put our bodies on the line. And the risen Christ beckons us still to follow him, follow him toward God's future, when Christ will be all-in-all and our own perishable bodies will put on the imperishable. As Richard Lischer has claimed,

> In a culture obsessed with improvement, preaching speaks an eschatological word. It announces God's open future that has broken into time in Jesus Christ. What a challenge! We preach

36. Moltmann, *Way of Jesus Christ*, 220.

37. See, for example, Rosner, "With What Kind of Body," 190–205.

to people exactly like ourselves—who want a better job, a bigger check, a happier marriage, a slimmer tummy, a longer life, a safer neighborhood, and a better government. But we have been given no word for self-improvement, only this majestic unveiling of a new age begun in Jesus Christ and awaiting consummation.[38]

Robin Meyers argues that for the earliest Christians, Easter was a "luminous apparition" and that stories of an embodied Christ are *ex post facto* inventions that arose only later as the church did battle with Gnosticism. "Remember," he says, "in Mark (the first Gospel) there are no appearance stories at all,"[39] as if the earliest Christians had no use for the bodily resurrection until later orthodoxy was threatened.

Ironically, though, this gospel with no appearance stories may be one of our best homiletical resources for proclaiming the resurrection. New Testament scholar Elizabeth Struthers Malbon has found a number of literary features in Mark's gospel that point to the "ideal reader" as a "re-reader," one who reads the gospel once with only partial understanding and then re-reads (or re-hears) it again and again with deepening comprehension. For example, Mark "opens with a sentence with no verb ('The beginning of the good news of Jesus Christ, the Son of God')." Malbon wonders, "Why would a complete narrative of the story of Jesus be called the *beginning* of the good news? Probably because the narrative is really incomplete, open-ended."[40] The open-endedness of Mark is an invitation to return to the beginning, to re-read the gospel in the light of the startling and unfinished ending. The author of Mark, says Malbon,

> . . . does not expect the disciples to understand the good news of Jesus Christ, Son of God, until it has been fully told, from baptism through resurrection, and fully heard—and heard again. The same expectation applies to the implied reader. Only in the echo is the sound true and clear.[41]

Meyers claims that there are no post-resurrection appearances in Mark, but taking seriously Malbon's view, one could say that there are nothing but post-resurrection appearances in Mark. As New Testament scholar David Bartlett describes it,

38. Lischer, "Interrupted Sermon," 178.
39. Meyers, *Saving Jesus,* 85.
40. Malbon, "Echoes and Foreshadowings," 228.
41. Ibid., 229.

> Readers [of Mark] are being directed to return to the beginning
> of the Gospel, which is set in Galilee, and to read or hear the
> text again knowing that it portrays not just the earthly Jesus but
> the authority of the risen Lord. The Gospel doesn't come to an
> abrupt end at all; it circles us back to the beginning. Every ser-
> mon on Mark, therefore, becomes a sermon on the power of the
> Risen Lord.[42]

So, preachers can themselves re-read Mark's Gospel, this time with a double frame. If we do, we will see there what we saw the first time, namely the earthly Jesus teaching and healing and casting out demons and preach-ing and forgiving sin and calling for all to follow him on the way to the cross. But we will also see what was hidden from our eyes the first time through and concealed from our vision before we traveled the whole way to the empty tomb and heard the stunning proclamation, "Do not be alarmed; you are looking for Jesus of Nazareth, who was crucified. He has been raised; he is not here" (Mark 16:6). As we re-read the gospel, we now see the risen Christ irrupting in the text, jutting through from the eschaton into our world and into our history, bodying forth still in the bodies of those who follow, bodying forth still the hope and glory of God wherever the gospel is preached and the sick are healed and the poor are cared for and the powers and principalities that hold our dying world in thrall are confronted in the power of the Spirit.

Bibliography

Ballentine, Samuel E., ed. *Oxford Encyclopedia of Bible and Theology.* New York: Oxford University Press, 2015.

Barth, Karl. *The Epistle to the Romans.* London: Oxford University Press, 1933.

Bartlett, David. "The Easter Texts: Hope, Comfort, Courage." *Journal for Preachers,* 29.3 (2006) 3–7.

Blount, Brian K. *Invasion of the Dead: Preaching Resurrection.* Louisville, KY: Westminster John Knox, 2014.

Bultmann, Rudolf. *Jesus Christ and Mythology.* New York: Charles Scribner's Sons, 1958.

———. *Kerygma and Myth by Rudolf Bultmann and Five Critics.* New York: Harper, 1961.

Davis, Stephen T. "'Seeing' the Risen Jesus." In *The Resurrection: An Interdisciplinary Symposium on the Ressurection of Jesus,* edited by Stephen Davis, Daniel Kendall, and Gerald O'Collins, 126–47. New York: Oxford University Press, 1997.

D'Costa, Gavin. *Resurrection Reconsidered.* Oxford: One World, 1996.

---

42. Bartlett, "Easter Texts," 7.

Goulder, Michael. "The Baseless Fabric of a Vision." In *Resurrection Reconsidered*, edited by Gavin D'Costa, 48–61. Oxford: One World, 1996.

Hauerwas, Stanley. *Unleashing the Scripture: Freeing the Bible from Captivity to America*. Nashville: Abingdon, 1993.

Jaspers, Karl, and Rudolf Bultmann. *Myth and Christianity: An Inquiry into the Possibility of Religion without Myth*. New York: Prometheus, 2005.

Lischer, Richard. "The Interrupted Sermon." *Interpretation* 50.2 (April 1996) 169–81.

———. "Why I Am Not Persuasive." *Homiletic* 24.2 (1999) 13–16.

McGill, Arthur C. *Suffering: A Test of Theological Method*. Philadelphia: Geneva, 1978.

Malbon, Elizabeth Struthers. "Echoes and Foreshadowings in Mark 4–8: Reading and Rereading." *Journal of Biblical Literature* 112.2 (1993) 211–30.

Meyers, Robin R. *Saving Jesus from the Church: How to Stop Worshiping Christ and Start Following Jesus*. New York: Harper Collins, 2009.

Moltmann, Jürgen. *The Way of Jesus Christ: Christology in Messianic Dimensions*. New York: HarperSanFrancisco, 1990.

Perkins, Pheme. *Resurrection: New Testament Witness and Contemporary Reflection*. Garden City, NY: Doubleday, 1984.

Rosner, Brian S. "With What Kind of Body Do They Come? (1 Corinthians 15:35b): Paul's Conception of Resurrection Bodies." In *The New Testament in Its First-Century Setting: Essays on Context and Background in Honor of B. W. Winter on His 65th Birthday*, edited by P. J. Williams, et al., 190–205. Grand Rapids: Eerdmans, 2004.

Spong, John Shelby. "The Easter Moment: Drawing Conclusions," *Beliefnet*. Online: http://www.beliefnet.com/Faiths/Christianity/2001/04/The-Easter-Moment-Drawing-Conclusions.aspx.

Taylor, Charles. *A Secular Age*. Cambridge, MA: Belknap, 2007.

Vanhoozer, Kevin J. *Remythologizing Theology: Divine Action, Passion, and Authorship*. Cambridge: Cambridge University Press, 2010.

Williams, Rowan. "Between the Cherubim: The Empty Tomb and the Empty Throne." In *Resurrection Reconsidered*, edited by Gavin D'Costa, 87–101. Oxford: One World, 1996.

The Holy Spirit and Preaching

THE WORD THAT MOVES

William C. Turner, Jr.

THIS ESSAY IS WRITTEN in honor of Richard Lischer, one of the foremost homileticians of our time. I use this term "homiletician" in the broadest sense. Lischer is a preacher, par excellence, and a teacher of preaching. He is trained in theology and, one might say, is one of the "father-founders" of the homiletics guild, and more specifically, of homiletics as a theological discipline. Homiletics appropriates disciplines dealing with effective communication, rhetoric, and elocution. But the trunk and taproot for Lischer are the theological disciplines, through which homiletics provides access to knowledge of God as revealed among the people of God.

As such, his work deals not only with the preparation for preaching—the work of interpreting the scriptures, including how the scriptures have been interpreted by the church; attending to systematic and dogmatic matters; and inspecting the world as a site that constitutes the destination of preaching. Beyond that, Lischer has paid keen attention to the way in which the moment of preaching itself is an instance of revelation and a means of *doing* theology.

Nowhere in his work are the gestures inside the preaching moment, which open revelatory space in the mysteries of God, demonstrated or highlighted more clearly than in his intersections with the preaching of the African American church. I am not saying that he himself has privileged these sites, but his work at these sites opens rich troves to mine for bringing into view the interrelationship between the Spirit and preaching. By amplifying his work at these sites and exploring suggested trajectories, I want to draw out the understated pneumatology in Lischer's work.

I shall ever recall a comment I made on a radio show sometime after Lischer's publication of *The Preacher King: Martin Luther King, Jr. and the*

Word That Moved America. Speaking with a radio talk show host in Greensboro, NC, I said, "Only a white man could have written that book." The person doing the interview looked at me in a quizzical manner. I could read his face. He did not understand the comment and perhaps thought I was being prejudicial or racist; so he pressed me to say more. I said to him, "Few black preachers or homileticians I know would have taken the time or expended the energy to write a book like his. So much of what Lischer did by way of technical analysis of King's work is what black preachers take for granted. It is the ether inhaled in the African American church. The way King articulated and delivered is so much taken for granted that one scarcely takes time to either learn or analyze it. Without such work we all would be deprived."

Hardly anyone preaching in African American traditions can be indifferent to the tropes, the patterns, the cadences. Deliberate decisions are made about what not to appropriate, but scarcely can there be indifference. As the ways of preaching that characterize African American preaching slip further into the past, the art form can easily be despised or lost. Or, it can be taken up as mere form to be mimicked without attention to how these cultural productions are fashioned into the body preachers inhabit.

Preaching is words, and yet it is more than words. A word itself is but a collection of alphabet arranged in such a manner as to signify some sound, but unless that sound is known and understood, it is but air that registers in the auditory system of another. It can be as the bard said, "full of sound and fury but signifying nothing."[1]

Preaching is words, and yet it is also more than words. By its very character, preaching evokes response. The response can produce resistance, or the response can motivate positive action. The sound should be certain. Like the note played on a musical instrument, preaching signifies something that is a matter of urgency, something of significance.

Richard Lischer has devoted his life to this task of preaching. A preacher himself of no mean ability, he has found acceptable words. To use the language of the ancient preacher, they are words "like goads."[2] They have changed minds and transformed hearts. They are as nails that fasten together the lives of many who were in need of refashioning. As a "master assemblyman," Lischer has taught the craft to many who undertook to learn it.[3]

In this essay I will go inside the work of Lischer and mine the understated pneumatological implications located in two rich, though easily

1 William Shakespeare, *Macbeth*, 5.5.27–28.

2. Eccl 12:11.

3. Eccl 12:9–11.

overlooked, lodes of his writing: 1) the subtitle of his book that sought to comprehend the preaching of Martin Luther King, Jr., *Martin Luther King, Jr. and the Word that Moved America*; and 2) the "Prayer for the Preacher," from James Weldon Johnson's *God's Trombones*, which serves as the epigraph for Lischer's book, *The Company of Preachers*. In these two lodes one finds the dynamic between Spirit and Word. The Spirit is like the inner coding of the seed of the Word: it gives ". . . seed to the sower and bread to the reaper."[4] Life is within it. This is the Spirit giving body to the Word, releasing the power that is inside. This power is nothing other than divine enablement bringing forth in time, space, and history what is the very mind of God. I am positing pneumatology as the "pneumatic tissue" of preaching.

Understated pneumatology characterizes the West in general. Indeed, the rich dynamic of pneumatology is often simply absorbed in other theological rubrics. Pneumatology is usually more implicit than explicit in Christology, ecclesiology, and the doctrine of the Word. But the Word in preaching is always accompanied by the Spirit. The Word is not reducible to the discrete fractions of auditions from the alphabet; rather it is more like their combination, which includes the spaces between them, the punctuation that interprets them, along with pauses, breaks, and gestures. But even more, the Word also includes tone, gesture, habits of the body. It is the result of all these combinations.

Still, the Word does not stop here; it also implies responses that are prompted when it is heard—whether acceptance or rejection. In all of these dimensions, the Word is accompanied by the Spirit, even when the Spirit is implied and not fully explicated.

Following a discussion of the understated character of pneumatology in homiletics, I will explore the two promising pneumatological lodes in Lischer's work. In each case I will probe through the lens provided by the African American preacher and the world from which that preaching emerges. From this perspective, it will be seen that preaching is speech accompanied by breath. The Word does not go forth void; it accomplishes what it is sent to do.

Understated Pneumatology

Consistently, it is said of pneumatology in the West that it is understated; and yet without it the entire theological project unravels. Whenever there is discussion of "doing preaching," it is always with the Spirit, even when the Spirit is implied and not fully explicated. The Spirit as the "inner motion of

4. Isa 55:10–11.

preaching" is consistent with the Word as "*dabar*"—namely, that it is accompanied by breath and accomplishes what it is sent to do.

One good example of how to make understated pneumatology explicit is Paul Opsahl's edited volume, *The Holy Spirit And The Life of The Church*. His work is a collection of essays by theologians in the Lutheran tradition to make explicit how pneumatology intersects with Christology. The essays trace the doctrine from what is given in the scriptures through the Patristic and Medieval Church and into the Reformation. Specifically, the collection is an effort to address issues posed by the charismatic movement within the Lutheran Church and to show congregations how to live together without the separations of the twentieth century. While showing openness to manifold manifestations, the accent nonetheless remains on preaching and the sacraments. The two sacraments, baptism and eucharist, are presented as the appointed means through which the Spirit works. In every case, the sacraments are accompanied by the preached Word.[5]

Lurking underneath this project is the question of how the Spirit gives body to a word that is spoken—a body of vitality, of motion that has the potential for power. How does one speak intelligibly of the Spirit at this boundary between the invisible and the visible? The description in creation is the very first image. All creation is in a state of "*tehom*"—without form, and void—until the hovering, brooding work of the Spirit (*ruach*) is performed. Only then is there the response of the creative word, ". . . Let there be . . ."[6]

The Spirit here shapes the inner motions of creation, without which there is no visibility coming forth, no observable performance. It is like the surges within matter that distinguish that which is inert from matter that possesses "*erga*"—energy: the enzyme, the capacity for growth, for fructification, exfoliation, reproduction.

In speaking of the Spirit one is not afforded the visual images as is the case with the first and second Trinitarian persons—namely, the Father and the Son. In one sense this is quite good. An overreliance on social roles can cause one to slip into great error concerning the divine persons. Nowhere is this problem more egregious than with the ancient presbyter, Arius, who seized upon the social roles that could be implied in the names Father and Son. By proceeding as he did, he inserted rank and temporality into his discourse. From roles that can be observed within human communities one

---

5. Opsahl, ed., *Holy And The Life*, 223ff. Other helpful texts that make pneumatology more explicit include Congar, *I Believe in the Holy Spirit*; Welker, *The Holy Spirit, Flame of Fire*; Macchia, *Baptized in the Spirit: A Global Pentecostal Theology*; Marshall, *Joining the Dance: A Theology of the Spirit*; Pinnock, *Flame of Love: A Theology of the Holy Spirit*.

6. Gen 1:1–3.

sees quite clearly that fathers rank above sons in matters of longevity and power. This led him to the erroneous conclusion that there was a time when there was no Son. But alas, the insertion of temporality in the life of God is the very seed for undermining confession of the Spirit's deity.[7]

Again, as feminist and womanist critique ably shows, overreliance on historical anchors can perpetuate the error in another direction. God as patriarch is quite different from God as Father (Abba) of the Lord Jesus. With pneumatology we have no such "problematic help" through the implications of a social role.[8]

Pneumatology takes the collection of Scriptural images and internal motions and fashions a discourse having its own logic. But this logic is utterly consistent with what we are to know about God. With the Spirit we are forced to attend ever so closely to the data that is given. Always, we remain within the realm of mystery—the boundary between the visible and the invisible. But this boundary is precisely where the Word has its effective motion. Accordingly, one is on much safer ground in speaking of the Spirit with images of vitality. The Spirit ever and always is about vitality, consistent with the confession that the Spirit is the Lord and giver of life. In this vital movement we find and follow this divine person.[9]

Whether it is with the creation, the breathing of life into Adam, or the formation of Israel at the foot of Sinai, what is at stake is some form that is inert and without consequence apart from the Spirit. Worse, without the Spirit the consequences can be utterly devastating. Jeremiah illustrated this devastating consequence when he charged Israel with forsaking the fountain of living water in exchange for brackish, broken cisterns that could hold no water. Likewise, the prophet Isaiah stressed the vital necessity of the Spirit, comparing the Spirit to streams that refreshed the land, making it fruitful and vibrant. Amos made the explicit reference to the Spirit as *mispat* (justice), flowing as an ever-living stream.[10]

7. The unsurpassed ancient treatise on the matter of pneumatology is Saint Basil The Great, *On the Holy Spirit*. He summarizes Cappadocian reflection that confuted ancient heresies denying the deity of the Spirit in the wake of the Arian controversy.

8. More is given on this matter in Elizabeth Johnson's work on the Trinity in her volume, *She Who Is*. Also, see the work of Sarah Coakley for how pneumatology looks without the lens of masculine and patriarchal biases. Studies like Valerie Cooper's *Word, Like Fire,* and Estrelda Alexander's *Black Fire* fasten on black women preachers who made explicit claims about the Spirit for their authority also help put tissue on the argument.

9. This approach to pneumatology expressly does not distinguish between the so-called dynamic and psychological metaphors. Rather, it follows a pattern like the one seen in George Montague, *The Holy Spirit: The Growth of a Biblical Tradition*. Montague mines the full range of texts and images.

10. Jer 2:13; Isa 32:15; Amos 5:24.

For Ezekiel the Spirit was like wind that moved through a valley of dry bones to reconnect them, resurrect them, and put flesh and sinew upon them as an image of God restoring Israel.[11] Positioned at the very boundary between where life is and is not, one sees the work of the Spirit that testifies to its very nature. The Word spoken in the Spirit's power is vital—it *moves*.

Lischer takes up preaching in the black church tradition as an instance of the Spirit fashioning and inhabiting encultured African American bodies to produce life-giving motions within the church and the larger culture. A "pneumatological lens" is afforded by the African American preacher and the world from which that preaching comes through the fleeting reference made to the "nommo" in the book, *The Preacher King*. The subtitle makes it plain that preaching "moved" America.[12]

The Word that Moved America

In King's preaching, as Lischer highlights, one is struck from the outset with this sense of the importance of power manifested in motion. What is brought into view is not mere rhetoric, not empty sound. This is not to diminish the beauty of King's oratory or the compelling nature of the analysis. But more was at stake. A surplus of meaning and content was present. It is not to be taken lightly that in King we have one who understood himself first and foremost as a Christian preacher. Nor should it go unstated that of all who dared to lift up and interpret this figure none before or after Lischer has so effectively taken seriously the power of preaching in the man named King. True, the work King did necessarily required organization, administration, strategizing, and coalition building. The enduring legacy has been translated into legislation and the election of persons to political office. Still, breaking the inertia of the times was the first moment. And in this moment it was the Word that moved.

King comprehended that what he was up against was more than bigotry, deeper than hatred, and more resistant than cultural norms. True, these maladies and many more were present. The wealth of a nation had been derived from the backs of slaves. A war had been fought to keep the patterns ensconced. The taproot, however, had to do with claims that were made about God. The deep and persistent question was whether or not persons of

11. Ezek 37.

12. Lischer makes explicit reference to "nommo" (also spelled "nummo") to account for ". . . the spoken word whose rhythms and prolific powers reflected those of nature itself." Here he is accounting for the submersion of King in the world of Afro-Christian preaching. See *Preacher King*, 39.

dusky hue were made in the divine image. One can see King's exploration of this inner spiritual world in strands of his preaching. This world gave rise to a set of values that could not be dislodged by reason alone.[13]

King knew that the power of the Word is more than rhetoric—more than the power of persuasive speech. In King's case the Word was spoken in public space—in the marketplace where issues of the nation and the world are adjudicated. In this space preaching required words that take residence in the pneumatic tissue supplied by the Spirit. The Word of preaching, King knew, gives life; it is ever to be a Word that moves. With King we are in the company of those who were clear about this matter.

As Lischer explicitly notes, the Word, in this sense, is characterized as *nommo* and has roots in the Dogon people of West Africa. With *nommo* we are not talking simply about striking the memory. The *nommo* or *nummo* situates one in a view of the world that gives explicit and detailed attention to the innermost motions of life. The *nummo* spirits were two homogenous products of god and developed in the womb of the earth. They were a pair and formed the substance of the life-force of the world, supplying all motion. This force, present within water, torrents, and storms, made creation possible. This pair excreted life, minerals, and the fibers inside plants. The account of their existence is an extensive excursion into the connectivity and inward consistency of the world that becomes visible.[14]

Marcel Griaule, the anthropologist who studied the Dogon, approached his work with the presupposition that he was considering the most primitive people of West Africa—savages and barbarians, if you will. After listening to the blind hunter Ogotemmeli who, after losing his sight, devoted himself to long and careful study, Griaule found a custodian whose knowledge was vast. As Griaule says of the Dogon, ". . . these people lived by a cosmogony, a metaphysic, and a religion which put them on par with the peoples of antiquity, and which Christian theology might indeed study with profit."[15]

I am not claiming that Lischer or King intentionally drew upon West African ontology. Nor am I suggesting some form of syncretism. Rather, I am claiming that a glimpse into the world that comprehends inward motions is crucial to the pneumatological project and might assist in describing how the work of preaching has the power to move.

13. King's understanding of racism was sobered both by his experiences in the south and north and by works like George Kelsey's *Racism and the Christian Understanding of Man*, and Howard Thurman's *Jesus and the Disinherited*.

14. Griaule, *Conversations with Ogotemmeli*, 16–23.

15. Ibid., 2.

We are not dealing exclusively with the rational faculty. No, it is more like dealing with the whole person. It is the domain that is underneath conscious reality, but that also implies saturation. The cultural inertia King sought to counter was a construction of the world that rested on a false ontology. Superior and inferior status were implied by skin color, hair texture, facial angle, and size of the cranial cavity. Texts were written to declare that of the four options the Negro must be a "beast," since he was neither fish, nor fowl, and to be human meant to be white.[16]

King understood that this false ontology required him to engage with enormous powers. Against these powers, rhetoric alone was insufficient. King, of course, did not despise rhetoric. He made powerful use of it, as Lischer amply shows. But he spoke not only from the pulpit, but also in the public marketplace where the issues of the nation and the world were being adjudicated. And he understood the enormity of the challenge. Using the language of the scriptures so prominently, refracted through the African American church, King was clear that the struggle was not against flesh and blood. It was against principalities and powers.[17] In sum, the disposition was, "Satan, we're going to tear your kingdom down." And something more than rhetoric is required for that challenge. King's preaching had to perform the work of deliverance from spiritual and physical bondage.[18] And for that calling the very Spirit of God must give vitality to a Word that *moves*.

Pneumatology and the Deacon's Prayer

The second lode worth mining is the Deacon's Prayer in James Weldon Johnson's *God's Trombones*, which serves as the epigraph for Lischer's *The Company of Preachers*. That prayer is a signification on preaching. Through the prayer one is pressed to know the nature of God's work in the life of the preacher. This work may be without the preacher's consent, even though one says he or she belongs to God in a special and unique way because of the calling.

The power of King's words to move a nation can be viewed with even greater clarity when set against the backdrop of the deacon's prayer for the

16. Such twisted reasoning supposedly was extracted from the scripture in 1 Cor 15:39. See Smith, *In His Image*.

17. Eph 6:12.

18. One can credit the work of Walter Wink with reinserting language of the powers into contemporary New Testament scholarship; Wink could find no other adequate account for the inertia he encountered during his involvement in civil rights campaigns led by King.

preacher. This prayer is a "membrane" over the pneumatology that is inherent in the theology of preaching known implicitly by this deacon. In this prayer the deacon demonstrates a sense of what preaching performs:

> And now, O Lord, this man of God, who breaks the bread of life this morning—
>
> Shadow him in the hollow of thy hand, and keep him out of the gunshot of the devil.
>
> Take him—this morning—
>
> Wash him with hyssop inside and without,
>
> Hang him and drain him dry of sin.
>
> Pin his ear to the wisdom post, and make his words sledgehammers of truth— beating against the iron heart of sin.
>
> Lord, God, this morning—
>
> Put his eye to the telescope of eternity,
>
> And let him look upon the paper walls of time.
>
> Lord, turpentine his imagination,
>
> Put perpetual motion in his arms,
>
> Fill him full with the dynamite of thy power,
>
> Anoint him all over with the oil of thy Salvation and set his tongue on fire.[19]

This prayer sets the preaching of any age within the perspective of the preaching of every age. It goes to the root—the heart and soul—of what preaching is, what it does, by putting tissue—body, if you will—on words that have been spoken in countless generations. One might say the Deacon's prayer is like a "poetic preamble" to what follows in *The Company of Preachers*. The setting of *God's Trombones* shows clearly that the divine assistance being requested is with the preacher's consent, although it may be going far beyond what she knows how to petition.

What is prayed for in the preaching moment discloses what is believed about preaching. In a serious way we can talk about this prayer as thick with images and having a vector intersecting modalities of beauty and pulsation. The prayer pulls open the work of preaching through images. But more, its presence and powerful operation hinge on prayer as petition and not demand. Preaching is a gift of God in favor of the people. As such it is not the property of the preacher. It is present within her or him only in the state of humility. A sign of that humility is that the preacher is prayed for by the deacon, who is the servant of the people, as well as the servant of God.

19. Lischer, *Company*, xvii, xviii.

Preaching is not a possession or a commodity to be bought or sold. It is not to be used for personal gain or even as warrant for lording over the people. Rather, it operates through acts of obedience to God in order to bless God's people.

The pneumatological implications of the prayer are manifold. One might even go so far as to say the prayer peels off the membrane and gives utterance to the Spirit's work. The preacher is portrayed as an oracle of God, immersed in divine effluvium. This is an immersion into the world of the Bible, the world of the Spirit—a world in which God is present and active, in spite of what appears on the scenes of human history.

One might say that making pneumatology explicit and preaching the Word are quite similar. They both look inside a text and context for meaning and insight that are present in forms, and they both peer under membranes not accessible to an eye that is limited by critical exegetical exercises. Such exegetical discourses and methods are designed to dominate the text, to cherish only "findings"; they often neither recognize nor appreciate gifts in the form of mysteries. But knowledge as revelation is *received* more than found.

Another way of articulating this approach is to use an expression I heard from a woman talking on the phone to a friend about another woman who, underestimating the keenness of her wit, was trying to outtalk her. She said: "I can look into the rock as far as she can pick." Seeing what is in the rock corresponds with what Charles Long calls "lithic imagination." This is where one pierces into the density of the "*lithos*" (rock) and brings out from its opacity what cannot be found by light reading or even probing.[20] One cannot set a limit as to how far one might go. Rather, what is at stake is continuing to probe, search, and to open oneself to the possibility of what might be received.

The work of the Spirit is implied throughout the Deacon's Prayer. The deacon, in a plea for protection, asks for a shadowing work in the hollow of God's hand. The prayer acknowledges that the word of preaching must be done in a danger zone, in the midst of those who might refuse what has to be said—scoffers, pretenders, or those with a contrary word who would position themselves in opposition. Unbelievers could be rife with fault to find. It must be remembered that during the time of this praying some might well be present to watch for an incendiary word. A prophetic word not in support of prevailing structures likewise would be a threat. So there was prayer for protection.

20. Long, *Significations*.

Overshadowing is reminiscent of the protection supplied to Moses by Yahweh on the mountain. He requested to see the face of God and was told that no one could see God's face and live. A similar overshadowing takes place on Mt. Tabor where Jesus is transfigured. It is a response to the disciples' request to build a tabernacle for Jesus, along with Moses and Elijah. The overshadowing is like a divine canopy.[21]

Along with protection, there is prayer for the purging of the preacher. A sanctifying work is sought so there will be no impediment. No discrepancy is to be left between the preacher's life and the preacher's message. Hence the petition for washing with hyssop. This is reminiscent of Psalm 51 where the petition to God is not only that the petitioner be purged, but that the Spirit not be removed. Instead, what is to be removed is any impediment to the gospel.

These powerful images in the prayer depict the servant of the Lord as one set apart and not to be mistaken. Accordingly, what was spoken would not be regarded as mere vocalization. Rather, the utterance was understood as being with power. Use was made of words, but they signified far more than that. This rich image communicates the awareness of a surplus that attends the auditions of one who speaks for God. As with the prophets, these words were so authorized as not to be withdrawn. No, these words went forth to perform with powerful accompanying speech.

By the Spirit the preacher was expected to have knowledge beyond that of the ordinary believer. This would be akin to a word of wisdom. It was to be received through the ear. The image of the wisdom post is the visualization of how such wisdom was imparted. The result would be to make the Word a sledgehammer that beat against the iron heart. What we have here is reminiscent of Jeremiah's claim that God's word breaks the rock in pieces.[22] The image here is of crushing power to reduce a solid rock into granules or even powder. Such effective power was needed for stubbornness, if it was perceived to be present in the people to whom preaching was given. But it also had reference to those who had opposition and would resist the voice of God.

The intensification of divine knowledge came through putting the eye to the telescope of eternity, looking on the paper walls of time. This goes beyond prescribed scripts and approved discourses. Such knowledge could narrate the fortunes of the people as God saw them, and enable them to see themselves as more than what was said of them. It is a similar case with the turpentining of the imagination: what is evoked might be compared to the

21. See Exod 33:17–23; Matt 17:5.
22. Jer 23.

Spirit performing like a resin that thins and loosens to distinguish between the Word of the Lord and the word of the land.

Finally, there is the prayer for the Spirit to take full control of the preacher. Here one sees the epiclesis in complete form.[23] The sense then may be of releasing the tongue from any thickness or stammering that might prevent intelligible speech. This would be consistent with the view that preaching is to be understood. The correctness of what was spoken was never to exceed clarity and plainness. The vernacular of the people was important. One might say that a premium was being placed on preaching as power to move, to lift, to change sullen dispositions, to create or enhance an attitude—a space, a *topos*—that resembled more authentically the world as God ordained it, and the world as it will be known when God's kingdom comes. A "turpentine imagination" renders the world as God views it, accessible by the Spirit, to the one who hears and believes—even if only for the moments of worship and ecstasy.

Lischer writes of preaching in this mode:

> Martin Luther King was the product of a preaching tradition that valued originality of effect above originality of composition. The United States is honeycombed with little clapboard Holiness and Baptist churches whose part-time preachers are the last folk poets in the land. They are black and white, literate and semiliterate, rural and urban, at home in the mining towns of Appalachia or the storefront churches of Atlanta. What they have in common is the process of apprenticeship to master preachers and the immediacy of the Spirit's power that inspires their words and moves their congregations. Most of these preachers speak the first part of their sermons, but their real power comes from the rhythmic chant with which they intone the main body and climax. They all religiously depend on the Holy Spirit but, just beneath and behind the Spirit, they celebrate an array of their own rhetorical skills. These include a prodigious memory in which they store thematic set pieces that they have "almost" memorized, the Spirit-given freedom to create new thematic sections on their feet, and the inspired gift of doing it all in poetic meter.[24]

Like the accompanying gifts of tongues and interpretation, this charism of speech would allow the preacher to speak in the idiom of the people so

23. Epiclesis is a prayer that calls down the Spirit. The prayer offers clarity concerning who performs the work. It is the Spirit of God, not the human person, no matter what the excellency of the gift.

24. Lischer, *Preacher King*, 114.

they might understand what was being said. Even if understanding were not achieved, there could be an even deeper resonance with the truth as "deep calls to deep." One can see this cooperation present in the companionship between Moses and Aaron. Moses claimed to be slow of speech and not gifted with utterance, but God promised to be with his mouth. In addition, God gave Aaron as his prophet to stand beside him and to be his interpreter when needed.

The oil of anointing recalls the saturation that gave copious covering to the priest of God.[25] Included in the mixture were spices (cinnamon, cassia, and aromatic cane). A pungent scent was left as a mark that could not be mistakable. The scene from Psalm 133 describes it as being poured on the head of the priest, descending to the skirt of the garment. The fragrance was a sign of the Spirit that set apart a prophet, a priest, or a king.

The Deacon's Prayer is thus like a pneumatological performance that could be called the first act of the preaching moment. The petition is for God to hang the preacher up, to drain him dry. This is a petition for the exhaustion of the preacher in the work that is given. Nothing was to be withheld in the preaching moment. What we have is not a picture of cool composure or self-control. Rather, it is an image of one who steps outside self.

In that ecstatic state, the preacher was not his own. Neither were the words to be merely his own. The preacher was not in control of the moment—to start and stop when he or she pleased. Indeed, to move the people, the preacher must first be moved. Priority was placed on a presentation that would persuade the people so they know that what they have heard is from God.

The Spirit and the Nurturing Word: Johnson's Mammy

The treasure chest of African American preaching opens many paths for connecting to this seminal image of the Spirit. The first is the Spirit's hovering over the chaos (*tehom*) during the creation. But that hovering takes on another form in the creation of Adam from the dust of the earth, where divine breath is blown into the lifeless form. There is perhaps no image more evocative of this life-giving moment than the poet's positioning of this Great God ". . . toiling over a lump of clay, and breathing in the breath of life."[26] Although there is no explicit reference to the creation of Adam in Lischer's work, the issue is in the treasure chest of African American preaching to

25. Its composition is detailed in Exodus 28.

26. Johnson, *God's Trombones*, 20.

which he gestures with the prayer from *God's Trombones*, as well as in the connection of King to that tradition.

In the larger work of Johnson, this God is depicted as a "mammy bending over her baby."[27] Through this image we can envision God the Spirit giving life. But even more, here we see God toiling with patience and tenderness. This image opens wide how the Spirit's nurture and guidance supply God's care for the world.

Here we see the tenderness, the toiling of God, in maternal images through which one can view both the nurture and guidance that exemplifies care for the world in preaching. The proverbial insult is God portrayed as a "mammy bending over her baby," breathing in the breath of life to turn dirt into a creature in the divine image. The institution of the black mammy suggests the prospect of the life-less creature, so helpless, being turned over to her custody. Here we have a poignant image of the way all human life is animated, incubated, and nurtured in its most vulnerable states.

There may be no image that presses more deeply into the mystery of the Spirit's work in fashioning and refashioning the creature. This is so whether one speaks physically or spiritually. Put another way, whether we are speaking of the creation of Adam as the human creature coming forth from the earth at the hand of God, or of Adam as the new creation in Christ, the interior or maternal work performed inwardly by the Spirit is without substitute.

Johnson presents the image of God as "mother" (mammy) bending over her baby, toiling over a lump of clay, into which "she" breathes the breath of life. Here is the penetration of the dirt by the breath (*ruach*) from which all life comes. In this nascent moment we are taken to the very boundary: before this breath there is no life; after it life abounds. Where there is life we find the Spirit bringing forth from nothing, bringing the visible from the invisible. These deep interior motions correspond to the vitality of the amniotic sac. There is correspondence between the womb and the bosom of God.

Johnson's bold and daring depiction corresponds to the image of Woman Wisdom in Prov 8:22–36. Theologian Donald Gelpi likens the Spirit to "Holy Breath." In this regard Gelpi's lead is a good one to follow, if not entirely.[28] Indeed, he is following the lead of early interpreters of the faith into the deep troves of the church to make explicit the connection with this Woman Wisdom who was with God in the beginning of God's works. To go a step further, one might even posit the Spirit "possessing" a woman walk-

27. Ibid.
28. Gelpi, *Divine Mother*, 9, 26, 45, 58, 215–18.

ing the streets, navigating the ways of life and death. Gelpi joins with others who bemoan the under-development of pneumatology in the West as one of the chief causes for atheism. He intimates that a pneumatology that explores the implications of feminine gender images does more adequate work than one that ignores these images.[29]

The image Gelpi most prefers is that of breath, as seen in Gen 2:7. This breath is the inner motion on the order of what is present in the incarnation of the Son. The body of obedience for the Son is fashioned in the womb of Mary. This work of the Spirit in incarnation is the paradigm for new life in Christ. In the New Adam believers are refashioned in the image of God and translated into the kingdom of the dear son. As in the womb of Mary, the Spirit causes Christ to dwell in the heart. The life we live is through faith in the Son of God who loved and gave himself for us. The Spirit as creator of the church fashions the body of Christ in the world.[30]

This begs the question: is this image of God as mammy a scandal, or is it an insight filled with revelation? It is scandal if the range of images that can be embraced is circumscribed by the literalization of God the Father as male—patriarch, monarch, master, Greek god, or powerful man. However, it is no greater scandal than that of the incarnation—namely, how the Spirit fashioned the womb of a teenage girl into a body of obedience and made of her the "mother of the Lord."

As a scandal that parallels the incarnation, such an hypostasization of God as "mammy" can reveal new insights into how God is source, giver of life, nourisher. Indeed, the image gives "tissue"—pneumatic substance—to ministries like preaching, healing, renewing, refreshing, filling, and comforting. There is a correspondence between God the Heavenly Abba who behaves toward the creation like a divine mother.

What we see through this image is the personification of wisdom as divine companion. While some take this Wisdom-Woman figure as proto-Christological, the range of reality that is opened may serve pneumatology better. The accent is on the inner motion that is more like circulation. It is movement that of its nature is choreographed and not random. Not set on

---

29. See Cooper, *Word Like Fire*; Higginbotham, *Righteous Discontent*; and Alexander, *Black Fire*. The ministry of Sojourner Truth is a case in point. Her name was Isabella Baumfree, and she travelled the land to cry out against slavery and the subjugation of women. She changed her name to signify her calling as she knew it. Her obsession was with the truth. From the streets of Durham the story is told of Mother Golda Brown who walked the streets, and said to anyone she encountered: "The Spirit of the Lord told me to tell you that Jesus is soon to come." Another woman who dressed in white was known as Heavenly Light. She wore white, never wore shoes, and went to any church she desired. She was never attacked or assaulted.

30. 1 Cor 12:12–14.

a course that yields collision, the searching is of the deep things of God. Existence is in another, where the exchange is mutual, as opposed to existence that is independent.

As with living water and subterranean springs, the Spirit is like the current inside the stream. There is inner consistency manifest in outward phenomena. Dew that saturates, mist coming up from the ground, vectors in the wind, combustion in fire, lumens in light are perduring marks and manifestations. As with vine, branch, and sap, the transitive properties pass over into and are received without substance being diminished. The Spirit can be manifest in the form that is entered. Such images are utterly consistent with tenderness and consolation. For one can then see how the life of God is communicated not only through formal command, but through inspiration and all grace-filled exchanges of energy, vitality, and power.

Speaking more specifically of preaching, one is hereby given a universe that is not limited to discursive speech for probing into the depths of the mystery that is participation in the very life of God. The Word is Spirit and life; the Word can dwell in the hearer richly. The Word sanctifies. It does not return void. Rather, it performs what it is sent to accomplish.

What one sees is the Spirit being with the Father from the beginning of God's ways—from eternity. In this image we see the Spirit as "eternal." But also, we see through this accent on Woman Wisdom the work of guiding, keeping from the path of destruction, the way that leads to endless despair. In this Wise Woman we see direction that is indispensable, but that can be obtained only where it is appointed, operating through the Spirit.

Pneumatology and Preaching

The lack of pneumatology in many formal accounts of preaching is notable. Yet the Spirit is the source of authority, especially when authority is not phallic. What is the authority for the Word that is spoken, and what shape does that Word take when it is subversive? What of a Word that moves and operates from underneath—disrupting, ungluing? I am speaking here of an undermining that unmasks where strands of phallic life come together, exposing the performance of race, class, and gendered reality. Here the Spirit is the transgressor of boundaries of every sort. Indeed, this is the deepest meaning of baptism as carrying one into the life of Christ and into the life of the other who likewise is a believer.[31]

Whether the view is that of the Spirit brooding over the *tehom* in creation, the Spirit penetrating the dirt from which all life comes, or the dirt of

---

31. Gal 3:28.

the womb, there is saturation with vitality. Once again, we are at the point where life is at its very boundary. Here we find the Spirit bringing forth the visible from the invisible. Moving within the *tehom*, or working within the amniotic sac, there is correspondence here between womb and bosom—deep interior motions from which life flows, to which life can be traced.

The axis between Christology and pneumatology is "the very axis of life." Here one finds the unsurpassed vital moment of bringing forth the visible from the invisible—where the visible is rooted in the invisible. This is the very intersection in which the church is birthed. The locus is consistent with the narrative that is the very content of preaching. Consistently the marker of this intersection is enmeshed in mysteries—like creation, incarnation, liberation, and transfiguration of the world as the home of God.

In the incarnation the word became flesh. The Spirit supplied the body for the Son's obedience. One sees this obedience in Mary who submits at the word of the angel.[32] Mary's obedience is likened to that of the preacher of righteousness in Psalm 40. The word spoken to guide and declare the righteousness of God took visible form in the Son.[33] However, this obedience was performed in a body of flesh. It came forth as preaching, teaching, and manifestation of power. It was consummated in death and resurrection. That same ministry is bequeathed to every believer who is fashioned by the Spirit into a body of obedience. With true obedience Christ dwells in the heart by faith in the Son of God.

In preaching the Spirit takes hold of human words and fashions them into words of life. These words plant faith in the heart and enable the good confession. They are words in which Christ is present to forgive and heal. They are words that give and encourage life. As such they possess spiritual tissue. They have power to move. The movements are inward, and they work toward outward motions. They possess power that is not wedded to magistrates. They well may confront the powers and transform them.

One can see in this tension how preaching and even pneumatology become excessively phallic when wedded too tightly to structures of authority, and in a manner that silences the voice of the woman or of others not perceived to be persons of power. Here I am pointing to the "unphallicized dimension of the Spirit." I am not saying that utterance is permitted to declare falsehood or defy rational discourse. Instead, I am affirming that the Spirit possesses a logic that is consistent with the very life of God. Put

32. Luke 1:35–38, 42, 43.
33. See the parallel in Heb 10:5 to Ps 40:7–10.

another way, preaching that is only rational cannot bear the weight of a word that moves.[34]

Indeed, within preaching there is the power to confront historical and scientific knowledges that are positioned against the gospel of God, which in essence is good news to the poor. One sees the performance of such preaching in the Old Testament prophets in their defiance of kings, priests, and sanctioned prophets, in their appropriation of poetry, drama, and metaphors. One sees it in the Lord Jesus where the miracle accompanied the message. One sees it in those sent out by the Lord, but not without the Spirit's power. The life of God is communicated not only through formal command, but through inspiration.

This extends beyond utterance that is only linear, rational discourse—fitting only patterns that are logical. Sermons that are only rational cannot bear the weight of preaching that moves. Such sermons are aimed at those possessing a structure that is accessible to those tutored in historical and scientific knowledges. This is the standpoint that dis-privileges the image, the metaphor—poetry, drama—often the very features of prophetic utterance. Jeremiah, for instance, prophesied with the sign of the soiled loin cloth. Isaiah discarded his clothes entirely and traversed the streets of the city with a yoke about his neck. Ezekiel cooked cakes with dung during his dramatic siege of the city. Such preaching moves beyond the linear and the rational to the mysterious and transformative movement of the Spirit.

When all is said and done, what we have in preaching is power that is consistent with the Spirit. The good confession is that the Spirit is the Lord and Giver of Life who proceeds from the Father (and the Son), who with the Father and Son is worshipped and glorified, who spoke by the prophets. Procession is movement. Like the blood that proceeded from the side of the lamb slain from the foundation of the world, the Spirit supplies the power to restore communion with God through Christ. Like the water that proceeds from under the throne in the New Jerusalem, there is power in the Spirit to heal the land and restore Eden. Only by the Spirit can there be transfiguration of the world as the home of God. It is a worthy project to explore the word that moves.

Bibliography

Alexander, Estrelda Y. *Black Fire: One Hundred Years of African American Pentecostalism.* Westmont, IL: InterVarsity Academic, 2011.

Congar, Yves. *I Believe in the Holy Spirit.* New York: Crossroad, 1997.

34. See Loder, *Logic of the Spirit.*

Cooper, Valerie C. *Word Like Fire: Maria Stewart, the Bible, and the Rights of African Americans*. Charlottesville: University of Virginia Press, 2012.

Gelpi, Donald L. *The Divine Mother: A Trinitarian Theology of the Holy Spirit*. Lanham, MD: University Press of America, 1984.

Griaule, Marcel. *Conversations with Ogotemmêli; an introduction to Dogon religious ideas*. London: Published for the International African Institute by the Oxford University Press, 1965.

Higgenbotham, Evelyn Brooks. *Righteous Discontent: The Women's Movement in the Black Baptist Church, 1880–1920*. Cambridge: Harvard University Press, 1994.

Johnson, Elizabeth. *She Who Is: The Mystery of God in Feminist Theological Discourse*. New York: Crossroad, 1992.

Johnson, James Weldon. *God's Trombones: Seven Negro Sermons in Verse*. New York: The Viking, 1927.

Lischer, Richard, ed. *The Company of Preachers: Wisdom on Preaching, Augustine to the Present*. Grand Rapids: Eerdmans, 2002.

———. *The Preacher King: Martin Luther King Jr. and The Word That Moved America*. New York: Oxford University Press, 1995.

Loder, James E., Jr. *The Logic of the Spirit: Human Development in Theological Perspective*. San Francisco: Jossey-Bass, 1998.

Long, Charles H. *Significations: Signs, Symbols, and Images in the Interpretation of Religion*. Aurora, CO: Davies Group, 1999.

Macchia, Frank D. *Baptized in the Spirit: A Global Pentecostal Theology*. Grand Rapids: Zondervan, 2006.

Marshall, Molly Truman. *Joining the Dance: A Theology of the Spirit*. King of Prussia, PA: Judson, 2003.

Opsahl, Paul D., ed. *The Holy in The Life of The Church: From Biblical Times to the Present*. 1978. Reprint, Eugene, OR: Wipf and Stock, 2001.

Pinnock, Clark H. *Flame of Love: A Theology of the Holy Spirit*. Westmont, IL: InterVarsity, 1999.

Smith, H. Shelton. *In His Image, but: Racism in Southern Religion, 1780–1910*. Durham, NC: Duke University Press, 1972.

Welker, Michael. *God the Spirit*. Translated by John F. Hoffmeyer. 1994. Reprint, Eugene, OR: Wipf and Stock, 2013.

The Promise of Law and Gospel

PREACHING WITH "UNCLIPPED WINGS"

Michael Pasquarello III

THIS ESSAY IS CONTRIBUTED with gratitude and in honor of Richard Lischer; teacher, mentor, and friend. My hope is that it may serve as a modest attempt at glossing one of Lischer's theologically insightful and practically challenging claims concerning preaching in our time:

> A vocation puts an end to you in order to disclose your true end
> ... Their call [of preachers] is marked by the grief of loss and the
> inexpressible joy of knowing that God wants them to speak ...
> For preachers, as for all Christians, the journey from death to
> prophecy begins in baptism. Those who are baptized into Christ
> are baptized into his death, buried with him, so that just as he
> was raised from the dead, we too might walk and talk—in new-
> ness of life. Our call follows the curve of his call.[1]

This eloquent description of our homiletic vocation is what we have come to expect from Richard Lischer. He has filled the offices of theologian, preacher, and teacher of preachers with a vocational integrity that has lent depth and wisdom to his life and work.

My initial introduction to Lischer's work was through *A Theology of Preaching* in which he identified theology as the most appropriate ground for preaching; theology as both doctrinal interpretation and theology as a personal quality, or *habitus,* of spiritual life and wisdom.[2] I am interested in the particular section of this book entitled "How Law and Gospel Work in Preaching," especially Lischer's description of law and gospel as "two tones" experienced by Christians with the gospel. "It is like listening to a bassoon

---

1. Lischer, *End of Words*, 31–32.

2. Lischer, *Theology of Preaching*, ix–x.

and a flute playing the same note," and he continues, "The fluidity of law and gospel points more to a method of listening than a doctrine."[3]

An important key to preaching law and gospel as promise is not only distinguishing their difference but also discerning their correlation, with a primary reality of their dialectical relation being death and resurrection. "Christian preaching follows the dialectic in its offer of human wholeness in which the identity of the old sinful, defeated person is put to death, and yet preserved and taken up into a new reality of life, forgiveness, and victory."[4] My aim is this essay is to revisit the dialect of law/gospel, death/resurrection as a promising way of discerning the vocation of preaching in the life of the church. It is worth noting, moreover, that law/gospel and death/resurrection are not what most popular books on preaching have encouraged pastors to consider as essential for their work during Richard Lischer's career.

In *The Great Giveaway*, David Fitch argues that evangelistic strategies designed to attract "seekers" or "the unchurched" tend to craft appealing presentations for drawing in the individual to hear a message that is intentionally kept simple, professionally produced, and entertainingly attractive by appealing to one's "felt needs." In addition, these strategies do not shy away from marketing programs that use self-fulfillment and novelty to present the gospel as personally beneficial, professional, and successful.

Fitch concludes that while this approach has proven effective for attracting large numbers of people, it also initiates seekers into a Christianity that forms them to be self-seeking. He describes this approach as tending toward "making the church into a mall where you get saved and then use the church to take care of all the needs a Christian might have."[5] In other words, Christians are trained to be consumers of Christianity and God. As Fitch points out, this presumably successful method may also make it very difficult, if not impossible, to expect such consumerist Christians to take up the cross in following the way of Jesus Christ (i.e., law/gospel, death/resurrection) since this would comprise a kind of "bait and switch" in the middle of the game.[6]

A survey of sermons at one of the largest most influential churches in North America shows an assortment of topics that follow a pattern of providing practical messages for consumption and use: adjusting to having children, marriage, jobs, apathy, abortion, debt, drugs, competition, boundaries, not measuring up, repetition, sloppiness, lust, anger, being passed by,

3. Ibid., 30.
4. Ibid., 31.
5. Fitch, *Great Giveaway,* 54.
6. Ibid., 54–55.

a spouse having an affair, growing older, and racism.[7] Christian Smith describes this use of the Bible in preaching as the "Handbook Model."

> The Bible teaches doctrine and morals with every affirmation that it makes, so that together those affirmations comprise something like a handbook or textbook for Christian belief and living, a compendium of divine and therefore inerrant teachings on a full array of subjects—including science, economics, health, politics, and romance.[8]

Smith argues this kind of biblicism has a long history in America which was driven by the sensibilities of post-revolutionary, nineteenth-century individualistic, republican democracy. He notes, however, that something of great importance is lost by strategies that turn the Bible into a useful religious manual to help contemporary people live more manageable lives by dealing with every conceivable question or problem—the good news of the gospel of Jesus Christ. Such an approach simplifies and reduces the Christian faith in order to demonstrate its relevance according to what is valued by the logic of the market and useful for the nation, economy, and well-being of autonomous individuals. Such strategies, moreover, have become for many pastors, congregations, and denominational leaders a virtual new "orthodoxy" that often goes unquestioned because of its promise to restore the church to the center of cultural influence and to decrease, or even reverse, long-term church decline.[9]

In a survey of nineteenth- and twentieth-century preaching in America, historian Hughes Old traces the roots of contemporary homiletic pragmatism to the revivalism that followed the Great Awakenings and then took more sophisticated forms in twentieth century liberal mainline Protestant preaching.[10] According to Old, although Charles Finney and Norman Vincent Peale are separated by a century in time, there is a particular kinship that characterizes their preaching as well as many others whom he includes in a discussion of "The Great American School." Old argues that it was Finney who established himself as the outstanding figure of an informal school of preaching that characterized the American pulpit for a century and a half. The optimism of the American frontier was the prevailing temper, disposition, and outlook. The place of Scripture in preaching was rather

7. Twitchell, *Shopping for God*, 242.
8. Smith, *Bible Made Impossible*, 5.
9. Stone, *Evangelism after Christendom*, 11.
10. Old, *Reading and Preaching*.

limited, serving only an instrumental purpose for the immediate goals of revival and reform.

The Bible could thus be approached as a source book of moral instruction and imperatives or as a simple plan of salvation. As debates over biblical authority increased in the growing conflict between religion and science, a simple gospel and moral code could still be derived from Scripture without having to deal with such weightier theological and interpretive matters. Old shows how there developed a kind of progressive evangelicalism less interested in the doctrine of its forbearers and more interested in ethical religion. Rather than adhering closely to Scripture, sermons proceeded topically as guided by the preacher's personal experience and opinion. Much attention was given to developing the rhetorical skills of the preacher so that one's personality and homiletic performance would serve to make the message attractive and effective.[11]

Old concludes that this turn to the human subject had the effect of transforming the church's traditional ministry of Word and Sacrament to preacher and sacrament, even as sacrament was decreasingly observed. Since what is valued is a focus on people and their needs, the study of human nature was most essential and human experience—rather than formal theological and exegetical study—is the best commentary on the Bible. The authority of the enlightened preacher was sufficient, since an inspired personality is what really counts.[12]

As the populism of the early nineteenth century gave way to the calls for social and moral reform in the early twentieth century, continuity remained in the underlying assumptions of preaching. Although the prominent preachers of mainline Protestant denominations brought considerable learning and skill into the pulpit, they continued to offer a much more sophisticated expression of revivalistic preaching while following a similar pattern. The gospel was made to fit the culture in a manner that would make it acceptable. Preaching should press for decision, understood as the exercise of one's choice to live in a disciplined way and to act for change that would bring about the betterment of the self and/or world.[13]

Old concludes that a significant factor which contributed to the rise of the Great American School was a loss of confidence in the spoken word of Scripture in preaching.

I don't believe it is inaccurate to say that many of the characteristics described by Old in his discussion are still with us: a preoccupation with

11. Ibid., 445–48.
12. Ibid., 540–58.
13. Ibid., 560–80.

cultural relevance, an inclination toward seeing the Bible as a source of sermon topics, the authority of personal experience and opinion, a focus on practical application for a utilitarian faith, the use of highly entertaining illustrations, a superficial reading of Scripture, minimal attention to doctrine, the inspiration of the preacher's personality, the use of marketing and business methods, and a strong appeal to the individual's power to choose in a manner well-suited for a consumer ethos.

In other words, we live in a time in which for many the nature of preaching has been redefined by a separation of faith and reason and theology and practice. Preachers are transformed into technicians whose work consists of packaging messages that promise personal benefits, cultural relevance, and social utility. Many would have us believe that we do not need the study of theology or Scripture to arrive at a common-sense spirituality filled with simple, practical solutions that can be taken home and applied for coping with the so-called "real world."

However, this popular, common sense approach to entrepreneurial, pragmatic, activist, and topically-driven problem solving has also obscured the centrality of preaching Christ and the conviction that Christ is the real purpose, center, and interpretive key to Scripture. But what if our approach to Scripture and preaching is measured by the proper subject of Scripture; the God who promises to be with the church through the presence of the risen Christ and the Spirit who creates and renews faith that works as a participation in God's life and mission?

Richard Lischer's promising description of law and gospel is more a matter of listening than a doctrine, principle, or method. Attentiveness to God speaking in the witness of Scripture as a form of prayer, the receptivity of faith by which the Spirit puts to death and makes alive. The form, shape, or pattern of our vocation and life follows the arc of the crucified and risen Lord whom we proclaim. Instead of a discussion on "how to" preach law and gospel, which could quite easily be treated as another abstract topic, I want to look at a particular example from the work of another Lutheran theologian, preacher, and teacher of preachers: Dietrich Bonhoeffer.

Bonhoeffer's 1935 lecture, "Contemporizing the New Testament," was given at a time when he was preparing to become director of the Confessing Church's underground seminary which was located at Finkenwalde in northern Germany.[14] The lecture seeks to show that the promise of law and gospel in preaching inevitably draws the preacher through death and resurrection. Contemporizing, or making relevant, the message of Scripture as a

14. Bonhoeffer, "Contemporizing the New Testament," in Barker and Brocker, *Works of Dietrich Bonhoeffer*, 413–33. For historical background on Bonhoeffer's work as director of the Confessing Church seminary see Bethge, *Dietrich Bonhoeffer*, 419–92.

witness to Jesus Christ is the promise of law and gospel—which is the work of God. True relevance in preaching begins where God is present in the word with the Holy Spirit as its primary principle or subject. The word of God is present to the church in the power of the Spirit, just as Christ comes to his people through the proclamation of the gospel in the Spirit's power to judge, command, and forgive. This way of reading and preaching was perceived as strange in Bonhoeffer's time; so strange, in fact, that he refers to it as "an alien gospel."[15] Understanding the strangeness of Bonhoeffer's construal of law and gospel will require a brief sketch of the demanding theological and political conditions under which he was working.[16]

As a means of expanding its power, the Nazi regime derived a strategy by which it sought to make Nazi doctrine compatible with Christianity. While this was named "positive Christianity," it was free from any particular confession and sufficiently vague to provide a place from which to attack any aspects of Christianity that were deemed "negative," meaning anything that stood in the way of the state's well-being. This reductionist strategy created an anti-confessional form of Christianity which was little more than a political theology and social creed that omitted any substance of faith. "It was, one might deduce, Christianity with no God, no Christ, no content; an . . . empty gospel."[17]

Preaching which sought to win favor for Hitler's positive Christianity had nothing in common with a form of authentic Christianity that said yes to the gospel, to Christ, and to Scripture as the witness of Christ. "Nazi religion was pagan, containing a pagan savior and creed. The creed knew nothing of sin, and its faith glorified violence. Nazism had no weakness, humility, love of neighbor, or thought of forgiveness. Hitler was the German savior and Jews were the devil incarnate."[18]

This Nazi "faith" was framed and presented as a "new gospel" and mandatory religion. It possessed a creed, a set of beliefs, and correlative virtues. German blood and soil were its new sacraments, the goodness proclaimed in every public venue, including churches, was that Hitler had come. This also meant for many that following the defeat of World War I, Germany, as a people and world power, was being resurrected. The exile from which the chosen people were returning was the shame and disgrace of defeat. The Christian scriptures, as a mythic or symbolic framework, provided a familiar narrative which could be used and contemporized as a world view to

15. Ibid., 417–19.

16. Stroud, *Preaching in Hitler's Shadow*, 3–46.

17. Ibid., 8.

18. Ibid., 9.

justify and sustain the German race over against its enemies. These included the Christian church and especially the Jewish people, since the two were linked as objects of Nazi hatred.[19] Michael Burliegh writes,

> The Nazis despised Christianity for its Jewish roots, effeminacy, other worldliness and universality. It appeared life denying to the life affirming, mobilizing entirely unwanted sentiments and values. Forgiveness was not for resentful haters, nor compassion of much use to people who wanted to stamp the weak into the ground. In a word, Christianity was "soul malady."[20]

Arguably, the greatest challenge was within the church, that of the German Christian movement, those who believed there was no compromise between Christianity and Nazism; that the two could be mixed into a new German gospel. This was a progressive movement in some ways, an attempt to bring the ancient faith of the church which was perceived by many as lifeless and meaningless, into the modern world of science and progress and to make the Bible contemporary to meet the crisis created by World War I.

This approach of reading the gospel and Scripture through the lens of Nazi ideology and hopes offered many Christians in German a unity of thinking and doing, faith and action, church and politics, religion and ethics. One critic of National Socialism compared living in Nazi Germany to "being a passenger on a train who is unaware that a bridge is being re-built—little by little and piece by piece—until it is no longer the old bridge but a completely new one." Nor was biblical interpretation immune to Nazi ideology. Rather than beginning with God, it took as its starting point the historical situation, human reason and desire, Germany's hopes, accomplishments and victories.

Pre-Nazi theology started with Hitler and worked its way up to God. This meant the reader was in charge of Scripture, a human-centered interpretation which opened the door to the idolatry of self-worship. This approach also meant that Scripture had to be made relevant by fitting the Bible into contemporary circumstances, historical events, and political programs. The divine word had to be separated from human words, a humanly controlled contemporization of Scripture that was dependent upon methodological skill rather than the promise of God in Christ who speaks through the sermon.[21]

The Barmen Declaration, which was framed in 1934 by the first Confessing Synod and led chiefly by Karl Barth, was a confessional document

19. Ibid., 10–11.
20. Cited in ibid., 19.
21. Ibid., 21–28.

that challenged the claims made on the church by the Nazis and the heretical teachings of the German Christians. At the same time, the document established the gospel of Jesus Christ as found in Scripture as the sole basis of the German Evangelical Church.

> Jesus Christ, as he is witnessed to in the Holy Scriptures, is the one word of God that we are to hear and in whom we are to trust and obey in living and dying. We reject the false teaching of the German Christians as if the church could and must recognize as the source of her proclamation in other events and powers, figures and truths as God's revelation outside and alongside this one word of God.[22]

One outcome of this confession was that preaching the gospel was affirmed as the central mission of the church. The "new religion" of National Socialism was to be exposed and challenged by speaking the "No" and "Yes" of the gospel in both judgment and mercy.

While seemingly far-removed from the theological and political circumstances of Germany in the 1930s, we who preach in the twenty-first century cannot help but marvel at such confidence in the spoken word. My hope is that such confidence in the proclaimed word of God may serve as encouragement toward discerning more clearly the vocation of preaching. Bonhoeffer's strong conviction and commitment to "preaching Christ" may assist us in reflecting on the ministry of the word, evangelism, and discipleship in a culture which easily reduces preaching to another form of human choice, activity, and productivity.

"Contemporizing New Testament Texts" was a timely statement for pastors of the Saxon Confessing Church. Bonhoeffer begins by offering two alternative ways of contemporizing or making relevant the New Testament message. On the one hand, this can mean that the biblical message must justify itself to the present, which was the urgent question posed by the German Christians to the church's theology and preaching. Bonhoeffer sees the form of this question as being rooted in the Enlightenment, the era of reason set free from faith, or rationalism, which continued to shape theology, including that of the German Christians. In other words, the demand of autonomous reason represents a human claim to the freedom of creating one's own faith and life.

The German Christians demanded the New Testament must justify itself before the forum of autonomous ways of thinking. According to Bonhoeffer, when this desire was successful they claimed to be Christian; when it failed, however, they claimed to be pagan. And while the forum before

22. Ibid., 8.

which the biblical message must justify itself changes over time—reason in the eighteenth century, culture in the nineteenth, the German people in the 1930s—the basic question remains unchanged: "Can Christianity become contemporary for us as we simply—thank God!—are now?" Bonhoeffer refers to this demand as a fixed and unquestionable "Archimedian Point." What must change is the Christian message which is required to pass through the sieve of one's knowledge or it simply will not pass. As he notes,

> *... whatever does not pass through is disdained and thrown away, so that one trims and prunes away the Christian message until it fits the fixed framework, until the eagle can no longer rise and escape into its true element and instead is put on display with clipped wings as a special exhibit among the other domesticated pets.*[23]

A form of Christianity that has been tamed to be usable will be a faith that in the face of honest scrutiny cannot maintain serious interest. Bonhoeffer's lecture is a strong indictment of this methodology, "This contemporizing of the Christian message leads directly to paganism, which means the only difference between German Christians and so-called neo-pagans is honesty."[24] This is not simply a matter of method but rather one of honesty. Missing is the courage to raise anew the question of the actual substance of the Christian message. Theological substance is eclipsed by the question of making contemporary or relevant, which Bonhoeffer compares to drinking murky water from a glass rather than investing the labor that is required to draw pure water. "Those who are thirsty have always found living water in the Bible itself, and in a substantially biblical sermon, even when such was quite out of sync with the times."[25]

Bonhoeffer proceeds to discuss the positive meaning of the question regarding the contemporizing of the New Testament message, ". . . the justification of the present to the message."[26] This means placing the present before the forum of the Christian message which requires raising the question of the substance, the "what" of the Christian message. His next assertion sounds strange in a time like ours, particularly when words such as "contemporary" and "relevant" are ascribed law-like authority, "True contemporization is found in the question of substance." In other words, the most contemporary move is simply putting forth the substance itself with

23. Barker and Brocker, *Works of Dietrich Bonhoeffer*, 413–14. Italics added.

24. Ibid., 415.

25. Ibid., 416.

26. Ibid., 417.

confidence that trusts in the spoken word, "The substance here is Christ and Christ's word; wherever Christ is expressed in the word of the New Testament, one has contemporization."[27]

This significant theological claim informs pastoral ministry, since the "present" is not a fixed, temporal determination. Rather, the "present" is determined through the word of Christ as the word of God. Moreover, the "present" is not a temporal feeling, interpretation, or worldview; it is the proclamation of the word by the Spirit's power which creates the "present." "Wherever God is present in the divine word, there one has the present, there God posits the present."[28] The subject of the present is the Holy Spirit and not ourselves, which is also why the subject of contemporization is the Holy Spirit.

Bonhoeffer insists that the substance of the New Testament should not be seen as the Bible but as Christ speaking to the church in the Spirit, which takes place through the word of Scripture rather than outside or alongside Scripture. Proclamation is thus rightly oriented to Scripture, an orientation to substance which is both a method and obedient trust in the substance of the Holy Spirit. This is an eschatological matter, moreover, in that the "present" is not determined by the past, that is, a return to the Bible as an ancient book in order to contemporize its message for "today." The present is determined externally, the future which is Christ and the Holy Spirit speaking today. There is a danger in moving from past to present, in attempting to define the present as something that resides within itself and bears its own criterion within itself. For this reason, the criteria for the authentic present is external to itself, in the future which is Scripture and the word of Christ who is attested there; a surprisingly "alien" and unfamiliar gospel.[29]

Proper contemporizing requires receptivity to the substance and allowing that substance to come to expression. A contemporizing proclamation must be an exegesis of Scripture. Its movement is not from Scripture to the present, but rather from the present to the word of Scripture where it abides and is drawn by the future from a false into an authentic present. Bonhoeffer concedes this will be incomprehensible for some. Yet if the present is found where Christ and the Spirit speak, it will require that preachers turn back to Scripture as listeners, "back to the cross of Christ." Not doing this is "untheological," a principle of contemporization that seeks to find in

27. Ibid., 417–18.
28. Ibid.
29. Ibid..

Scripture something eternal, a meaning, an ethical norm or essence which can be applied to the present and the individual "today."[30]

Bonhoeffer describes the process by which Scripture is brought before the forum of the present and made to yield to familiar forms of knowledge, norms, principles, ideas and truths, "They themselves know where the word of God is and where the word of human beings is."[31] What cannot be used, or what will not conform to the present, is left to the past and viewed as something that is not eternal or divine. For example, the doctrines of sin and justification are temporally bound and past, whereas the struggle for the good and pure is eternal. In the same manner, the ethical teaching of Jesus is eternal, while the miracle stories are temporally bound. The fighter Jesus and his death are expressions of the eternal struggle of light against darkness, while the suffering, defenseless Jesus should not concern us. And the doctrine of grace is eternal, while the Decalogue and commandments of the Sermon on the Mount are no longer useful.[32]

Bonhoeffer's assessment of the German Christians' method of contemporizing exposes the presumption that those who live in the present are capable of distinguishing the word of God from the words of human beings and extracting it for their use. The criterion for such judgment resides in either reason or the conscience and in one's cultural or ethnic experiences. Thus, "The norm of contemporizing resides within us: the Bible is the material to which this norm is applied."[33] Bonhoeffer's assessment leads to an alternative path or way of interpretation. The whole of Scripture is the witness of God in Christ for which the point of every passage is to make the character of this witness available. It is God who evokes the word in contemporary fashion by the Spirit who is the principle of contemporization. Textual exposition of Scripture is substantive as a witness of Christ, while such exposition possesses the promise of Christ's presence.[34]

Stranger yet is Bonhoeffer's discussion of application as the work of the Holy Spirit rather than that of the preacher. What makes Scripture concrete in the life of a congregation is Christ and the cross; the contextual work of the sermon belongs to the Spirit who speaks the judgment, command, and forgiveness of Christ as lord, judge, and savior. In his rejection of preaching that addresses the particular experiences, identities, and expectations of listeners, Bonhoeffer states, "Precisely by not taking seriously in an ultimate

30. Ibid., 419.
31. Ibid., 420.
32. Ibid., 420–21.
33. Ibid., 421.
34. Ibid., 421–22.

sense the so-called concrete situation of the congregation, one is able to see the true situation of human beings before God."[35] Preaching cannot raise itself above the witness of the New Testament by adding something eternal, something that claims to transcend the New Testament, and still hope to make it concrete.

Although Bonhoeffer's lecture seeks to expose and challenge, it also offers help and encouragement. As he states,

> The New Testament is the witness of the promise of the Old Testament as fulfilled in Christ. It is not a book containing eternal truths, teachings, norms, or myths, but the sole witness of the God-human, Jesus Christ. In its whole and in its parts, it is nothing other than this witness of Christ, Christ's life, death, and resurrection.[36]

Christ is not an eternal idea or essence, but the unique Son of God whose history fills the entire New Testament. This means all texts, not just a select group, bear witness to his uniqueness and historicity which is the common character of the New Testament witness. Christ himself is the One who performs the miracle, speaks the parable, issues the commandment, and through such speaking calls and binds human beings to himself.

The interpretation of Scripture in preaching, therefore, does not distinguish between doctrinal and historical texts, God's word and human words, since all bear witness to Christ. "The New Testament is not something in itself but witnesses to something else; it has no inherent value, but value only as a witness to Christ." Nor is the New Testament a book of wisdom, teachings, or eternal truths but rather is ". . . the joyful cry. This Jesus is the Christ!" Because God's word in Christ is the source of the good of the text, the Bible does not function as a preacher's source book of topics, principles, or examples but ". . . a witness to the present Christ, the crucified, resurrected Lord who calls to discipleship . . . Contemporizing means Christ alone speaks through the Holy Spirit . . . Christ steps toward us."[37]

Contemporizing is practiced best by interpreting the New Testament as the unique witness to the historical and living Christ. This is a matter of freedom, the freedom of exegesis unbound from the burden of proof and liberated for the praise of the scriptural witness to Christ. Such homiletic freedom is bound by service to the word which includes the use of language in preaching; the "contemporary" does not possess the authority of law, but rather functions as a more modest and appropriate means of mediating

35. Ibid., 423.
36. Ibid., 424.
37. Ibid., 425–26.

the word. The same is true in choosing texts for preaching. This will not mean asking what the congregation wants to hear, what happened during the week, or what questions are on their minds. In the freedom that serves the word, approaching these questions will be oriented theologically. "The congregation is always asking in its mind, whether it knows it or not, about the entire Christ, and only the proclamation of the entire Christ will be able to address those questions."[38] This will require questioning that leads to proclaiming the entirety of the New Testament witness to Christ instead of any topic, truth, or idea of a preacher's own choosing.

Bonhoeffer concludes with three primary concerns related to the fullness of Christian proclamation: grace and discipleship, the church and world, and the Good Samaritan. While Protestant tradition holds that Christians live from grace alone, proclaiming grace should not be an obstacle to Christ and the call to discipleship. Costly grace must be proclaimed as grace that is the obedience of faith. The New Testament witness to Christ is not a commodity but inseparable from the call to follow him. The doctrine of grace calls the church to live in the world and empowers its members to serve by participating in its affairs. Grace does not make the church a spiritual and invisible witness to other-worldliness.[39]

As a pilgrim people the church is called to live by simple obedience in the world. The proclamation of Christ is a witness of the whole Christ in the world; the Lord and his body, the church, over which the cross stands visibly. The witness of the New Testament message to Christ creates the church as a community that exits to serve and welcome people from all places and classes who suffer violence, injustice, and who have been abandoned. Significantly, Bonhoeffer cites Prov 31:8, "Speak out for those who cannot speak," which raises a more urgent matter, "Perhaps here the decision of whether we are still a church."[40] The matter of contemporizing is thus inseparably linked to the church's credibility before the word and the world, that is, the urgency of credibility rather than comprehensibility.

The primary challenge in proclamation is not that of providing comprehensibility according to contemporary ways of understanding but is maintaining the credibility of the church: "Because the church and the pastor speak differently than they behave; because the existence of the pastor no longer differs from that of the citizen." The freedom of the gospel makes credible in that the life of the one who proclaims, is itself a mediating element. Credibility and contemporizing are therefore inseparable. Bonhoeffer

38. Ibid., 430.

39. Ibid., 431–32.

40. Ibid., 433.

ends the lecture on this sobering note: that the pastors of the Confessing Church should "ask ourselves whether through our own lives we have not already robbed our scriptural word of credibility."[41]

Bonhoeffer's view of contemporization, the dynamic reality of law and gospel spoken and enacted by Christ himself in the Spirit's power, is predicated upon the church's primary disposition as a listening community. Law and gospel is not a tool, principle, doctrine or method in the hands of preachers. Nor is law and gospel a version of the "next new thing" which promises to work if only applied with the right skill and technique. The work of the Word and Spirit is not implemented by a program but must be received as a promise and gift; the real and eloquent Spirit-enlivened speech of Christ who speaks today as lord, judge, and savior.

In our time the work of Richard Lischer has demonstrated the promise of law and gospel in preaching. Broken open to a listening church for the sake of the world, the truth of Scripture is made credible when the biblical witness is understood to be at the disposal of Jesus Christ who is present in the spoken word and addressing himself to his followers. In preaching, the voice of the Risen Lord calls into being faith and the new life of obedience which is the Spirit's work. The promise of law and gospel thus shapes the vocation of preaching and those who preach and listen according to the reality by which they have been called and sent to proclaim: the death and resurrection of Christ. If preaching is a reenactment and participation in the defeat and victory of Christ, then something in us must die *so that the eagle can rise and fly with unclipped wings.*

Bibliography

Barker, H. Gaylon, and Mark S. Brocker, eds. *The Works of Dietrich Bonhoeffer.* Vol. 14, *Theological Education at Finkenwalde* 1935–1937. Translated by Douglas W. Stott. Minneapolis: Fortress, 2013.

Bethge, Eberhard. *Dietrich Bonhoeffer: A Biography.* Edited by Victoria J. Barnett. Rev. edn. Minneapolis: Fortress, 2000.

Fitch, David E. *The Great Giveaway: Reclaiming the Mission of the Church from Big Business, Parachurch Organizations, Psychotherapy, Consumer Capitalism and other Modern Maladies.* Grand Rapids: Baker, 2007.

Lischer, Richard. *The End of Words: The Language of Reconciliation in a Culture of Violence.* Grand Rapids: Eerdmans, 2005.

———. *A Theology of Preaching: The Dynamics of the Gospel.* Rev. edn. Eugene, OR: Wipf & Stock, 2001.

Old, Hugh Oliphant. *The Reading and Preaching of the Christian Scriptures in the Worship of the Church.* Vol. 6. Grand Rapids: Eerdmans, 1999–2013.

41. Ibid.

Smith, Christian. *The Bible Made Impossible: Why Biblicism Is Not a Truly Evangelical Reading of Scripture*. Grand Rapids: Brazos, 2011.

Stone, Bryan. *Evangelism after Christendom: The Theology and Practice of Christian Witness*. Grand Rapids: Brazos, 2007.

Stround, Dean G., ed. *Preaching in Hitler's Shadow: Sermons of Resistance in the Third Reich*. Grand Rapids: Eerdmans, 2013.

Twitchell, James. *Shopping for God: How Christianity Went from In Your Hearts to In Your Face*. New York: Simon & Schuster, 2007.

The Gospel and the Missional Church

SIGNIFICANT PREACHING AND THE AGENCY OF GOD

Clayton J. Schmit

If anyone is in Christ, there is a new creation.
—2 CORINTHIANS 5:17

THE ESSAYS IN THIS book focus on how the gospel of Jesus Christ is foundational for all Christian preaching and theology, and they address the issue from many points of view. Surprisingly, as interest grows in a recent movement in theology, the *missional church movement,* it finds itself susceptible to the gravitational pull of an expression of theology that mitigates the power of the essential good news of the death and resurrection of Christ. This essay seeks to offer a caution against losing sight of the gospel in the missional conversation. It considers the ways that Christian preaching announces what is central to our Trinitarian faith, the promises of God in Christ, and what preachers need to bear in mind in order to foster *missional* congregations that engage their communities while responsibly engaging Scripture and theology. It will do so by addressing two matters. The first is a reflection on Richard Lischer's *three tones of preaching* and how they relate to the Divine-human drama that preaching proclaims. Second, it offers a caution and suggests direction for those who preach in contexts of missional engagement.

The Three Tones of Preaching
and the Divine-Human Drama

Christian preaching, if it is to reach those who have ears to hear, needs to contend honestly with two critical domains. One is the long arc of the theological drama that is revealed to us through the scriptures. The other is the life, emotion, and experience of the listener. The sermon occurs at the intersection of these two considerations. When preaching misses the former, the preacher loses the capacity to speak in God's behalf. When preaching misses the latter, the sermon becomes insignificant.

The Significance of Preaching

Aesthetic philosopher Suzanne K. Langer said that all genuine art has *significant form*: it is "the essence of every art; it is what we mean by calling anything artistic."[1] Art's significance, she reasons, is its capacity to symbolize human feelings in all their richness, depth, and complexity.

If Christian preaching is to contend with God's dramatic engagement with creation and with the complex experiences of human life, it needs to have a sense of significant form. It achieves that by being a form of art that resonates with the feelings and experiences of its listeners. Preaching is "the preacher's attempt to create a form that, growing out of a scriptural text or biblical idea, expresses some aspect of what the preacher takes to be an important connection between God's Word and what is going on in the hearts and lives of God's people."[2] Preaching engages people with the narrative of what God has done and draws them into that drama, taking into account all their fears, joys, hopes, anxieties, uncertainties, ambivalences, assurances, and so forth. When preaching is honest about human feeling and experience, it has the power of poetry, to create a simulation of life that is recognizable, relevant, and resonant. It accomplishes what Charles L. Bartow describes as creating "a world real enough for people to enter, to believe in, to be changed by."[3]

Preaching as art may have a sense of plot (as Eugene L. Lowry urges).[4] It also reveals the greater arc of the Divine-human drama. This arc, which

1. Langer, *Feeling and Form*, 24.

2. Schmit, *Too Deep for Words*, 85.

3. Bartow, *Preaching Moment*, 14.

4. Lowry developed the now famous idea of homiletical plot in two books, *The Homiletical Plot: The Sermon as Narrative Art Form* and *The Sermon: Dancing on the Edge of Mystery*.

Jesuit theologian Hans Urs von Balthasar calls *theo-drama*, can be described in Trinitarian terms: God initiates the drama, then sends the Son on a mission that is played out through his life, Passion, death, and resurrection; the human part of the drama unfolds as believers are sent by the Holy Spirit to be part of Christ's mission in the world.[5] God's people become engaged as co-missionaries with Christ and the Spirit. This suggests that they become committed (co-mitted) to the activity of God. The theo-drama "is *live performance* in solidarity with others of Christ's all-encompassing mission to the world," as one writer summarizes von Balthasar's thought.[6] As preaching reveals the great drama, it engages listeners both in the humanity of the plot and in its unfolding performance,[7] of which they become a part. Performing the gospel is key to the interests of the missional church, whereby God's people are sent to engage the mission of God already present in their communities. This is, as we will see in the second section of this essay, the essential movement of the *missional* church. The significance of preaching is that it connects the drama initiated by God to listeners who are shown that their own lives, experiences, and emotions are part of God's unfolding theological plot.

Always at the center of the Divine-human drama, what Richard Lischer calls "the long, twisted story,"[8] is the full mission of Christ. Critical for both von Balthasar and Lischer is the centrality of the cross and resurrection. Without them, for Lischer, the preacher has no power to preach and can make no connection with the real concerns of human life, such as "the alienation, loneliness, anxiety, sin, and evil that cluster around" death.[9] For von Balthasar, the liberal-critical approach to the story of Christ—which overlooks, at best, and often denies the death and resurrection of Jesus— "ends up 'functionalizing' Christ as an exemplary means to the end of human moral goodness and social betterment."[10] Critically, Lischer insists that omitting these central elements from preaching has the result of producing moralistic sermons, preaching that denigrates the role of Jesus within the

5. While rarely cited by those engaged in the missional conversation, von Balthasar's understanding of the movement of the theo-drama is strikingly parallel to the theological movement articulated by the missional theology literature.

6. Quash, "Theo-drama," 144. Italics in the original.

7. For rich explorations of the notion that Christians perform the gospel, see Stanely Hauerwas, *Performing the Faith: Bonhoeffer and the Practice of Nonviolence*; Samuel Wells, *Improvisation: The Drama of Christian Ethics*; and Kevin J. Vanhoozer, *The Drama of Doctrine: A Canonical Linguistic Approach to Christian Theology*.

8. Lischer, *Theology of Preaching*, 50.

9. Ibid., 44.

10. Chapp, "Revelation," 13.

drama to a person that demonstrates an exceptionally high standard of good behavior.

The Three Tones of Preaching

Lischer maintains that preaching has three essential tones: *analysis, transition,* and *integration.* In his classroom teaching, he uses synonyms for these tones: the *law tone,* the *gospel tone,* and the *new obedience tone.* Each of them is typically present and balanced in effective sermons. The sermon's analysis examines where people have fallen short of the law's expectations. The transition demonstrates how the gospel represents the promise and power of God to overcome human failure to follow the law. The integration moves from proclaiming the good news to a new understanding of how the law points toward ways in which God's saved and empowered people can engage in performing the gospel in their lives and communities.

A critical problem occurs when the second of these tones is overlooked, or is treated so lightly that it is not heard as something that trumps the law tone.[11] The result is moralistic preaching. "Moralism preaches the Christian virtues without Christ-the-core, and when the congregation asks, 'To whom shall we turn to become such people?' moralism offers for our imitation 'Jesus Man of Genius,' . . . or 'The Greatest Possibility Thinker That Ever Lived,' . . ."[12] or, in a more timely reference, Jesus, The Exemplary Community Organizer. Moralistic preaching omits (or understates) the gospel tone that is the source of Divine power for integration, for being a new creation that freely performs the Word in Christian action. It is only through the proclaimed gospel that the hearer is sanctified. When this happens, Karl Barth asks, "how, then, shall all things not be made new?"[13] Moralistic preaching is the opposite of good news for the listener. It is bad news when the example offered up for imitation is Jesus' unattainable model of perfection. It is bad news when the motivation to imitate this excellent behavior comes from one's own personal resources—for we are powerless to achieve his high standard. And, it is bad news when a sense of martyrdom shames people into action.

The good news is what Peter Storey once called in a sermon the *great never-the-less of God.* It sounds like this: we have fallen short of God's expectations; never-the-less, God forgives us. In preaching, proclamation

11. In preaching, Karl Barth argues, "sin has to be taken seriously, but forgiveness even more seriously." Barth, *Homiletics,* 52.

12. Lischer, *Theology of Preaching,* 63.

13. Barth, *Homiletics,* 74.

of the great-never-the-less of God lies between the law tone and the new obedience, overcoming the former and empowering the latter. The great never-the-less is the key to preaching the theo-drama. It provides the essential "clue to resolution," or the "aha!" in every homiletical plot.[14] It allows for preaching to be honest about the human condition and to explore fully the human condition with all its experiences and emotions. Proper preaching announces that, judged by the law, we are liberated and empowered by God's promise, and freed to engage in the great co-mission with Christ.

In the homiletics classroom, I warn my students: Take a careful look at end of your sermon. If it piles imperatives upon the listener, it is likely to be a moralistic sermon.[15] When the sermon concludes with "therefore you should, . . . we must, . . . you ought to, . . . we need to," and so forth, that is a strong signal that the sermon has mislaid the gospel tone. What Bartow says of poetry also applies to the good news: "it is an 'is,' not a 'must,' or an 'ought,' or a 'have to.'"[16] The good news is always in the indicative. The sermon's new obedience tone is not new if it is shouted in the imperative voice. It is merely a louder restatement of the old imperative, the law.

To prevent moralistic preaching, we need clearly, boldly, and resolutely to proclaim the good news, the promise, the hope. Notice here that I *am* speaking in the imperative. But, I speak it to the preacher so that the preacher does *not* speak it to the hearer. In teaching preaching, I have arrived at a single cardinal rule. Every other attempt at saying, "always do this," or "never do that," has been proven false by someone who violated the rules with good effect. The one standing rule is simple: *always proclaim the good news*.[17] If the preacher does not do this, there is no reason for the preacher to speak. I call this rule the evangelical imperative.[18] Each time he or she stands to deliver a sermon, it is incumbent upon the preacher to

14. Lowry, *Homiletical Plot*, 47–61.

15. So pervasive is the tendency toward moralism that in his own teaching, Lischer says that nearly half of the sermons he reads are moralistic. Lischer, *Theology of Preaching*, 63.

16. Bartow, *Cries of Earth and Altar*, 105.

17. I do provide one rhetorical allowance for the violation of this rule. The preacher may choose, as a element of sermon design, to omit proclaiming the good news in a Good Friday sermon. The assumption is that anyone who attends to preaching at worship at a Good Friday service is more than likely to attend proclamation of the triumphant good news at Sunday's Easter celebration. In this case, the Good Friday sermon and the Easter proclamation are of one rhetorical piece.

18. Lischer, similarly, calls this the "gospel imperative," however its use is nuanced. "The gospel indicative contains an imperative, else it purveys cheap grace." Yet, for him, too, the new obedience is not shouted with a legalistic tone. Rather it takes the form of a promise: "what the law ordains is fulfilled in us." Lischer, *Theology of Preaching*, 57–58.

proclaim some aspect of the Bible's good news or promise. I once asked Peter Storey, one of the champions against South Africa's apartheid system, to speak to my preaching class on the subject of prophetic preaching. He gave a powerful exhortation to my students to have the courage to speak prophetically. Yet, he also said this: "The night before you preach, read through your sermon. If it does not contain the good news, tear it up!"

The Performative Power of the Word

"If anyone is in Christ, there is a new creation," St. Paul said. In homiletics class, Lischer often points out that in Paul's Greek, there is an absence of a predicate in this phrase. "If anyone is in Christ: new creation." (Famous chef Emeril Lagasse might say, "If anyone is in Christ: BAM, new creation!") Lischer uses this as an example of Joseph Sittler's adage, "where grammar cracks, grace erupts." Eruption is the right word for what happens linguistically in Paul's statement. When these words, and other statements of good news like them, are proclaimed, what they promise springs into being. The old becomes new. To echo Barth, at the trumpet sound of the promise, how could things not become new?

Declaring the good news in preaching is a liturgical example of what is linguistically called a performative utterance.[19] Performative utterances accomplish the action of which they speak precisely as the words are spoken. To say, "I bet you five dollars," is to effect the wager. To say, "I declare you my friend," is to enjoin the friendship. These utterances rely on the power or the intent of the speaker to fulfill them. In liturgical settings, for the minister to say, "I baptize you," is to employ the power of God to initiate a person into faith. To say, "your sins are forgiven," is to invoke God's forgiveness even as the words are spoken. These are powerful proclamations. They do not call upon our own agency to fulfill them. They call upon God to make good on the promises spoken in God's behalf.

In preaching, the same effect takes place: to proclaim the good news is to bring the liberating and transforming power of God to bear upon the listeners. To declare, "in Christ there is a new creation," is to loose the Spirit of God in the generation of a liberated people of God. This principle is at the center of the second tone of preaching. The transition is effected when the promise is announced. It may be incomplete—rarely do we see total transformation in the space of one sermon. But, the work of God is initiated by

19. Schmit, *Too Deep for Words*, 43–59.

the preacher's voice. It is God's self, acting through what Bartow calls "God's human speech,"[20] speech that is activated according to God's promise.[21]

To summarize, I contend that proclaiming the good news in preaching is the preacher's evangelical imperative. Without it, no fitting proclamation occurs. Yet, while the preacher must or ought to do this, the preacher must or ought *not* impose imperatives upon the listener. The gospel tone along with the new obedience is in the indicative. The integration for the listener comes when the transforming power of the spoken promise brings about freedom and joy for the listener to be committed to Christ's mission. Even as the good news is an expression of who God is, obedience is or becomes an expression of who God's people are. The imperatives are for the preacher in preparing the sermon. The indicatives are for the sermon and its listeners.

The Fluidity of the Law and Gospel

The law and the gospel, the classic dialectic, are part of the same coin. In order for the good news to ring true, it needs to be understood in light of the law. Barth observed "the Law is nothing else than the necessary form of the Gospel, whose content is grace."[22] To observe (both in terms of perceiving and living into) the law and the gospel as people of faith is to spin the coin and see its two faces blur into a singular sphere. The liberated believer moves fluidly from acknowledgment of sin to confession; from confession to absolution; from forgiveness to worship; from worship to love, from the desire to love back to failure, and so forth, as the coin spins. Every step, whether forward toward love or backward toward iniquity, is part of the one journey of grace.

The three tones of preaching function within this fluidity. The law judges us and shows us our need for Christ's saving love. The gospel liberates us from the law and empowers us for love. The new obedience occurs in response to the liberation and empowerment of the Holy Spirit to return to the law's way of life with joy and zeal, no longer to be judged by it, but to be what we are: part of Christ's mission. People who hear this kind of preaching are secured by the gravitational pull of this constantly spinning sphere.

There are dangers associated with introducing discontinuity between the law and the gospel in preaching. One of them is quite well known. To

20. Bartow, *God's Human Speech.*
21. Barth, *Homiletics,* 72.
22. Barth, "Gospel and Law," 80.

preach the law and the gospel without the integrating new obedience is to propose Bonhoeffer's *cheap grace*.[23]

> The essence of grace, we suppose, is that the account has been paid in advance; and, because it has been paid, everything can be had for nothing.... Cheap grace means the justification of sin without the justification of the sinner. Grace alone does everything, they say, and so everything can remain as it was before.[24]

Preaching that promotes cheap grace is that which encourages comfort without transformation. It speaks the good news without urgency. It spoils the grammar of grace: turning the indicative of *new obedience* ("Because of God's grace . . . this is therefore what you can do. Become what you are!"[25]) from what grammarians call a *realis mood* (indicating that something *is* the case) to an *irrealis mood* (indicating something that *is not* the case). Putting it in Paul's language, cheap grace means that in Christ, there is *no* new creation. Only the former self remains, basking in the balm of a perceived righteousness. Without the urgent resolve of the good news announced in preaching, the listener may drift toward defeating the power of transformation by denying the need for repentance. Cheap grace may be satisfying to experience. But it does not edify and it certainly does not honestly attend to the human condition. Proper preaching has significant form: it contends with the reality of human experience and brings to awareness what God has done along with the expectations that such grace bears. It squarely declares the human role within the theo-drama.

A second danger is to introduce discontinuity in the sermon between the law tone and the new obedience tone (omitting or understating the promise). This, as we said above, is the key to moralist preaching. But it might also be called *extortionate law*, to play on Bonhoeffer's image. Without the gospel tone, the law that judges us pushes us to the law of what we must become, without the liberation of the gospel. The old law and the new obedience become one and the same, judgment in sheep's clothing. If cheap grace is receiving the good news while ignoring the cost of its call to response, extortionate law is taking on the full burden of the law, disregarding the high cost that Jesus paid to liberate and empower Christian love. In such preaching, one might justly conclude (as when buying a new car): Jesus paid far too much for what he got. In a listener's response to the moralistic sermon, what is intended to be the new obedience (in Christ,

23. Lischer, *Theology of Preaching*, 57.
24. Bonhoeffer, *Cost of Discipleship*, 43.
25. Lischer, *Theology of Preaching*, 49

all things are new) becomes rather the *listener's* obedience which is called for by the preacher whose sermon does not attempt to loose the liberating power of the gospel by proclaiming it in full voice. Instead of Christ's burden being light, the full burden of the law falls upon the shoulders of the listener. When the gospel is left unspoken, or underspoken, it has no power to affect transformation in the listener. Even though Christ paid the full price, such preaching offers a form of law that makes Christ's death unnecessary.

In moralistic preaching, Christian virtue is preached, with Jesus as the first example. His excellent behavior could quite easily have continued on had he avoided paying the exorbitant price of going to the cross. We might have been left with gospels filled with more years of stories of his moral example. Moralistic preaching might also offer others—Ghandi, Mother Theresa—as fitting exemplars, people who may have paid high prices in providing their moral examples, but achieved them much more cheaply than dying on the cross.

The theological problem for those that listen to moralistic preaching is that virtuous activity is not the same thing as spiritual transformation; that is something that only occurs when the power of Christ through the Spirit of God is loosed and at work in the lives of disciples. Moreover, such preaching is dishonest about the human condition (and thus, insignificant). It suggests that the person *can* obey. The whole point of Christian preaching and teaching is that the human person cannot obey. "I can will what is right," Paul said, "but I cannot do it" (Rom 7:18). For this, Christ died.

Promoting extortionate law is the problem with moralistic preaching. It is also a danger for preaching in a missional context.

The Gospel and the Missional Church

Since the 1950s[26] missiologists have been noting a change in the Western and North American religious context. While Christianity is growing explosively throughout Africa, Asia, and South America, its growth has largely stalled in the regions from which missionaries were once sent. The consensus is that we are now the mission field and that the *missio Dei* is something to be engaged in our own communities. Darell Guder summarizes: it has become "a truism to speak of North America as a mission field" and an "obvious fact that what we once regarded as Christendom is now

---

26. Craig Van Gelder traces the so-called missional movement back to 1952 when Wilhelm Anderson proposed a new look at the theology of mission at the International Missionary Council at Willingen, Germany. Van Gelder, *Essence of the Church*, 33.

a post-Constantinian, post-Christendom, and even post-Christian mission field."[27] Patrick Kiefert speaks of this age as a "New Missional Era."[28] Engaging the missional literature has led me to conclude

> that all churches, whether they know it or not, exist in a missional era. They need, therefore, to have a missional thrust to their ministry if they are to survive—or to thrive. Just as in the apostolic age, the mission field is directly outside the door of the church, regardless of whether the congregation is located in Moshi, Tanzania, or Memphis, Tennessee.[29]

The missional movement has gained cachet in the North American theological conversation of the last two decades. It has engendered books on missional theology and the nature of the missional church, and it has fostered considerable activity known as missional engagement. Churches across North America are eagerly embracing the new missional era and shaping their ministries to be engaged with what God is doing in their local communities. There is a good deal of consonance between missional engagement and von Balthasar's discipleship and its co-engagement with the mission of Christ in the world, wherein liberated people become the performers of their share of the theo-drama.

Of the many books that provide guidance for those involved in missional outreach, few have arisen to address the pastoral matters of how to shape worship in missional communities,[30] how to engage in pastoral care,[31] and how to preach to missional congregations. Of specific concern here is the lack of literature addressing the question of preaching in a missional context. The field is not completely barren, but as will be shown, there may be weeds growing even before fruitful plants are brought to harvest.

The missional impulse is for congregations to embrace what God is doing in their neighborhoods. The movement outward is fertile. It broadens congregational perspective, opens church doors to the community, creates partnerships with local agencies for doing ministry, engages congregants

27. Guder, *Missional Church*, 27.

28. Kiefert, *We Are Here Now*, 28.

29. Schmit, *Sent and Gathered*, 40.

30. There are at least two recent books addressing worship and missional church: Schmit, *Sent and Gathered*, and Meyers, *Missional Worship, Worshipful Mission*.

31. At least one book on the relationship between missional engagement and pastoral care is currently in process. Mary Sue Dreier serves as Professor of Missional Theology and Pastoral Care at Lutheran Theological Southern Seminary of Lenoir-Rhyne University. She intends to demonstrate that pastoral care in this new missional era needs to be equally focused on care of congregants and a congregation's care for its community.

with those who are not and may never become members of the congregation, provides encouragement for people of all ages to be involved in active
ministry, brings the talents and skills of local people into the sphere of local
congregations, makes for more diverse worshiping communities, increases
cultural awareness as communities change ethnically and demographically,
and so forth. The benefits of missional engagement may not be measured
in increased church attendance—this is no church growth movement—but
can be seen in unquantifiable things like deepening spirituality, increased
discipleship, greater understanding of Scripture, and the joy of being engaged in mission with Christ.

As with all aspects of faith life, congregations bear the responsibility to
ground their missional activity on Trinitarian theology and sound doctrine.
A centerpiece of congregational theological formation has always been, and
urgently needs to be its Scriptural preaching. Preachers in missional contexts have the unrelenting responsibility to proclaim the gospel in order to
ground the outward moving discipleship of Christian people in the liberating force of the Spirit's power. A major thrust for nearly all of the missional
writers is the sense that mission is the Spirit's sending of God's people into
action. As noted above, for preachers to proclaim the promise is to release
the Spirit's power to shape God's people and send them out in love. A leader
in the missional movement, Darrell Guder, puts it this way:

> Scripture's authority resides in the ongoing event in which Christ
> is encountered in scriptural testimony as God's word; that Word
> can be heard and listened to, and by virtue of the Holy Spirit's
> empowering, responded to and obeyed. Faith and discipleship
> emerge as the Scriptures work with their distinctive authority.[32]

For preachers whose sermons are founded on a theology that balances law
with gospel and obedience, their congregations are likely to be fed on the
nourishing word of God's love, forgiveness, and empowerment. Where there
is an imbalance in a preacher's theology of proclamation—especially where
preaching veers toward moralism—there is a critical homiletical danger
that can play out in unhelpful, perhaps even dangerous ways in missional
congregations. If the thrust of moralist preaching is Christian virtue and if
the impulse of the missional movement is community engagement, there
is a ripe arena for neo-heresy. Virtuous behavior and social engagement
are drawn to one another, even as works and righteousness seem morally
linked. But Christian virtue will not save us. Christian action will not save
us. Only Christ, who ignites Christian love, both saves and sends his people

32. Guder, "Missional Hermeneutics," 119.

out in service to the world. The surety for congregations, whether involved in missional outreach or not, is the same. It is Christian preaching that proclaims the fullness of the gospel that moves disciples from law to grace to love.[33]

The danger is that people can move so quickly to social engagement that they fall back into expressions of the old social gospel that is moralistic at its core. As H. Richard Niebuhr famously described it, the social gospel is characterized as "A God without wrath," that "brought men without sin into a kingdom without judgment through the ministrations of a Christ without a cross."[34] In moralistic preaching, social obedience overtakes spiritual empowerment. Christ is robbed of his cross and we are left only with law. Jesus is seen not as one who died to liberate people, but as the exemplar for community engagement. What Would Jesus Do is the guiding question in pursuit of his moral vision. The virtue of doing good things is its own reward, and as the law to love is being fulfilled, it comes at the cost of denigrating Jesus' death and resurrection as the central theme and action of the divine–human drama. Moving into social action without hearing the good news means that God's people do not find themselves in the arc of the theodrama. They are, rather, caught up in virtuous behavior that is discontinuous with what God has done and is doing in the world. While good work may be accomplished, the hazard is that the people of God cease to see the hand of God at work in them. Altruism becomes the idol that is honored and sought.

Getting our Homiletical Theology Right

The solution to this potential problem is, as stated above, preaching in missional communities that connects the activity of God's people with the action of God in the far-reaching plot of God's loving God's people. Where can mission-minded preachers find resources for this work? Slowly, books on preaching in the missional context are being produced. But, the reader needs to be discerning. Textbooks with the word "missional" in the title do not necessarily represent the Spirit sending force that Guder, Van Gelder, Kiefert, and other leading scholars have in mind when using the term. One

33. The surety for balancing spiritual formation and Christian action lies not only in proper preaching, but also in celebration of Christian sacraments. Both preaching and sacraments are part of the means of grace that the missional theologians refer to as the centering that occurs in worship prior to the sending of believers into the world in love and service.

34. Niebuhr, *Kingdom of God in America*, 193.

recent book stands as a critical example: *Choosing the Kingdom: Missional Preaching for the Household of God* by John Addison Dally. At the time of this writing, it is one of the only books on preaching that strictly contains the term *missional* in its title.[35]

In this book on missional preaching, Dally begins with a proper understanding of what it means for the church to be engaged in the mission of God. He gives a brief and accurate history of the term *missional* and urges the reader to comprehend that the church today exists in a missional era. He observes that much preaching offered by seminary trained preachers today is of the *docent* variety, whereby preachers "inform the congregation about a biblical or theological subject."[36] Dally argues that preachers need to rethink their approach to preaching, modeling themselves after Jesus' own preaching. As he points preachers in this direction, we begin to see him start the reader on a journey that eventuates in a theologically tenuous position. Jesus' preaching may indeed be worthy as a model for preachers today, but seeing Jesus' work merely as a model for ministry today is precisely the shoal that missionally minded congregations must avoid.

As Dally unfolds his argument for rethinking the common approach to preaching, we find him making exhaustive biblical references. Surprisingly, they are almost entirely confined to gospel pericopes relating to the life and earthly ministry of Jesus. He avoids the Passion narratives (except for a few brief references within which he finds descriptions of the kingdom of God); his argument makes no use of the resurrection of Christ, the sending of the Holy Spirit by Jesus, the coming of the Spirit in Acts, the results of the Spirit moving among God's church in Acts, and the interpretation of the death and resurrection of Christ in the epistles. Tellingly, historical Jesus scholarship and writers such as John Dominic Crossan, famously of the Jesus Seminar movement,[37] inform the author's scriptural interpretation. Basing his case entirely on the personal acts of the so-called historical

35. Another is Al Tizon, *Missional Preaching: Engage, Embrace, Transform*. Most recently, Patrick W. T. Johnson has produced *The Mission of Preaching: Equipping the Community for Faithful Witness*, a book derived from his 2013 Princeton Theological Seminary dissertation entitled "Preaching for the Witness of the Christian Community: Toward a Missional Homiletic." Neither of these fine books suffer from the uncertain theology of preaching that lies at the heart of Dally's work.

36. Dally, *Choosing the Kingdom*, 22.

37. The Jesus Seminar, founded in 1985 by biblical scholar Robert Funk, was committed to the search for the historical Jesus through liberal-critical interpretation of the gospels. Against seven interpretive canons, the words and works of Jesus were evaluated. The accounts of the miracles and sayings of Jesus that spoke of his messianic mission were presumed to be additions of later writers who obscured the image of the true itinerant preacher of Nazareth.

Jesus implies that the goal of the sermon is to create listeners who believe that Jesus' most significant work was accomplished before his death on the cross. Also revealing is this question posed by the author: "The reader who has followed me this far may well have some questions. Is this book simply an argument for preaching the historical Jesus rather than the Christ of faith, and thus for a style of preaching limited to the most liberal end of mainstream Christianity?"[38] This is a question the book fails to address. The reader is left to draw his or her own conclusions and there is much given to form an opinion that writer *is* espousing a social gospel view of missional action.

The implication of a theology of preaching that is unmoored from the realization that God alone acts through preaching becomes explicit in Dally's description of the Christian assembly. He urges the reader to understand the political implications of the New Testament word *ekklesia*. Like the First Amendment of the American Constitution that guarantees the right of citizens to assemble, Dally reasons, the Greek word suggests a democratic sense of agency.[39] He argues toward an understanding of preaching that places agency for understanding the sermon and the scriptures on the people of the assembly. He urges preachers to "get out of the way," to relinquish their own hegemonic agency, to press people toward realizing their own personal agency in being a part of the kingdom of God.

What is troubling about this approach to preaching is the impoverished theology that discounts the fact that preaching is God's activity, spoken by God's chosen witnesses, people whose own words are void of any power for proclamation or transformation. In other words, properly seen, the agency in preaching, and in its resultant Christian action, is God's. It is neither the preacher's nor the people's agency. Barth provides the strongest correction here, arguing in a voice that is not unfamiliar with enticing pull of the historical Jesus campaign, nor the effects of the social gospel.

> Preaching is an attempt that is made with human means. In all circumstances, then, it is made with inadequate means. There is nothing here upon which to rely. But through God, who raises up the dead, who calls into being that which is not, this attempt, this action, is undertaken as a good work insofar is it takes place under God's command and promise and blessing. [40]

Equally troubling is a theology that insists that being engaged in God's kingdom is centered on the choice of congregants rather than on the

38. Dally, *Choosing the Kingdom*, 41.

39. Ibid., 81.

40. Barth, *Homiletics*, 73.

8

sending power of the Holy Spirit, a proper claim that is central to all responsible writers on the subject of missional theology. At its core, the missional movement is a Trinitarian movement which declares that the Father sends the Son and the Father and Son send the Spirit. The activity of the Spirit to center people in worship and send them into faithful action is foundational for work of the missional movement. It needs also to be foundational for a theology of preaching that functions in missional communities.

Fortunately, there are theologically responsible voices to be found. The newest voice to enjoin the conversation is Patrick W. T. Johnson. In his 2013 dissertation, Johnson observes of Dally's approach: "The theological substitution Dally makes is that he replaces Jesus Christ with the kingdom of God, essentially saying that the preacher proclaims what Christ preached instead of preaching Christ."[41] By preaching Christ, he means the fullness of the Christian witness with the death and resurrection at its center. To preach Christ is to understand that the transition point in sermons, Lischer's new obedience, springs from the power of Christ unleashed on the cross, and not from the democratic agency of a people who choose for themselves what to believe and where to serve. To preach Christ is to center God's people in God's word and intention. For the hearers, at the proclamation of Christ, grace erupts as they become new creations living for the world.

With the work of Johnson and others that may emerge, we can hope that those seeking pastoral guidance for preaching in missional communities will find encouragement for proceeding from the same strong theological foundation from which the missional movement has emerged. The gospel is at the center of the missional movement. It must be at the center of its preaching. It is the preacher's evangelical imperative to make certain that the outward movement of missional congregations is grounded in the essential good news of the gospel of Jesus Christ.

Bibliography

Barth, Karl. *Community, State, and Church.* Garden City, NY: Doubleday, 1960.
———. *Homiletics.* Louisville: Westminster John Knox, 1991.
Bartow, Charles L. *Cries of Earth and Altar: Poems That Couldn't Be Helped.* Eugene, OR: Cascade, 2014.
———. *God's Human Speech: A Practical Theology of Proclamation.* Grand Rapids: Eerdmans, 1997.
———. *The Preaching Moment.* Nashville: Abingdon, 1985.
Bonhoeffer, Dietrich. *The Cost of Discipleship.* Translated by R. H. Fuller. New York: Simon and Shuster, 1959.

41. Johnson, "Preaching for the Witness," 230.

Chapp, Larry. "Revelation," in *The Cambridge Companion to Hans Urs von Balthazar.* Cambridge: Cambridge University Press, 2004.

Dally, John Addison. *Choosing the Kingdom: Missional Preaching for the Household of God.* Herndon, VA: The Alban Institute, 2008.

Guder, Darrell L. *Missional Church: A Vision for the Sending of the Church in North America.* Grand Rapids: Eerdmans, 1998.

———. "Missional Hermeneutics: The Missional Authority of Scripture." *Mission Focus: Annual Review* 15 (2007) 119.

Hauerwas, Stanely. *Performing the Faith: Bonhoeffer and the Practice of Nonviolence.* Grand Rapids: Brazos, 2004.

Johnson, Patrick W. T. "Preaching for the Witness of the Christian Community: Toward a Missional Homiletic." PhD diss., Princeton Theological Seminary, 2013.

———. *The Mission of Preaching: Equipping the Community for Faithful Witness.* Downers Grove, IL: Intervarsity, 2015.

Kiefert, Patrick. *We Are Here Now: A Missional Journey of Spiritual Discovery; A New Missional Era.* Eagle, ID: Allelon, 2006.

Langer, Suzanne K. *Feeling and Form.* New York: Charles Scribners and Sons, 1953.

Lischer, Richard. *A Theology of Preaching: the Dynamics of the Gospel.* Nashville: Abingdon, 1981.

Lowry, Eugene. *The Homiletical Plot: The Sermon as Narrative Art Form.* Atlanta: John Knox, 1980.

———. *The Sermon: Dancing on the Edge of Mystery.* Nashville: Abingdon, 1997.

Meyers, Ruth A. *Missional Worship, Worship Mission: Gathering as God's People, Going Out in God's Name.* Grand Rapids: Eerdmans, 2014.

Niebuhr, H. Richard. *The Kingdom of God in America.* New York: Harper & Row, 1959.

Quash, Ben. "The Theo-drama." In *The Cambridge Companion to Hans Urs von Balthasar,* edited by Edward T. Oakes, SJ and David Moss, 143–57. Cambridge: Cambridge University Press, 2004.

Schmit, Clayton J. *Sent and Gathered: A Worship Manual for the Missional Church.* Grand Rapids: Baker Academic, 2009.

———. *Too Deep for Words: A Theology of Liturgical Expression.* Louisville: Westminster John Knox, 2002.

Tizon, Al. *Missional Preaching: Engage, Embrace, Transform.* Valley Forge: Judson, 2012.

Van Gelder, Craig. *The Essence of the Church: A Community Created by the Spirit.* Grand Rapids: Baker, 2000.

Vanhoozer, Kevin J. *The Drama of Doctrine: A Canonical Linguistic Approach to Christian Theology.* Louisville: Westminster John Knox, 2005.

Wells, Samuel. *Improvisation: The Drama of Christian Ethic.* Grand Rapids: Brazos, 2004.

Gospel Wisdom for Ministry

SERMONS FOR THEOLOGY STUDENTS

Ellen F. Davis

FOR SEVERAL REASONS IT seems apt to use sermons preached to theology students as the basis for an essay in honor of and in conversation with Richard Lischer. First, it is my privilege to share with him the daily work of instructing those who are preparing for professional ministry; during one term, we taught a course together on preaching the Psalms. Second, theology students are the "congregation" to whom most of my sermons have been addressed for nearly three decades. Third, my own work as a preacher has from the outset grounded my thinking and practice as a teacher of the Old Testament in several seminaries and divinity schools. Here I set two recent sermons—not coincidentally, on psalms—in the new context of a literary conversation with Lischer's Lyman Beecher Lectures, delivered at Yale University Divinity School and published as *The End of Words: The Language of Reconciliation in a Culture of Violence.* Those lectures, like my sermons, were delivered to theology students and graduates. However, both the sermons and the lectures aim to illumine more broadly the place of scripture in the Christian life.

When, toward the end of my own seminary study, I realized that my primary vocation is to teach Scripture, I realized also that preaching is a more important part of my vocation than I had previously recognized. For it is through sermons—my own, and also the "classical" sermons from ancient, Reformation, and modern preachers that I study and assign to my students—that I discover and rediscover, always with some surprise, the reach of the Bible into the lives of Christians. I speak of the Bible's reach, not its relevance. Calling a biblical passage relevant is sometimes the faint praise that serves as a warrant for treating the text as a springboard from which to make a quick leap into another story with which the preacher feels more at ease. Often enough that comfortable story is a personal reminiscence; likely it is told in what Richard Lischer calls the "secular codes"[1] of our general culture: psychology, politics, entertainment and sports, universal moral truths, and sometimes plain moralism. When the preacher leaps away from the particular language and narrative world of the Bible into something that appears to be more relevant, the sermon's depth dimension is most often lost. As Lischer says (with reference to Erich Auerbach),

> The "background" of the story is precisely the dimension that has gone missing in contemporary preaching, which in many instances appears two-dimensional, restricted to an intensely personal relationship between God and the individual. The necessary background can be recovered only if preaching rediscovers its true narrative framework in scripture and tradition.[2]

The alternative to springboard preaching is to leap into the center of the gospel story as told in both the Old Testament and the New and to speak from there. It is to help a congregation make sense of a story that comes from a world not our own, to make sense of a strange text on its own terms, in the peculiarities of its thought. That kind of preaching demands much more of both preacher and hearer; it requires slow reading, careful listening to both text and preacher. People engage in that kind of inconvenient preaching, from both pulpit and pew, only when they feel that they have to—as Lischer says, when they hear Scripture "as if it were addressed to our particular community and as if our lives depended on its conclusions."[3] That is the kind of reading that he calls theological exegesis, which is nothing other than ordinary Christians—the church—reading the Bible as our own book. If it is arduous, it is also invigorating, even exhilarating, because it opens up new dimensions on both sides of the homiletical engagement. Lischer says that preaching at its best is "an imaginative expansion into realms not easily discerned on the printed page."[4] In the first instance, he is speaking of the expansion of the text, but it is equally true of Christian lives. Preaching that is theologically and exegetically serious, rather than convenient, expands and clarifies the dimensions of the world in which careful listeners may live their faith.

The two sermons that follow are attempts at that kind of preaching. Although I speak here of the particular challenges faced by those entering into professional ministry, the ways I handle the text are not peculiar to

1. Lischer, *End of Words*, 93.
2. Ibid., 94.
3. Ibid., 68.
4. Ibid., 86.

seminary settings. All Christians face the core challenge of embodying the gospel message in its many dimensions and countless faithful forms. The first sermon (on Psalm 119) was a commencement address; the second (on Psalm 91) was delivered a few months later and in a different place, in a service of welcome at the beginning of a new academic year. Both biblical texts treated here are classified as "wisdom psalms"; they speak in a teacher's voice, offering basic instruction in the life of faith. Although that genre may not be frequently preached, it should be. As is typical of wisdom literature, these two psalms illumine basic concepts and practices—prayer, trust, fear, and love of God—that are indispensable for understanding innumerable other biblical texts, and even more, for understanding what it is to be human in the presence of God.[5]

Read, Pray, Trust[6]

A Sermon on Psalm 119

I thank you, both Class of 2014 and Faculty, for this undeserved honor of being your preacher this evening, as you enter into your majority (so to speak) in ministry. The honor to me is undeserved, because with respect to much of what lies ahead for you, I am clueless: I don't belong to the Reformed tradition, as most of you do, and I have never been a pastor, as most of you will be. Therefore I focus now on what we do share: We are all people of prayer, or at least people trying to pray, trying to do our part in maintaining a life–giving relationship with God. And, speaking for myself, it isn't easy, nor is it clear most of the time whether we are doing a decent job. Sad to say, what it is to be in relationship with God tends to get murky, muddled after you leave seminary, where there were clear standards of expectation on things such as chapel participation, as well as a great deal of guided theological reflection, which is the name of the game you've been playing here for several years. But now you will be mostly on your own in tending your relationship with God—unless you find a really good spiritual director, which I would heartily recommend.

So now I bring before you the most skilled spiritual director I know, the genius of poetry and prayer who has given us the 119th Psalm. Biblical scholars call it a wisdom psalm, and having lived with it now for some years, I believe this might be the single best lesson on spirituality in the whole Bible. It is of

5. Each sermon text is followed by a brief comment, which brings the sermon into conversation with Lischer's Lyman Beecher Lectures.

6. Delivered at the 2014 commencement ceremony at Western Theological Seminary, Holland, Michigan.

course a very long psalm, and there is a reason for that, because spirituality is not the kind of thing that lends itself to quick study. This psalmist is taking us on a slow winding journey of 176 fairly repetitive verses; in the course of our travel together we are gradually being inducted into a spirituality for the long haul, one that can sustain us now and for the rest of our lives. As I thought about what this psalm might say to you, I realized that it has particular resonance for those in the Reformed tradition, because the spirituality in which it instructs us is so deeply rooted in Scripture. It is teaching us, you might say, an intimate hermeneutic, a way of reading scripture that draws us into profound and loving relationship with the One whose voice we may hear on every page, if only we know how to seek out God through the written word and hold fast to what—or who—is disclosed to us. In short, the psalmist is teaching us how to read, pray, and trust.

In the manner of the best teachers in every age and setting, the psalmist teaches by sharing with us his own struggles—in this case, his struggles to find God in the words of a text. The psalmist presents himself to us as a young man, though he could be an older man remembering what it was like to be young. In any case, we see him as a young Torah student, and that means he is a lot like us—more like us than he is like other folks we know from the Bible: Moses, say, or Abraham, or Elijah. Like us and unlike them, this psalmist does not experience God as a 3-D, speaking character who says, "Leave here; go there; do this now." Our psalmist doesn't hear God speaking out of the fire, or in the thunder of Sinai, or even in a still, small voice, giving directions that are unmistakable, if not always logical. Our psalmist was not present at Sinai, when the divine finger inscribed the commandments—black fire on white fire, as the rabbis say. Those holy words have cooled down by his time; the psalmist knows them pretty much the same way we do, as black ink on parchment or paper. And so he has the same difficulty we have: How on earth can you learn to read in a way that enables you to find the reality of God in a book, even if you call it a holy book?

This is a tough situation, spiritually speaking, although I suppose we are all sort of used to it by now. Yet the greatness of the psalmist is that he does not try to get used to it. He is honest enough, and desperate enough for a living connection with God, that he repeatedly cries out for hermeneutical help: "Open my eyes that I may see wonders in your *torah*, your teaching." He believes there is a real connection to be made through these texts, though often it is maddeningly elusive. "Do not hide from me your commandments," he pleads. "I cling to your testimony, Adonai; do not put me to shame" (v. 31). Acute longing and vulnerability is the tone of the whole psalm: "My eyes pine for your speaking" (v. 82); "My *nefesh*, my soul, my whole being, clings to the dust" (v. 25); it "dissolves in anguish" (v. 28)—now that's vulnerable.

Our young psalmist is reading scripture the way people of my generation and many before read love letters. Electronic communications have probably eclipsed the ancient drama of the love letter, but for centuries, reading a love letter was a common, yet never ordinary, experience. Probably for most people it was their sole experience of reading a text with total attention, in a state of utter vulnerability. Imagine: You might wait weeks, even months, to hear from the beloved. You planned your days around the mail delivery; you ran to the mailbox; sometimes you approached it with trepidation. When the letter finally came, you went to a quiet place and read it over and over; you returned to it for days. When you knew every word, you added it in the bundle of letters, tied up with a ribbon, and put it in a shoebox. Sometimes those letters were kept for generations, especially if the romance emanated in marriage and children. But sometimes, after a painful break, you threw them away—or better, you ceremoniously burned them, and then you were physically ill. "My soul, my *nefesh*, my whole being, dissolves in anguish."

Don't tell me the poet of this psalm is a legalistic pedant. A lot of people think so, but they cannot have read his words. Our psalmist is melting with unfulfilled longing: "My whole being dissolves." This psalm is the Song of Songs of the Psalter. That is, it is one extended expression of longing that meets with an answering passion, yet is never sated. Intense longing—that is what makes for a passionate reading of texts, for a hermeneutic of intimacy, whether you are reading love letters or Torah. Moved by intense longing, you try to connect with another heart and mind, a life that seems essential for your own life. You never get tired of reading every word, over and over, carefully probing every ambiguity, playing with every hint that points to more than is actually written. Our psalmist, whether young in years or young in heart, is a playful reader—but this is the serious play of a child. If you read this psalm carefully, you will run across that word over and over: "Your *Torah*, God, your Teaching, is my *plaything*" (*sha'ashu'ai*, v. 174; cf. vv. 16, 24, 47, 77, 92, 143, etc.). I have noticed that most translators try to come up with something more grown-up sounding than the word "plaything," and that's too bad. The point is, the psalmist never gets tired of Scripture, any more than a child gets bored with her favorite toy.

Reading God's Word like this is the farthest thing from a head-trip. This is heart-reading, and it changes a body. It will change yours, if you stay at it. "You widen my heart," the psalmist prays (v. 32). Poring over words that come from God and reveal God, you may feel your own heart stretching. "You widen my heart"—that is a sign of health, of spiritual athleticism—and "I *run* in the way of your commandments." It is good when God widens your heart, but still, it is painful. How could it not be painful to have your heart stretched? An older priest, a wise and compassionate woman, tells a story from some years ago. She had gone to see a psychiatrist because she was struggling with depression. She was depressed about the state of the world, the terrible suffering and inhumanity she witnessed or read about. "Why do you let these things bother you?" the psychiatrist asked. "You can't do anything about them. The aim of therapy is to be well adjusted." That remark was clarifying for her; it was even healing, although not in the way the psychiatrist had intended. She recognized it as the counsel of despair, and not the word of the gospel. "We certainly can do something about these things," she said; "we can bring them in prayer before God." The aim of prayer, like the aim of poring over God's word in Scripture, is to let our hearts be stretched to embrace the world, to embrace its agony and nurture its difficult hope. The aim of prayer is by the grace of God to develop a more capacious heart for the world in its suffering, not to be "well adjusted," that is, conformed to the world in its sickness.

The psalmist, our director, reads Scripture with a lover's passion and prays like an athlete in training. But there is something more here, something that makes this psalm not just a keeper but a lifeline; it has the capacity to guide us through a lifetime in ministry. What is most distinctive here is the persistent note of vulnerability, utter vulnerability before God. You could call it "trust in God," and that would be perfectly accurate, but the spiritual genius of this psalmist is to show us that the flip side of trust is vulnerability. Trust is the disposition of heart and mind that characterizes those who are vulnerable; if you are in control of a situation or a relationship, then you don't need to trust. Now let's be honest: most of us would prefer to be in a situation where it is not really necessary to trust God, where we are sailing along with a fair wind at our back. It is when the wind is against us that we are forced back on trust in God. And that is where the psalmist is: "The way of trust have I chosen" (v. 30), he says; "I have trusted in your word" (v. 42).

So total is his choice for trust that the final stanza of the psalm is pure supplication: "Save me . . . , I long for your rescue . . . , I have wandered like a lost sheep." Stop right there. What kind of way is that for an authoritative biblical teaching to end? "I have wandered like a lost sheep." This, the very last line, is where we come to the real shock-value of this psalm, where it totally violates our good professional sense. You don't publicize your cluelessness and then expect people to take you seriously; as we all know, you need to project self-confidence if you are going to succeed in ministry. "I have been wandering like a lost sheep"—this is biblical wisdom? Would you post that on your Facebook page?

Yet that final line of the psalm up-ended and re-directed the life of one person whose work is known to us; it eventually became the impetus for half a century of fruitful ministry. "I have been wandering like a lost sheep; seek your servant"—that line haunted the eighteenth-century slaver John Newton until he finally renounced the slave trade and began to study for ministry. There is a faint echo of the line in his most famous hymn, *Amazing Grace*: "I once was lost but now am found." You don't need to be as lost as Newton was to discover in this psalm the wisdom essential for any ministry that is to be fruitful over the long term, namely the difference—no, the total incompatibility between *self*-confidence and trust in God.

Self-confidence may be widely promoted as a professional asset for pastors, but the Bible represents it quite differently. From a biblical perspective, relying on your own strengths is a mode of arrogance. Repeatedly, our psalmist talks about the people from whom he needs to protect himself—the ones who aren't thinking about God as they confidently pursue schemes that work to their own advantage; he calls such people "the arrogant" (vv. 78, 85, etc.). Our psalmist would tell us that we need to choose: either self-confidence, which is a form of spiritual blindness, or the way he himself has chosen, radical trust in God.

As we consider the consequences of that choice for ministry, my attention is arrested by one particular moment of both declaration and supplication. First the psalmist's declaration: "I trust in your word" (v. 42). And then the plea that follows from that: Do not take any word of truth entirely out of my mouth (vv. 42–43).

All of us here should become practiced in that plea; it belongs on our own lips. Think about what we are called to do. Whether it is pastoral ministry, preaching or leading worship, teaching, counseling, chaplaincy, spiritual direction, or community work, all of us with a theological education bear the responsibility regularly to speak some word of truth about God and human life with God. In other words, we need to speak about things that are vastly beyond our understanding. If we imagine that we are in a strong position to speak authoritatively about God, if we are perhaps afraid to admit how much we do not know, or how much we ourselves may struggle with confusion and doubt, even as we keep turning back to God to try again—in other words, if we choose the way of *self*-confidence over the way of vulnerability and trust in God, then we are likely to be among those arrogant of whom the psalmist says, "They twist, they manipulate me with lies" (v. 78).

Unfortunately, some of us know about that manipulation: what it is to have someone who claims to be an authority on the things of God—a minister or teacher or spiritual guide—mess with your mind and heart. Sustained exposure to that kind of deceptively confident manipulation is damaging; it takes a long time, sometimes years, to recover your spiritual health. How different is the ministry of someone like our psalmist, who chooses the way of trust and thus invites others into a genuinely safe space, where it is all right to be uncertain, even about important things; where all—even we who are "in authority"—can be vulnerable before God and one other. Whenever two or three or more gather thus in Christ, a little truth about God may be spoken and shared, and gradually we may grow together into the true body of Christ.

Therefore, Western Seminary graduates of the Class of 2014, this is our prayer for you:

- that you may foster the creation of safe, nurturing spaces for the body of Christ to grow, each of you in the ministry to which you are now called;
- that you may be sustained in that ministry by the practice of reading scripture with a lover's eye, with your heart and not only your head;
- that through reading, prayer, and truthful sharing of the Christian life, God will stretch your heart wide to embrace the world in its pain and faltering hope.
- Above all, we pray that you may have the courage to lose your *self-confidence* and to trust in God—the courage to be wide open in vulnerability to God and neighbor.

And let all the people of God say: *Amen*.

Sermon Comments

Richard Lischer writes of the preacher's "love affair with the Bible,"[7] which reaches its culmination when the preacher "speak[s] the book," taking it on her own lips.[8] This means that it is finally the tone of the *text*, and not the personality and mood of the preacher, that determines the nature of the sermon. Following Augustine, the most influential of Christian rhetoricians, he affirms that "each text of scripture has its own style and therefore suggests the manner in which it should be preached."[9]

This particular sermon takes its direction from what I hear as the psalm's distinctive tone: intense yearning for intimacy with God. Like countless religious Jews through the centuries, the psalmist seeks that intimacy through Torah, God's written word—described here, remarkably, as a "plaything." My reading of the psalm as both playful and intimate departs completely from the view of the psalm once standard among Christian commentators that it expresses or leads toward a legalistic piety that is at variance with the gospel. It is hard not to hear a measure of anti-Judaism in Artur Weiser's judgment that the "theology of the law" expressed here

---

7. Lischer, *End of Words*, 50.
8. Ibid., 76.
9. Ibid., 77.

"carries with it the germs of a development which was bound to end in the self-righteousness of the Pharisees and scribes."[10]

The tone of yearning generated by and focused on God's word led me to the metaphor of the love letter, which anchors the sermon. In a criticism of the overuse of sermon illustrations, which tend "to take over the sermon and detract from the gospel,"[11] Lischer identifies as one alternative the use of a "master metaphor":

> Unlike the illustration, the metaphor is . . . essential to the sermon, for in a mysterious way metaphor encompasses the apparent contradiction of specific instances and abstract ideas. An illustration confirms to its hearers something they already know. A metaphor discloses a reality that at some level the hearer has not imagined.[12]

Here the image of the love letter points to a way of reading Scripture that is totally involving of heart as well as head, that leads beyond self-absorption and (mere) *self*-confidence to trust in God. Ironically, although self-confidence is generally considered to be the sine qua non for success in professional ministry, trust in God is a mode of vulnerability that enables genuine openness to God and neighbor.

Stuck on God[13]

A Sermon on Psalm 91

Gathered as we are to celebrate the feast of Saint Bartholomew, don't feel bad if your first instinct is to say, "Pardon my ignorance, but what did Bartholomew do? Just what sort of sainthood are we celebrating here?" That would be an astute question, because we have no biblical evidence beyond the bare fact that he is one of the twelve who accepted the intimate companionship of Jesus, one of the eleven who "stood by [Jesus] in [his] trials," as Luke puts it (Luke 22:29). Bartholomew made it to the end and beyond with Jesus, and therefore he must have participated in the spate of healing miracles and the spread of the new faith that followed the resurrection, again according to Luke (Acts 5:12–16). Nonetheless, he is a disciple without a pedigree or a personal

10. Weiser, *Psalms*, 741.

11. Lischer, *End of Words*, 110.

12. Ibid., 119.

13. Delivered on the opening day of classes 2014, to the Anglican Episcopal House of Studies at Duke Divinity School. The liturgical date was the Feast of Saint Bartholomew.

story, biblically speaking. (Of course there are post-biblical stories about Bartholomew that run in various directions and therefore leave us wondering if they are all simply conjecture. Did he really found churches in India and also Ethiopia and Mesopotamia, before he was flayed alive in Armenia—and if so, who was his travel agent?) Yet as far as the New Testament is concerned, Bartholomew is a completely blank slate, unlike most of the other disciples. We have no family names or stories about parents and siblings; we don't know where he met Jesus or the character of his relationship with the Teacher; there are no clues about his personality.

In a word, the Evangelists do not seem to regard Bartholomew as special in any way. Could it be that that is what makes him the right saint for us on this opening day of the year—for many here the opening of a new chapter of life? As far as the Evangelists are concerned, what is important about Bartholomew is that he followed Jesus and stayed with him, even if afterwards no one could remember anything that distinguished this disciple from the others who remained faithful. Could it be precisely his unstoried faithfulness that gives *us* a way into the story of discipleship? Just because we know nothing about him as an individual, we can imaginatively Photoshop our own faces onto Bartholomew's shoulders and through him take our place in the family album—that is, in the church's multi-generational and multi-faced, but often anonymous, story.

Bartholomew gives us a way into the Christian story that does not depend on my special qualities or yours, any more than it depends on his. Take that as good news for you personally, if you are beginning this year with your competitive instinct fully engaged, as is common in the church and in our wider culture, and even in this school. Bartholomew in his unstoried sainthood lifts from us the pressure to be more devout or self-sacrificing than the next faithful person, more successful in mission or more recognized in preaching, maybe to be a better theologian (that's my own unholy aspiration)—in sum, to be known as just a *little* more special than the others whom Jesus loves and calls to serve him in this place. Bartholomew tells us that the point is simply to accept the companionship of Jesus and stay with him, to the end and beyond. You do that, and let others tell whatever stories they want about your qualities and achievements, or tell no stories at all. From the standpoint of eternity—and that is the perspective from which you should be learning to think in your years here—from the standpoint of eternity, it makes no real difference. What matters is the *church's* story, the story of Christian discipleship "from generation to generation in the Church, and in Christ Jesus, for ever and ever."[14]

14. *Book of Common Prayer*, 102; cf. Eph 3:21.

Bartholomew testifies to nothing more nor less than the singular value of sticking with Jesus through thick and thin. I am guessing that is why those who crafted the lectionary were inspired to associate him with the anonymous believer of Psalm 91, of whom God says, "Because he is passionately-attached to me, I will rescue him" (v. 14). "Passionately-attached" is the best translation I can think of for the Hebrew verb *hashaq*; the familiar translation, "because he is bound to me in love,"[15] seems a shade cool for this kind of driving devotion—so intense, you couldn't let go even if you thought that might be a good idea. *Hashaq* denotes attachment, both religious... and not. It is the biblical word for what we call "falling in love" (Gen 34:8; Deut 21:11)—initially at least, an attachment involving more passion than sense. So for instance, the Canaanite prince Shechem goes *hashaq* for Dinah, daughter of the patriarch Jacob (Gen 34:8)—and the result is disastrous. So when we hear that the anonymous believer in the psalm has gone *hashaq* for God, we should assume that this is a highly consequential attachment, though not necessarily a convenient one. Possibly some of you know what it is to be passionately but inconveniently attached to God.

So this is a psalm about someone who is really stuck on God. Not coincidentally, it is also about someone in serious trouble: arrows flying about, plague and pestilence stalking the streets, people dropping right and left. In these dire circumstances, the protagonist of our psalm takes refuge in God; she sets up shop in the hiding-place of the Most High, makes himself at home in the shadow of the Almighty (Ps 91:1). This is a poem—a song, if you like—about fear-management, about handling fear and not yielding to the impulse to cut and run (Ps 91:5). It comes to us this evening via the lectionary as a gift of the Spirit, because handling fear is one of the crucial skills you will need, first in Divinity School, and then in every form of ministry to which you are called for the rest of your life.

You'll need to learn to handle fear, not primarily because people who frequent divinity schools and churches are unusually threatening—although that is a hypothesis worth exploring on another occasion. But the point for us now is that the very nature of God's call requires that you learn to manage your fear. God calls people to serve in situations where the forces opposed to God seem to have the upper hand. Death, hatred of self and others, idolatry, willful ignorance, self-absorption, greed—aren't these the conditions that call forth the work of ministry? You walk into the middle of a situation where God is out-numbered and out-gunned, so to speak. You confront the evil within yourself as well as the evil coming at you, and with all your puny might and whatever integrity you can summon, you testify to a different and by no

---

15. Ibid., 720.

means obvious reality. Of course that is scary. If you think the outcome of your testimony and your labors is uncertain on this side of death, you are right. And now that you have accepted a call to ministry of some kind (whether or not you know what kind), you can expect to have this experience over and over again. I am guessing that some of you are ahead of the game: It is only the first day of class, and already you are experiencing some fear. If that is your situation, then congratulations; you are a quick study. Your fear is a sign that you have not entirely missed the point of the new thing that God is doing in your life.

It is because fear is a constitutive part of ministry that the Bible gives nuanced treatment to the whole phenomenon. If you are feeling afraid, then take comfort in the Bible, which has anticipated this and charted the territory for you. If you are feeling afraid, take heart; you are in a position to understand the assurances of God as we hear them in Scripture, over and over again. And the crucial thing those assurances disclose is this: if you are feeling afraid, then you are in exactly the right position to learn how to open yourself to God more fully.

Here is a curious point of biblical theology: God often says, "Don't be afraid"—a sure sign that there is good reason to be afraid. Yet even more often the biblical writers and Jesus himself *commend* fear, specifically "fear of God,"/ *yir'at Elohim* in Hebrew; this is biblical shorthand for being wholly open to God. Some translators want to tone down the phrase by rendering it "reverence for God," but it is a mistake to disguise the gut-grabbing sense of it. Fear of God is not simply well mannered piety of the kind we Anglicans display rather well. No, living into the fear of God is a fully embodied, wholehearted, total-life experience. Fearing God means fearing nothing but the loss of God, as one beautiful prayer puts it.[16] That reckless, total spiritual openness is something into which disciples may grow, usually over many years. If we do grow fully into it, if we should become saints, I suppose it will be only through painful experience and difficult confrontation with our own evil.

As our psalm shows, being totally open and passionately attached to God means gradually giving up all your ordinary fears and the self-protective behaviors that go with them. Once he got stuck on Jesus, the unstoried disciple Bartholomew must have spent the rest of his life in fearsome situations. He stuck with Jesus as the pressure against the Master began to mount in Jerusalem. He was among the apostles testifying publicly to Jesus the risen Messiah, after he had been executed by the Empire. For teaching about Jesus in the Temple compound, the apostles got themselves arrested, imprisoned, and flogged (Acts 5:17–40).

16. Collect for the Eighth Sunday after the Epiphany, *Book of Common Prayer*, 216.

"Because he is passionately-attached to me, I will rescue him," says God in our psalm; "I am with him in trouble . . . ; I will show him my salvation" (Ps 91:14–16). Likely Bartholomew and his companions knew this psalm, and no doubt they came to understand through following Jesus that being rescued by God does not mean putting trouble behind you. Rather, it means that God is with you in trouble; Bartholomew and the company of faithful disciples see God's salvation in the resurrection of their murdered Teacher and Lord. In short, being rescued, being "saved," means experiencing God's faithfulness in the midst of trouble and thus discovering your own capacity to stick with God, because you fear nothing so much as the loss of God. That is what we pray for you this evening, beloved of God in Christ, as you enter into this year, into your studies in this place. May you be stuck on God through thick and thin (you'll experience both here). And one thing more: May you, like Bartholomew and the other disciples of the newly risen Christ, count it all, count all of it as joy (Acts 5:41). Amen.

Sermon Comments

This sermon is a literal instance of reading the Bible "with the church . . . , with the saints," as Lischer puts it—although he does not mean only those saints who appear in the church calendar.[17] Preached on the Feast Day of Saint Bartholomew at a service at the beginning of the academic year, the sermon sets Psalm 91 in the context of the saint's life. It is just because we know so little about Bartholomew that he is a sort of stained-glass saint, transparent to the life of every faithful disciple, and that made him the ideal focus of a sermon preached largely to incoming students, who did not yet have any story or any established "personality" in their new Christian community. Therefore focusing on Bartholomew brought the sermon down to the most basic common denominator of what it is to be a Christian: it is simply to be with Jesus, as Bartholomew was—"passionately attached" to God in Christ, to use the language of Psalm 91.

The preceding sermon used a master metaphor as an alternative to the typical and often superfluous sermon illustration; this one uses a second narrative alternative, which Lischer calls "the focal instance." Rather than competing with the biblical text for our attention, it enables us to see more clearly what the text is saying. "The focal instance means to say, in effect, 'This is the message of God's grace; and this is what that grace looks like

---

17. Lischer, *End of Words*, 67.

when it intersects the lives of real people.'"[18] Perhaps I was drawn to preach on the psalm, among the several lectionary texts for that day, because the psalms lend themselves especially well to that kind of narrativizing; they may even require it. The secret of preaching the Psalms is discovering their narrative potential, hearing how they highlight moments in the ancient and ongoing story of those who pray to Israel's God. That is why the ancient theologians who shaped the psalter inserted superscriptions that connect various psalms with key moments in David's life (e.g., Psalm 51), which is one of the Bible's most fully developed narratives. Thus they provided guidance for anyone who might pray the psalms, preach them, and try to live into the faith they express.

The language of the psalms is condensed and vivid, the "maximal speech" of poetry,[19] and so it is true to their character to concentrate on one or two words or concepts. Here, the compelling idea of passionate attachment to God, conveyed by the verb *hashaq*, is linked with the central biblical theme of setting aside fear as we ordinarily experience it and embracing the fear of God. Although we do not like to admit it, the fear born of self-absorption is a constitutive and often disabling element of seminary life and of ministry. In showing us what life looks like when we set that aside and give ourselves passionately to God, the psalm obliquely invites us to claim the consuming yet life-giving fear that is characteristic of the saints.

Bibliography

The Book of Common Prayer . . . According to the use of The Episcopal Church. New York: Church Hymnal Corporation, 1979.

Davis, Ellen F. *Wondrous Depth: Preaching the Old Testament.* Louisville: Westminster John Knox, 2005.

Lischer, Richard. *The End of Words: The Language of Reconciliation in a Culture of Violence.* Grand Rapids: Eerdmans, 2005.

Weiser, Arthur. *The Psalms: A Commentary.* Old Testament Library Series. Philadelphia: Westminster, 1962.

18. Ibid., 111.

19. See Davis, *Wondrous Depth*, 23–28.

Preaching the Gospel of Hope

HOW THE PROPHETS NAVIGATE BETWEEN
OPTIMISM AND DESPAIR

Charles L. Aaron

WE WINCE WITH EMBARRASSMENT when we see the pictures now. Headbands, shoulder-length hair, bell-bottom jeans, and peace signs seemed cool in the sixties. Even though I missed by a few years the opportunity even to look like a hippie, I remember feeling a sense of solidarity with that particular counter culture. I certainly enjoyed the music. The decade's defining anthem filled the air each time I turned it up. Bob Dylan's "The Times, They Are a Changin'" captured the mood of the day. With biblical allusions to the role reversal of first and last, the song announced inevitable progress, as inescapable as a rushing flood. Declaring a populist, bottom-up movement with the role of politicians limited to standing aside to avoid injury, the song celebrated the end of the old and the sprouting of the new.

Many people fretted over the rapid social changes of the sixties, but the young saw potential for a culture less materialistic, less divided, more peaceful. If Dylan provided artistic interpretation, the obvious religious leader of the push for change and justice was Martin Luther King, Jr. Starting at least with the bus boycott in Montgomery, Alabama, in the fifties, King rose to national prominence with his eloquent, majestic speeches and sermons. Even with the difficulties of confronting racism and injustice and the predictable backlash at his attempts, King insisted, at least publicly, that change could occur. In one essay he reflected on his attitude while engaging in the struggle, "People are often surprised to learn that I am an optimist. They know how often I have been jailed, how frequently the days and nights have been filled with frustration and sorrow, how bitter and dangerous are my adversaries. They expect these experiences to harden me into a grim and desperate man. They fail, however, to perceive the sense of affirmation generated by the challenge of embracing struggle and surmounting obstacles."[1] In his most famous speech on the Washington mall he outlined his dream of the end of racial discrimination and the healing of the wounds caused by injustice.

To say that King projected a tenaciously positive hope for change does not suggest a sunny avoidance of reality. Especially toward the end of his life he faced the intractable nature of evil and injustice. As Richard Lischer notes, his later sermons reflected his growing awareness of resistance to change. In Lischer's words, "When he is not sad in these sermons, he is uncharacteristically angry with those who have obstructed his programs or deserted him. His rhetoric becomes more confrontational, more prophetic in nature."[2]

Nevertheless, King embodied the hope for cultural transformation of the civil rights movement of the fifties and sixties (one errs in assuming that the civil rights era has passed; it continues today). Even on the night before his murder, he declared his conviction that the "promised land" remained a realistic destination. For at least a time, part of the American populace embraced a vision for something new and different: for equality, justice and community.

Three Forms of Prophetic Hope

That attitude bears some similarity to a strand of the prophetic literature of the First Testament. Preachers often oversimplify the message of the prophets. One often hears the term "prophetic preaching" referring to sermons on controversial issues or sermons that address injustice. Certainly, the prophets did engage in controversy, and did address injustice. Underlying their calls for just treatment of the poor lay the conviction that the community could achieve justice. Although many biblical scholars conclude that the historical Amos, for example, simply announced God's abandonment of Israelite society in part because of its lack of justice, the final form of the book that bears his name urges the establishment of justice with the expectation that Israel can fulfill that expectation. So Amos declares, "Fallen, no more to rise, is virgin Israel, deserted on her land, with no one to raise her up" (5:2).[3] Yet the same chapter later exhorts, "Seek good and not evil, that you may

1. King, *Testament*, 314.

2. Lischer, *Preacher King*, 162.

3. Common English Bible. All biblical quotations will be from the CEB unless otherwise noted.

live; and so the Lord, the God of heavenly forces, will be with you just as you have said. Hate evil, love good, and establish justice at the city gate. Perhaps the Lord God of heavenly forces will be gracious to what is left of Joseph" (vv. 14–15). The final form of the book of Amos expects that Israel can achieve justice.[4] In the words of one First Testament scholar writing about the prophets, "It was possible to act justly in the courts and in the economy. If they had not believed this, their criticism of their contemporaries and the judgment they announced upon them would have made no sense. Without a hint of utopian fanaticism, they assumed that concrete acts and decisions and policies which expressed justice were attainable."[5]

One passage in particular embodies this hope for real change in present circumstances. The church often mistakes Isaiah 11 for a prediction of the birth of Jesus. In reality the prophet expressed hope that a leader would arise in the prophet's own time. With nearly superhuman abilities this leader would create a fair and equitable society in which the poor and the meek receive justice. The leader accomplishes his mission because of the divine spirit resting on him. The passage does not present a realistic picture of what one human being can accomplish, even with the aid of the divine spirit. The fanciful nature of the passage comes more clearly into light in vs. 6 when the realm of nature loses its violent quality, with even lions turning into vegans. One has trouble articulating exactly what Isaiah 11 envisions. Despite the unrealistic nature of the passage, however, the prophet holds out deep hope for this creation. God can work astonishing things within this world. The prophet assumed a different process than did Bob Dylan. The folk singer envisioned a bottom-up change, unaided by political leaders. The prophet believed that God would work through a leader with the flow of justice moving downward.

The prophet's expectations never materialized. In fact, the various messages of the prophets failed to find fertile ground. Hosea could not turn the people from their idolatry. Isaiah son of Amoz could not produce the obedience that prevented the people being devoured by the sword (1:19–20). The Assyrians (owners of the sword Isaiah warned of) and the Babylonians conquered the northern and southern kingdoms respectively. These defeats caused profound theological questioning among the people of Israel and Judah. The production of the First Testament likely arose as a way to seek understanding of these devastating events.

When Cyrus the Persian conquered the Babylonians and allowed the people of Judah to return to their homeland, the prophet whom scholars

---

4. See Coote, *Amos Among the Prophets*.

5. May, "Justice," 8.

have come to call Second Isaiah offered some of the most beautiful poetry ever written to help the people understand how God acted in the opportunity to start anew. With the familiar words, "Comfort, comfort my people! says your God," the poet brings new expectancy to the long exiled people (Isa 40:1). This prophet, likely one who had studied the prophecies of the original Isaiah, assured the discouraged people of Judah that returning from exile would result in a renewed relationship with God and prosperity (cf. 54:7–8, 55:13). The new community would experience internal harmony and safety from outside attack (cf. 54:13–15).

The prophets, then, offered hope in three different ways in three different circumstances. First, they offered the hope that the people, if instructed in their identity, could produce a just society. Then, Isaiah offered a mysterious hope that, with proper leadership inspired by the divine spirit, the people could enjoy a deeply satisfying justice and harmony. Finally, the poet of Second Isaiah believed that perhaps the experience of defeat and exile, followed by the outpouring of divine love, would create a new awareness in the people of their mission and potential for living in community.

Apocalyptic Hope

All three levels of hope failed. The returning exiles encountered obstacle after obstacle. Conflicts arose between the returnees and those who had stayed behind in Jerusalem. These conflicts created strife in the community and undermined a sense of solidarity among God's people.[6] The Persians treated the people of Judah better than the Babylonians had, but the people still had to play by the Persian rules. Eventually, of course, Alexander the Great conquered the Persian Empire, spreading Hellenistic culture across the land. In the second century BCE, the people faced a grave threat. Antiochus IV, a Syrian leader, arose and attempted to use Hellenization as a means of unifying his dominion. Antiochus punished viciously any resistance to Greek culture. He did not exempt the people of Judea from his program, punishing observance of Yahwistic faith with unspeakable cruelty. He destroyed copies of the Torah. He had families who circumcised their babies killed and the babies hung around the necks of their dead mothers. He turned the temple in Jerusalem into a shrine for Zeus (cf. 1 Macc 1:54–64; 2 Macc 6:2).

The book of Daniel reflects the attempt of the people of Judea to resist Greek culture, both in the third century and during the time of Antiochus in the second century. Daniel represents the full expression of apocalyptic theology within the First Testament. Apocalyptic theology drew upon

6. See Hanson, *Dawn of Apocalyptic*, 95.

traditions of myth from earlier periods of Hebrew thought. Dreams and visions revealed reality. Faithful Yahwists should endure persecution and martyrdom because God would reward such heroism in resurrection (see 2 Macc 7). Daniel 12:2 contains the first clear, unambiguous reference to resurrection in the First Testament. With the affirmation of resurrection, the fulfillment of hope is located beyond the boundaries of history in an afterlife. Daniel does not describe life in resurrection, but affirms that hope lies there.

In summary, the prophetic literature of the First Testament struggles with the affirmation of hope for harmony and justice within history. Can God's people create a society in which all people find fairness and the opportunity to thrive? The prophets proclaimed the divine will for justice and care for the poor. In an interesting but ambiguous passage, Isaiah provided an image of a ruler filled with the divine spirit that could do what people on their own could not. In both cases, the prophets held out hope for justice in this life, that is, within the history of Israel. Their words did not produce a just society. The experience of exile and return did not produce a just society. In the second century BCE obedience to God led to death and punishment. The idea appeared that God's rewards and the possibility of justice existed in an afterlife, in resurrection.

Hope in Contemporary Preaching

This brief sketch of the changing understanding of hope within the prophets serves as a background for talk of hope in the contemporary church. Within American society, the fervent hopes of the sixties for an end to racism and injustice have faded. At the time of this writing, racial tensions have flared over police shootings and a choking death of African-American men by law enforcement officers. I do not intend in this article to assign blame or take sides, but to grieve over the continued conflict and distrust. Writing about one of those shootings, the 2014 death of Michael Brown in Ferguson, MO, *New York Times* columnist Charles M. Blow said, "The frustration we see in Ferguson is about not only the present act of perceived injustice but also the calcifying system of inequity—economic, educational, judicial—drawn largely along racial lines." Blow then cites the poem "Harlem" by Langston Hughes and asks, "What happens when one desists from dreaming, when the very exercise feels futile?"[7] Blow summarizes the sense that progress in racial justice and reconciliation has moved slowly and only on the surface. The hope experienced in the sixties has morphed into frustration and

7. Blow, "Frustration in Ferguson," 2.

despair. Poverty rates remain discouragingly high. Political polarization has created deep animosity between the two parties and their supporters. War and terrorism have created fear and distrust between nations and ethnic groups.

In the midst of this situation, how does the church proclaim hope? We can no longer assume that youthful exuberance will translate into new, pervasive attitudes and practices. We do not look at the evidence around us and sing that things are changing for the better. In the face of despair and cynicism, what can the church offer to evoke a sense of hope?

I think that Christian preaching divides into three categories. This scheme oversimplifies, just as most do, yet perhaps it helps us think about the way we understand sermons. Sermons seek one of three purposes.

1. Some sermons preach an apocalyptic word about eschatology. These sermons find hope in resurrection, beyond history. This purpose of preaching finds consistency with the book of Daniel and with Paul, who wrote in Rom 8:18, "I believe that the present suffering is nothing compared to the coming glory that is going to be revealed to us." Corruption and suffering mark this world. The church maintains its witness, drawing on the Spirit to sustain it (cf. Rom 8:26).

2. Other preaching offers an existential message that seeks to help people find healing and meaning in the midst of suffering and the turmoil of the world. This form of preaching finds hope in individual or communal wholeness.

3. Liberative preaching remains committed to the goal of creating change within history. Liberative preaching motivates the church to address injustice with the explicit goal of raising awareness and forming new, more egalitarian structures that resist oppression and exploitation. In the words of Rebecca S. Chopp, writing on liberation praxis, "Finally, praxis as the understanding of human reality means that humans must and can intentionally create history, transforming and shaping reality for the improvement of human flourishing."[8]

Each of these three ways of proclaiming hope from the church has much to commend it, but each has drawbacks as well. The death and resurrection of Jesus direct the attention of the church to the general resurrection. The Second Testament consistently and confidently affirms the resurrection and the future establishment of God's dominion beyond history. With the

---

8. Chopp, "Latin American Liberation Theology," 177.

brokenness, pain, sorrow and death of this world, the church offers hope for God's peace and true justice in the resurrection.

Finding hope in the resurrection raises the question of where to find hope within history. If we focus only on resurrection, do we abandon hope for changing things now? Must we live with extreme poverty, deep alienation among people, despair and oppression until the eschaton? Do those who live in relative comfort use the resurrection as an excuse to avoid working for justice now?

Existential preaching offers important healing and purpose to those who have experienced trauma or just the everyday weariness of life. Existential preaching affirms God's care and love for people who have felt loneliness, grief, abandonment, abuse and failure. Existential preaching gives new meaning to life's difficult experiences. Existential preaching runs the risk of becoming too individualistic, however. Existential preaching must not ignore social structures and the effects of poverty, oppression and injustice in causing despair and alienation within people.

Liberative preaching draws upon the powerful strand within the prophetic tradition that spoke up on behalf of the poor and disenfranchised. Liberative preaching takes seriously the call of Jesus to do ministry among the "least of these" (cf. Matt 25:31–46). Liberative preaching believes that people can change and expresses genuine confidence that people can live and work together now, within history. Yet liberative preaching may not take seriously enough the intractability of sin within creation. The church must do serious reflection on the declaration of Eph 6:12, "We aren't fighting against human enemies but against rulers, authorities, forces of cosmic darkness, and spiritual powers in the heavens." However one understands the language of powers and the demonic in the Second Testament—as metaphor, or a description of some ontological reality—this language speaks to the deep-seated nature of the evil within creation.

Isaiah 65:17–25 and Radical Renewal

I want to commend a passage of scripture that can inspire a sound theology of hope for the church. The passage represents a transition point between traditional prophetic eschatology and apocalyptic theology. Near the end of the book of Isaiah, a book full of majestic poetry, comes a passage that presents as good a description of the divine will for creation as any part of the Bible. Isaiah 65:17–25 portrays God's radical act to renew all of creation, in which "radical" means getting to the root of the problem.

The poem starts exuberantly: "Look! I'm creating a new heaven and a new earth." The English translation of "Look!" draws attention, reflecting the Hebrew grammar. The word for "create" evokes Gen 1:1, and describes God's ability to act freely, decisively and dramatically. The opening verse does not call for the sweeping away or destruction of the present creation, but a "make over," a total refreshment and regeneration of this creation.

The assurance that "past events won't be remembered" might speak of psychological healing. Memories of conflict, anger or trauma typically linger. These memories leave their own stubborn wounds. The poem thus moves quickly from a cosmic scale to a personal one. God will refresh all that exists and heal the memories inside our own heads. Repeatedly the prophet mentions joy, with calls to "rejoice," or "be glad." The divine cosmic act will find its place in the human heart.

When I preach on this passage I usually tell my congregations that I will translate verse 18b from Hebrew into "American," and then I offer the rendering, "I'm creating Washington, DC, as a joy." That part of my sermon usually evokes snickering! We can hardly imagine the bickering, posturing and dirty pool of our political system rejuvenated into a source of joy, even with divine help! The name "Jerusalem" in the First Testament carries many connotations. It had political importance as well as a reputation as the "heart and soul" of the land. The temple in Jerusalem represented the presence of God among the people. As a political and religious center, the city generated loyalty as well as feelings of conflict and strife. Isaiah 65:18 promises unmitigated joy from the city as part of God's renewal.

Addressing the beginning and ending of life, the poem promises a healthy life expectancy. Whatever a society's statistics about infant mortality, the death of a baby represents heartache and lost potential. If we allow ourselves to consider all that the child will miss, the grief might seem unbearable. A person who dies prematurely also misses many opportunities and the chance to enjoy the fruit of labors. In the new creation, babies have the chance at life, and the middle aged will reach the "golden years." The poem does not mention death or "Sheol" as an active, destructive force as earlier parts of the book do (see Isa 5:14), but the poem promises that death, even if still inevitable, will not score too early or easy a victory.

My service on the North Texas Jobs with Justice Worker Rights Board has taught me how oppressive the world of labor can become. Undocumented workers can put in a full week of hard, sweaty, muscle-aching work, but receive no remuneration at the end of that week. Because of their status, they cannot file a complaint. Even with the legal complications put aside, many workers face exploitation at the hands of employers.[9] The passage advocates for labor that leads to satisfaction. Laborers can enjoy the fruit of their labor. An online article described a situation similar to the scenario in the passage: cacao workers eating chocolate for the first time.[10] The prophet does not promise a day at the beach, but work which results in dignity, respect and fulfillment.

With surprising brevity, the poet touches on the divine human relationship. God will answer the prayers and calls of people before they speak them. God will take initiative to enter into fellowship with people and to meet their spiritual needs. God will hear and respond. When we consider the plea of the psalmist, "How long will you forget me, Lord?" we see the power of this promise (Ps 13:1). People will experience no delay in their cries or prayers. God will anticipate prayers and respond to those who seek favor and communication.

God's act of new creation will redeem the realm of nature. Predatory beasts will coexist with their former prey. Zoologists have revealed the cruelty inherent within the animal kingdom. Primates enforce order within a group through intimidation. Ants practice a form of slavery. Felines torment rodents. Elephants endure juvenile delinquency. The prophet may not have known of these behaviors, but he knew the danger within the animal world. That danger will fade away in God's act of new creation.

The poem promises renewal for all of creation. God's "holy mountain" will become a place of peace, of shalom. God's creative act will touch all aspects of life, from health to work to politics to ecology to faith. Because the passage offers a comprehensive picture of the divine will for all of creation, it provides a foundation for hope that transcends the hopes of individuals. Each individual might hope for success and happiness, but the passage describes an all-encompassing hope for God's creation.

This passage from late in Isaiah sounds wonderful. We can take delight in the promises. The passage offers important theological insights as well. As stated above, the passage represents a transition from prophetic eschatology to apocalyptic theology. It draws on many of the themes of Isaiah 11. The prophets of the eighth century used fiery rhetoric to motivate the people to create a just and fair society. Apocalyptic theology pushed hope beyond history into a resurrection life, where the wrongs of this creation were made right. In the resurrection the ways that life thwarted God's will were overcome. Isaiah 65:17–25 represents what scholars call "proto-apocalyptic" writing. In evaluating the place of Isaiah 65 in the development of

9. See Ehrenreich, *Nickel and Dimed*.

10. Barclay, "These Ivory Coast Cacao Farmers."

apocalyptic theology, Paul Hanson writes, "The essential characteristics of apocalyptic eschatology are drawn together into a coherent whole in Isaiah 65: the present era is evil; a great judgment separating the good from the evil and marking the crossroads between the present world and the world to come is imminent; a newly created world of peace and blessing ordained for the faithful lies beyond that judgment."[11] The passage falls between the expectation of earlier prophets that the community could achieve justice within history, and apocalyptic theology that expected hope only beyond history.

Preaching Hope

Apart from the beauty and majesty of its promises, the passage contains important theological insights for preaching hope. The passage recognizes the deep entrenchment of evil within the creation. The First Testament often depicts this evil within creation as the forces of chaos that threaten to wreck God's creation (see Isa 24:21; Ps 77:16). Occasionally, the authors portray mythological scenarios of battles in the heavenly places that affect life on earth (see Dan 10:12–14). Exodus considers the human arrogance that challenges the divine will. YHWH must use the power of creation and nature to break Pharaoh's stubbornness so that the people can leave Egypt. The Second Testament, of course, uses the language of the demonic and of unclean spirits. Regardless of precisely how the contemporary church and synagogue understand this kind of language, it reminds us that the evil in the world does not respond to logic and reason. The prophets used a variety of strategies to convince the people to pursue justice and righteousness. Apocalyptic theology considers the corruption of God's creation so pervasive that only in a resurrection beyond history can God overcome that corruption. This proto-apocalyptic passage from Isaiah 65 understands that only God's action can overcome the deep-seated evil that saturates the creation. Nevertheless, it does not give up on this creation. The passage affirms that God continues to work in this world, in this creation.

On the one hand, preachers cannot affirm the exact picture painted by Isaiah 65. Preachers cannot proclaim that if only the church did its ministry with enough passion and effectiveness, it could create this kind of world. On the other hand, preachers cannot exhort the church to wait for God to fulfill this vision becoming reality within history. Neither hard work nor patience—nor the two together—will allow the community of faith or the world to live into this vision. Nevertheless, this vision from the prophet

11. Hanson, *Dawn of Apocalyptic*, 160.

provides theological substance for the preaching of hope by the church and synagogue. The church offers the hope that the elements of this vision represent the divine will for creation. God wills the healing, fulfillment, justice and reconciliation of this poem. God does not will the status quo of infant mortality (so the death of a baby is not "God's will"), worker exploitation, traumatic memories, environmental carelessness or divine/human alienation. In whatever way one understand the corruption of creation—as the presence of demonic forces, as an incompleteness within creation, as a metaphor for the frustration of trying to bring about change—the poem affirms that only God can overcome this corruption. The full healing of creation will happen in God's time, from God's action. The poem affirms God's continued action within the creation toward this end.

The poem challenges those who preach an apocalyptic word about resurrection to act and work within this creation. The poem challenges those who assume that the church can transform the world with enough effort to take seriously the forces arrayed against change. The poem challenges those whose sermons offer individual therapy and meaning-making to recognize the impact of exploitation on the wellbeing of people. The poem addresses the individual human psyche, but places it within the larger context of health, employment and environment.

If the church and synagogue take seriously the theological substance of this poem, preachers will preach a hope that looks ultimately to what God will do beyond history, and looks also for the ways God works in creation within history. Such preaching will not be naïve about the ways that demonic forces in the cosmos, the darkness of the human heart, and the fragility of life prevent the church from fashioning a world that fulfills the vision in Isaiah 65. Nevertheless, the community of faith can offer the world the promise that the death, exploitation, trauma, and alienation of this creation do not represent God's eternal will. God will create a time and place of shalom, justice, and joy beyond what we see. And even as we hope for such a world beyond history, we look for and participate in God's present work toward wholeness in this creation. Working together, God and the community of faith form pockets of justice, relationships of grace, and expressions of joy within the hardship. The relative justice and celebrations of God's presence bear witness to what God will do in the fullness of God's dominion.

Of the many people I know who live out the call to hope and to work in situations that could lead to despair, I choose to commend Dr. Isabel Docampo, a faculty member in the intern program in supervised ministry at Perkins School of Theology and ordained Baptist minister. She has worked among a remarkable variety of people, many of whom lived on the margins of life. In a private conversation at a coffee shop, she answered my questions about where she found hope in the midst of suffering, sadness, and even violence.

I assumed that a woman who had ministered in El Salvador, facing fear and horror, could explain hope to me. Immediately after 9/11 she helped form a group of women from different faiths, including Jewish and Muslim women who met with Christian women to dialogue and learn from one another. After the thirty-four-day war between Hezbollah and Israel in the summer of 2006, the group experienced inevitable tension. Despite the temptation to disband, the women decided that they could not let each other go, and that God would not allow them to let go of each other. They concluded, "Something beyond us called us to come together."

Dr. Docampo told me about Christians she knows who show courage and hope in small ways and in more far-reaching ways. One of the students whom she supervised on internship ministered in Brazil. She worked on a project for the street children, working with traumatized children. Such a ministry can leave one burned out and despairing. Yet the student found hope in her on-site supervisor, herself a former street child. She discovered that she could experience hope in the faces of the children themselves. She realized that something beyond her called her to do that kind of ministry. She found hope in each child she could help. She recognized God's presence in those children. At Grace United Methodist Church in Dallas, Docampo became acquainted with a young man from Burundi, who had to flee to the United States. His family was divided by political strife. He had to leave his parents and family behind. Yet he finds joy playing drums at the church. Those who know him feel inspired by his sweet spirit, from a man one might expect to be bitter. His smile, his participation in church and his music reflect his courage, his faith and his hope.

A well-respected pastor in Washington, DC, exemplifies hope in the face of despair. The Rev. Edgar Palacios is an internationally recognized Baptist pastor and peacemaker who has received numerous awards for his ministry. He served as executive secretary of the National Council of Churches in El Salvador and executive director of the Permanent Committee of the National Debate for Peace in El Salvador. He is currently pastor of Calvary Baptist Church in Washington, DC. Dr. Docampo presented him to me as her friend, the man behind the awards and accolades. After being placed on the Salvadoran government's death list in the 1980s, he came to the US as an exile, and now ministers to other exiles. His wife, also a Baptist pastor, now deceased, worked with women affected by domestic violence. His community admires him because he treats street people and the "least of these" with the same respect that he treats the politicians whom he lobbies on behalf of his country. Those who know him say they do not see bitterness in him, only righteous anger. He exudes the influence of the Holy Spirit in his life.

The proclamation of hope by the community of faith points ultimately to what God can do in renewing the creation. Eschatologically, God will establish a creation that bears the marks of the vision of Isa 65:17–25. In the interim, the community of faith works to form models of justice and peace in this creation. Some of those models will have a small influence, like one young man who drums in one church in Dallas. Others models will have an impact on those in power, such as the lobbying work and bold ministry of the Rev. Palacios.

The proclamation of the community of faith must offer hope. Without hope people descend into cynicism and despair. Preaching cannot offer a naïve hope that ignores reality. If the pulpit offers the hope that the community of faith can usher in by its own effort something like the vision of Isaiah 65, it will produce only disappointment. If preaching points only to eschatology, it will disengage from this world. Preaching can offer ultimate hope beyond history in God's new creation and resurrection. Preaching can also advocate for courageous resistance to injustice, oppression, violence and sorrow. This creative resistance can form pockets of justice, love and joy that bear witness to Isaiah's vision and the affirmation of God's redeeming power in the rest of scripture. This proclamation of creative resistance can sustain the community as it looks for God's work in creation and waits for the ultimate fulfillment.

Allan Boesak lives out the courageous resistance that I suggest should form the basis of the proclamation of hope of the community of faith. He knows firsthand the pitfalls of offering hope in too facile a manner. Writing from the South African context, he declares,

> When Hope has taught us to speak, shall we then speak her language without fear, challenging the language of meaningless religiosity, patriotic uniformity, and political conformity? For if there is one thing that we have learned through our struggles and our faith, it is that the language of hope is first the language of suffering and pain; of truth and anger and courage; of protest and confrontation and endurance—before it is the language of comfort, uplifting, and joy. It screams before it soothes. The language of hope is a language that scorches the tongue of the powerful, the arrogant, and the violent. In the mouths of the deceitful, the comfortable, and the complacent, it grits like sand between the teeth. On the lips of the faithful it is a balm. Speaking of hope should disturb us before it comforts us.[12]

12. Boesak, *Dare We Speak of Hope?* 33–34.

Richard Lischer advocates three theological movements in every sermon. He uses the terms analysis, transition, and integration to designate these movements. Analysis is both the mirror of futility and the judgment of God. Transition recognizes that God has done for us what we cannot do for ourselves. Integration moves the hearer to do and become in different ways because of God's action.[13] Hope in preaching comes from the analysis that we live in a world marked by injustice, oppression, poverty and suffering. Even if we could eliminate these things, we do not. The brokenness of creation works against us. The transition affirms that God wills health, community, fulfillment and relationship for creation. God will bring about full shalom in God's time and place. God continues to work in the creation as it is. The community of faith integrates this divine grace and power by continuing to work for justice and peace in spite of the obstacles against full realization. The community shows courage in facing backlash and resistance. It expresses joy at the ways in which models of justice, even small ones, appear within a world of hurt. It continues to trust in God even in the face of setbacks and slow progress. The community refuses to give up or to abandon the oppressed. It banishes despair. The community of faith may not accept the optimism of Bob Dylan's anthem. However, it does not surrender the struggle. The community of faith knows that even if the times do not change, the times should not change it.

Bibliography

Barclay, Eliza. "These Ivory Coast Cacao Farmers Had Never Tasted Chocolate." *The Salt: NPR*, August 1, 2014. Online: http://www.npr.org/sections/thesalt/2014/08/01/336919715/these-ivory-coast-cacao-farmers-had-never-tasted-chocolate.

Blow, Charles M. "Frustration in Ferguson." *The New York Times*. August 17, 2014.

Boesak, Allan Aubrey. *Dare We Speak of Hope? Searching for a Language of Life in Faith and Politics*. Grand Rapids: Eerdmans, 2014.

Chopp, Rebecca S. "Latin American Liberation Theology." In *The Modern Theologians: Introduction to Christian Theology in the Twentieth Century*, edited by David F. Ford, 173–92. New York: Basil Blackwell, 1989.

Coote, Robert B. *Amos Among the Prophets: Composition and Theology*. Philadelphia: Fortress, 1981.

Ehrenreich, Barbara. *Nickel and Dimed: On (Not) Getting By in America*. New York: Holt Paperbacks, 2001.

Hanson, Paul D. *The Dawn of Apocalyptic: The Historical and Sociological Roots of Jewish Apocalyptic Eschatology*. Revised edition. Philadelphia: Fortress, 1979.

---

13. Lischer, *Theology of Preaching*, 31–33.

King, Martin Luther, Jr. "A Testament of Hope." In *A Testament of Hope: The Essential Writings and Speeches of Martin Luther King, Jr.*, edited by James M. Washington, 313–28. San Francisco: Harper, 1986.

Lischer, Richard. *The Preacher King: Martin Luther King, Jr. and the Word that Moved America*. New York: Oxford University Press, 1995.

———. *A Theology of Preaching: The Dynamics of the Gospel*. Rev. edn. Durham: The Labyrinth, 1992.

Mays, James Luther. "Justice: Perspectives from the Prophetic Tradition." *Interpretation* 37 (1983) 5–17.

Singing the Story

THE GOSPEL ACCORDING
TO THE SPIRITUALS

Luke A. Powery

IF ONE BROWSES THE corpus of work produced by Richard Lischer, one will observe the ways in which his scholarship is historical, cultural, pastoral, and theological. He touches on themes of culture and preaching, ministry and memoir, death and lament, community and reconciliation, and the hope of the gospel. These are just a few, but it is the last—the gospel—which forms the heart of his writings, and in particular, the gospel story centered on the life, death, and resurrection of Jesus Christ. Through his years of teaching and preaching, Lischer might as well have said, like the early Black preachers and creators of the spirituals, "You can have dis ole world but give me Jesus," a phrase called "the narcotic doctrine"[1] of Black religious folks during the time of slavery. Lischer's classic study of the Rev. Dr. Martin Luther King, Jr., represents not only the preeminent work on King's preaching, but also Lischer's embrace and deep appreciation for Black preaching in general.

Given the core gospel theme at the center of Lischer's work and his keen interest in the cultural expression of Black preaching traditions, this brief essay will explore how the spirituals, the musical genre created by enslaved Africans in the United States, sing the gospel story. Elsewhere, I argue how the spirituals are musical sermons, and thus can serve as teachers of preaching even for today.[2] This essay will not make that same argument; rather, it is assumed when I speak of spirituals, I am talking about preaching. After a brief discussion of the spiritual origins of song, I will discuss

1. Johnson, *God's Trombones*, 3.
2. See Powery, *Dem Dry Bones*.

three major themes of the gospel story presented by the spirituals followed by an exploration of why singing the gospel is important. It will become clear that the gospel story should not only be spoken but also sung.

Divine Origins of the Spirituals

One cannot truly comprehend the significance of *singing* the gospel story from a cultural perspective without learning about High John de Conquer. In her book, *The Sanctified Church,* anthropologist Zora Neale Hurston tells an important story from African American cultural history about this figure.[3] Here is some of what Hurston writes.

> [High John de Conquer] was not a natural man in the beginning. First off, he was a whisper, a will to hope, a wish to find something worthy of laughter and song. Then the whisper put on flesh. His footsteps sounded across the world in a low but musical rhythm as if the world he walked on was a singing-drum. . . . The sign of this man was a laugh, and his singing-symbol was a drum-beat. . . . It was an inside thing to live by. It was sure to be heard when and where the work was the hardest, and the lot the most cruel. It helped the slaves endure. . . . He had come from Africa. He came walking on the waves of sound.

There are many stories about how the enslaved received freedom through High John de Conquer. "The best one," according to Hurston, "deals with a plantation where the work was hard, and Old Massa mean. . . . So, naturally, Old John de Conquer was around that plantation a lot."

"'What we need is a song,' he told the people after he had figured the whole thing out. . . . Us better go hunt around. This has got to be a particular piece of singing." However, the slaves were scared to leave because they knew how Old Massa would treat any slave who attempted to escape. Their fear did not stop High John. He came with a big black crow for them to travel on in their search for a song. They traveled to hell looking for "a song that would whip Old Massa's earlaps down." But the song was not in hell thus they decided to visit heaven.

When they reached heaven, they were "given new and shining instruments to play on" and they "walked up Amen Avenue and down Hallelujah Street," both of which were tuned to sing bass, alto, tenor, and soprano, respectively. "You could make any tune you wanted to by the way you walked. . . . Old Maker called them up before His great work-bench, and made them

---

3. Hurston, *Sanctified Church,* 69–78.

a tune and put it in their mouths. It had no words. It was a tune that you could bend and shape in most any way you wanted to fit the words and feelings that you had. They learned it and began to sing."

Just about that time, Old Massa began to call them and scream. They returned to the plantation with a new song and laughter, both an advantage in their minds. They picked up their hoes as they "broke out singing as they went off to work. The day didn't seem hot like it had before. Their gift song came back into their memories in pieces, and they sang about glittering new robes and harps, and the work flew . . . ."

This cultural vignette suggests the divine origins of the gift of song. The "Old Maker," God, made them a melody for survival. Moreover, it is significant that when speaking of the religious slave songs, the spirituals, an ex-slave makes an even greater and specific claim. He says:

> Us ole heads used ter make them on the spurn of de moment, after we wressle with the Spirit and come thoo. But the tunes was brung from Africa by our granddaddies. Dey was jis 'miliar song . . . they calls 'em spirituals, case de Holy Spirit done revealed 'em to 'em.[4]

According to this account, the "spirituals" are called such because they stem from the Holy Spirit. Like the story of High John, they have divine origins thus are not to be taken for granted and easily dismissed. The spirituals are musical revelations of the Spirit proclaiming the gospel story. These historical musical sermons are the roots of centuries of musical preaching within African American settings. Black preachers have been called "God's trombones" pointing to the musical homiletical tradition. From early chanting slave preachers, to whoopers like Caesar Clark and C. L. Franklin, to King's musical speech that quotes spirituals, to contemporary preachers who also have singing careers such as Shirley Caesar, Andrae Crouch, Marvin Winans, Donnie McClurkin, and Marvin Sapp, one can observe the rich heritage of singing the gospel that began with the spirituals, the word of God in song. These few examples of singing preachers affirm what others have proclaimed, "I got the word in me, and I can sing it, you know"[5] or, what Shirley Caesar herself has said in an interview, "I sing my sermons and preach my songs."[6] Preaching is musical, especially within African American culture, and the spirituals embody a distinct expression of this

4. Callahan, *Talking Book*, 61.

5. See Davis, *I Got the Word in Me.*

6. Gilkes, "Shirley Caesar," 12–16.

proclamatory tradition, not only musically but also in the ways they tell the gospel story.

The Gospel Story Sung by the Spirituals

Before the blues, jazz, gospel, and hip hop, there were the spirituals, musical paintings of the human soul. I write about these songs, but writing is no substitute for actual singing and inhabiting them through sound in order to have a better picture of the story they tell. These songs are meant to be heard and felt, taking a cue from James Weldon Johnson who writes of the spirituals, "the capacity to feel these songs while singing them is more important than any amount of mere artistic technique."[7] Nonetheless, in naming some of the spirituals and their lyrics, it is important that one imagine their soundscape because sound is fecund with meaning, even theological meaning. For this essay, I focus on the lyrics and not acoustics per se, but this should be sufficient in grasping the gospel story they proclaim with melody and word.

W. E. B. Dubois reminds us in *The Souls of Black Folk* that African peoples brought "a gift of story and song" to America.[8] The spirituals are stories, including the gospel story, told through songs created by the unknown Black bards. A 1922 poem titled, "O Black and Unknown Bards" praises them.

> O Black and unknown bards of long ago,
> How came your lips to touch the sacred fire?
> How, in your darkness, did you come to know
> The power and beauty of the minstrel's lyre? . . .
>
> What merely living clod, what captive thing,
> Could up toward God through all its darkness grope,
> And find within its deadened heart to sing
> These songs of sorrow, love, and faith, and hope?
> How did it catch that subtle undertone,
> That note in music heard not with the ears? . . .
>
> There is a wide, wide wonder in it all,
> That from degraded rest and service toil
> The fiery spirit of the seer should call

7. Johnson and Johnson, *Books of American Negro Spirituals*, 29.
8. Dubois, *Souls of Black Folk*, 275.

These simple children of the sun and soil.
O black slave singers, gone, forgot, unfamed,
You—you alone, of all the long, long line
Of those who've sung untaught, unknown, unnamed,
Have stretched out upward, seeking the divine . . .

You sang far better than you knew; the songs
That for your listeners' hungry hearts sufficed
Still live,—but more than this to you belongs:
You sang a race from wood and stone to Christ.[9]

This poem celebrates the creators of the spirituals. Those "black slave singers, gone, forgot, unfamed . . . untaught, unknown, unnamed." It is a miracle
that these songs were produced in the fiery furnace of inhumane slavery.
There are many known names of fame in Christendom and the music industry. But the spirituals reveal that there are musical stories that have come
down in human history through the unknown, the unwanted, and the unfamed. The spirituals point us to a gospel of the underside. We do not know
their name or face, but they have contributed to the history of the world,
including the church's proclamation. They might be unknown but what they
have given is well-known—a musical story of the gospel of sorrow and joy,
sung "from wood and stone to Christ." These Black bards have graced us
with a musical homiletical history, and it is through their lyrical melodies of
suffering, faith, and hope that we hear the story of the people of the African
diaspora and the gospel story of God. The story sung by the spirituals is a
"haunting echo"[10] that still reverberates down the acoustical corridors of
human history. Three prominent themes echo the gospel story through the
spirituals.

Gospel of Suffering and Death

Soon-a will be done a-with the troubles of the world
Troubles of the world, troubles of the world
Soon-a will be done a-with the troubles of the world
Goin' home to live with God

No more weeping and a-wailing

9. Johnson and Johnson, *Books of American Negro Spirituals*, 11–12.
10. Dubois, *Souls of Black Folk*, 264.

No more weeping and a-wailing
No more weeping and a-wailing
I'm goin' home to live with God

I want t' to meet my mother
I want t' to meet my mother
I want t' to meet my mother
I'm goin' home to live with God

I want t' meet my Jesus
I want t' meet my Jesus
I want t' meet my Jesus
I'm goin' home to live with God

First, the unknown Black bards sing a gospel story of human suffering and death. The lyrics of the hymn, "Lift Every Voice and Sing," reveal the gloomy past of Black people. "Stony the road we trod, bitter the chastening rod, felt in the days when hope unborn had died. . . . We have come over a way that with tears has been watered, we have come treading our path through the blood of the slaughtered." There have been many troubles, much weeping and wailing in the world, yet God encounters the people in the valley of despair and death. Through the lens of the spirituals, God works in the midst of pain and does not avoid situations of suffering. The historical oppression of African peoples in the Americas has been described as "terror."[11] From the cruel "Middle Passage" of slavery to the so-called New World in the belly of slave ships, music came in the form of human moans and shrieks, surrounded by the aroma of filth and stench of death. Life was so degrading that one person writes that in the belly of the slave ships, "Lament danced and swayed under the watchful eyes of the crew."[12] In this context, the gospel was in the groan.

This is a history of struggle for survival as Africans in America, where dehumanization ruled through such devices as chattel slavery that caused a "social death," alienation from society. Blacks were viewed as beasts, objects for study, property to be sold and stripped, and "entertainers" who would at many times, wear "rope neckties" (lynching).[13] This is why Billie Holiday, the jazz great, could sing:

Southern trees bear strange fruit,

11. See Pinn, *Terror and Triumph*.
12. Holmes, *Joy Unspeakable*, 75.
13. Pinn, *Terror and Triumph*, 15, 21, 31, 52.

> Blood on the leaves and blood at the root,
>
> Black body swinging in the Southern breeze,
>
> Strange fruit hanging from the poplar trees.[14]

As property, Black bodies could be physically marked through branding (sign of possession) and whip-scarring (sign of punishment); these were signatures of slavery, naming Blacks as *other*, on the borderlands of human existence.

The spirituals are musical memorabilia created on the anvil of misery, and they demonstrate the presence of the gospel even in hell. It is not surprising then that the spirituals have been called "sorrow songs"[15] and that a slave could sing and shout:

> No more auction block for me, No more, No more, No more auction block for me, Many thousand gone. No more peck o' corn for me, No more, No more, No more peck o' corn for me, Many thousand gone. No more driver's lash for me . . . No more pint o' salt for me . . . No more hundred lash for me . . . No more mistress' call for me . . . . Many thousand gone.

The enslaved sang, "Oh, freedom all over me . . . An' be fo' I'd be a slave, I'll be buried in my grave, an' go home to ma Lawd an' be free."

They desired to be free from the bitter bonds of slavery. For many, death was better than life thus they sang, "Death, oh death, oh me Lawd, Death, oh death, oh me Lawd. When-a me body lay down in de grave, Den-a me soul gwine shout fo' joy." For many, life was and is the blues. The old past has been a deadly past, a bloody past, a tear-filled past, a history of great suffering. African American slave Christians were martyrs who "bore witness to the Christian gospel despite the threat of punishment and even death at the hands, not of 'pagans,' but of fellow Christians."[16] The ballads of the Black bards sing a sorrowful story under Egyptian-like oppression while calling for freedom from their unjust Pharaohs.

> When Israel was in Egypt land
>
> Let my people go
>
> Oppressed so hard they could not stand
>
> Let my people go
>
> Go down Moses

---

14. These words are from a song called "Strange Fruit," written in 1937 by Abel Meeropol, a Jewish schoolteacher in New York.

15. Dubois, *Souls of Black Folk*, 264.

16. Raboteau, "Blood of the Martyrs," 23.

Way down in Egypt land

Tell ole Pharaoh

Let my people go.

Through the spirituals, we remember the death and suffering of innocent people, even the Christ because Jesus was the personification of the slaves' own suffering. They sang:

Calvary, Calvary,

Calvary, Calvary,

Calvary, Calvary,

surely he died on Calvary.

His death embodied their own as they knew what it meant to hang from trees. "Were you there when they crucified my Lord? Were you there they nailed him to the tree? Were you there they pierced him in the side? Were you there when the sun refused to shine? Were you there when they laid Him in the tomb?" The suffering of Jesus was their suffering. This story was a serious one and was never meant to be humorous because this musical homiletical memory is moist with human blood.

Howard Thurman, in his work on the spirituals, *Deep River*, writes:

> for the slave, freedom was not on the horizon; there stretched
> ahead the long road down which there marched in interminable
> lines only the rows of cotton, the sizzling heat . . . it must be inti-
> mately remembered that slavery was a dirty, sordid, inhuman[e]
> business. When the slaves were taken from their homeland,
> the primary social unit was destroyed, and all immediate tribal
> and family ties were ruthlessly broken. This meant the severing
> of the link that gave the individual African a sense of *persona*.
> There is no more hapless victim than one who is cut off from
> family, from language, from one's roots.[17]

Not only did slavery destroy bodies, it destroyed and disrupted relationships. This points to a second major theme echoing the gospel story in the spirituals.

Gospel of Community

Sometimes I feel like a motherless child

Sometimes I feel like a motherless child

17. Thurman, *Deep River*, 35.

Sometimes I feel like a motherless child

A long ways from home

A long ways from home

A long ways from home

A long ways from home

Second, the unknown Black bards sing a gospel story that yearns for and affirms the human community. The spiritual above, "Motherless Child," expresses an extreme sense of disconnection and alienation from family ties. Not to have a mother and not to be at home expressed radical estrangement. Many of the spirituals focus on "going home" because "home was an affirmation of the need for community."[18] Home was where mother, father, sister, and brother were. The enslaved wanted to be united with them. There was a deep yearning for community and right human relations, which is what the gospel is always working toward.

The enslaved were denied their humanity, but they sought to reclaim their own humanity; they focused on God delivering them while making a universal call for deliverance of every individual and community.

Didn't my Lord deliver Daniel, deliver Daniel, deliver Daniel?
Didn't my Lord deliver Daniel, and why not every man? He delivered Daniel from the lion's den, Jonah from the belly of the whale, and the Hebrew children from the fiery furnace, and why not every man? Why not every man?

This includes the enslaved and even the slave master. There is an affirmation of the human spirit.

You got a right, I got a right, We all got a right, to the tree of life
. . . You may hinder me here but you cannot dere, 'cause God in de heav'n gwinter answer prayer. You got a right, I got a right, We all got a right, to the tree of life.

We all have a right to life just by the very fact that we are human—this is the tune of their gospel. The slave was denied life but was still willing to offer life to their oppressors. The slave preacher had one crucial insight— every human is a child of God, created in the image of God. The preacher validates the human spirit, and in the same manner the spirituals do not deny anyone their human dignity. Peter Paris notes that slave Christianity was an alternative to slaveholding Christianity because its theology and anthropology were "thoroughly nonracist."[19]

18. Cone, *Spirituals and the Blues*, 59.
19. Paris, "When Feeling," 115.

The enslaved could sing "dere's room for many a mo" and "all can go" on God's train because it is big enough and wide enough to include everybody as somebody.

> Git on board, little chillen,
> Git on board, little chillen,
> Git on board, little chillen,
> Dere's room for many a mo!
>
> De fare is cheap, an' all can go,
> De rich an' poor are dere,
> No second class aboard dis train,
> No diffrunce in de fare.
>
> Git on board, little chillen,
> Git on board, little chillen,
> Git on board, little chillen,
> Dere's room for many a mo!

This particular spiritual presents a sense of human equality—the rich and poor are there, there is no second class and no difference in the fare. Even though there is an affirmation of the self ("no second class there") this does not mean there has to be a negation of someone else. One's freedom to be human does not necessitate the enslavement of another. From the spiritual's perspective, the gospel story proclaims that we are all children of God, part of the human community, bound to God's law of love. As the spiritual says, "O gimme yo' han', Gimme yo' han', All I want is de love o' God; Gimme yo han, gimme yo' han'; You mus' be lovin' at God's comman.'" To give one's hand to each other shows that we need each other in this world, and it is a sign of love for one another. We need to "walk together children" in order not to get weary.

In addition, although there is a radical inclusiveness of humanity embedded in the story told by the spirituals, there is not a cheap acceptance of another's rejection or hate. There is some tension between this apparent embrace of all humanity into God's community and insight into the fact that those who mistreat others might not be going to heaven:

> I got a robe, you got a robe, all o' God's chillum got a robe. When
> I get to heab'n I'm goin' to put on my robe, I'm goin' to shout
> all ovah God's heab'n, heab'n, heab'n, Everybody talkin' 'bout
> heab'n ain't goin' dere . . . .

Another example of this sentiment is expressed in "Scandalize My Name":

> Well, I met my sister/brother/preacher de other day, Give her/him my right han', Jes' as soon as ever my back was turned she/he took 'n' scandalize' my name. Do you call dat a sister/brother/'ligion? No! No! you call dat a sister/brother/'ligion? No! No! you call day a sister/brother/'ligion? No! No! scandalize' my name.

One cannot scandalize my name and still be my brother or sister. Mistreating others was a misuse of one's freedom and an assault on the human community. Love was and is key. Singer Tina Turner asked, "What's love got to do with it?" The enslaved would answer: everything.

The gospel impulse toward genuine community is so prevalent in the spirituals because they can be viewed as a "collective exorcism"[20] of selfish individualism. The very nature of these songs points to a communal ideal. The spirituals are folk songs/sermons with no specific author or actual place of origin, but created by individuals, the unknown Black bards, within a community for the community. They are anonymous, a fact that points to the priority that these tunes had for the collective expression of the community's thoughts and feelings. Their aim was to give voice to the community's concerns, not an individual's. They were "our songs" and "our stories." They are at their heart a musical, communal interpretation of the gospel of God. As the African proverb goes, "I am because we are."

This affirmation of community is expressed further through the call and response performance of many of the spirituals, a musical trait stemming from Africa. There is a leader who sings or calls and then the community responds. For example, in "Wade in the Water," the leader sings "See that band all dressed in white" and then the community sings, "God's a-gonna trouble the water." The leader calls again, "The leader looks like an Israelite" and then the community sings, "God's a-gonna trouble the water." Then everyone sings together, "Wade in the water, wade in the water, children, Wade in the water, God's a-gonna trouble the water."

Whether through their performativity or lyrically, the spirituals promote a gospel of human community that includes all people. Despite the obvious suffering that can make people "weary at heart," Dubois asserts, "Through all of the sorrow of the Sorrow Songs there breathes a hope—a faith in the ultimate justice of things. The minor cadences of despair change often to triumph and calm confidence."[21]

20. Kirk-Duggan, *Exorcizing Evil,* 336.
21. Dubois, *Souls of Black Folk,* 186.

Gospel of Hope

Swing low, sweet chariot,
Coming for to carry me home
Swing low, sweet chariot,
Coming for to carry me home

I looked over Jordan, and I what did I see
Coming for to carry me home?
A band of angels coming after me
Coming for to carry me home.

Third, the unknown Black bards sing a gospel story of robust hope in God. The hymn "Lift Every Voice and Sing" has a verse that captures the theocentrism that is the heart of the faith of Black people: "God of our weary years, God of our silent tears, Thou who hast brought us thus far on the way, Thou who hast by thy might, led us into the light, keep us forever in the path we pray. Sing a song full of the hope that the present has brought us, facing the rising sun of our new day begun, let us march on till victory is won." The spirituals preach a God present in all of life's circumstances, so present that God continues to lead us home to the eternal light of victory. Even if many of the spirituals did not change to triumph in their overall movement, one can still discern hope in these songs because as Pauli Murray reminds us, "hope is a song in a weary throat."[22] Singing itself is a sign of hope. But these spirituals of the Black bards are more explicit about hope many times because of their faith in God.

In his 1855 autobiographical narrative, *My Bondage and My Freedom*, Frederick Douglas, an ex-slave, says of the spirituals, "Every tone was a testimony against slavery, and a prayer to God for deliverance from chains."[23] God was deemed to be a deliverer of the weak and oppressed. "God is a God! God don't never change! God is a God an' he always will be God!" What God did in the past, God was believed to do in the present. "He's jus de same today, Jus' de same today, an' de God dat lived in Moses'/Daniel's time is jus de same today." There was a firm belief in the continual work of God in history despite the apparent odds. One could be on the auction block and still sing, "Over my head I hear music in the air . . . There must be a God somewhere." The enslaved were confident in the presence of God thus could sing a gospel story of hope.

22. Murray, "Dark Testament: Verse 8."
23. Douglass, *My Bondage and My Freedom*, 99.

A critical part of their hope was a tremendous trust in "King Jesus." "He is the King of Kings and Lord of Lords, Jesus Christ, first and the last, No man works like Him." Jesus causes the enslaved to keep moving along in life despite painful circumstances. "Keep a-inchin' along, Massa Jesus is comin' bye an' bye." Because of Jesus, they believed that no one could ultimately stop them.

> Ride on, King Jesus,
> No man can a-hinder me,
> Ride on, King Jesus, ride on,
> No man can a-hinder me.

Though there are spirituals that exemplify hope due to the presence of "King Jesus" in the present or anticipated future, there is a "mixed texture" of sorrow/joy or lament/celebration in many of the spirituals echoing the reality of the crucifixion and resurrection of Jesus Christ. The gospel is a joyful sorrow that rings through the spirituals. The spirituals are true representations of life—both true to human suffering and to the reality of God simultaneously. These songs are, in the words of Thurman, "born of tears and suffering greater than any formula of expression. And yet the authentic note of triumph in God rings out trumpet-tongued!"[24] There is a hope that "trouble don't last always" even in the midst of apparently hopeless situations.

One begins to hear this dogged faith while in despair in such spirituals as "I've been 'buked an' I've been scorned, Dere is trouble all over dis worl', Ain' gwine lay my 'ligion down." Despite the trials, they could sing "My soul's been anchored in de Lord." A more explicit example of this mixed texture of African-American spirituality is found in this spiritual:

> Nobody knows the trouble I see,
> Nobody knows my sorrow,
> Nobody knows the trouble I see,
> Glory hallelujah!

There is obvious trouble and sorrow but the musical preacher still declares, "glory hallelujah." In addition, the enslaved were so assured of the grace and power of God that they give an answer to the prophet Jeremiah's query in the Bible, "Is there no balm in Gilead?" The enslaved answer:

> There is a balm in Gilead to make the wounded whole,
> There is a balm in Gilead to heal the sin-sick soul.

24. Thurman, *Deep River*, 28.

> Sometimes I feel discouraged and think my work's in vain,
>
> But then the Holy Spirit revives my soul again.

> There is a balm in Gilead to make the wounded whole,
>
> There is a balm in Gilead to heal the sin-sick soul.

Despite the pain, there is hope for healing. Suffering is acknowledged but so is the possibility of healing and deliverance. The spirituals reveal that the gospel is not about happiness but always about hope.

Moreover, a glaring demonstration of hope in the spirituals is the motif of heaven. "Heaven" may not be a popular topic these days except at funerals, but the spirituals make it prominent.

> I am a poor pilgrim of sorrow,
>
> I'm tossed in this wide world alone,
>
> No hope have I for tomorrow,
>
> I've started to make heaven my home.

> Sometimes I am tossed and driven,
>
> Lord Sometimes I don't know where to roam,
>
> I've heard of a city called heaven,
>
> I've started to make it my home.

The enslaved would encourage each other and preach to each other: "Hold out yo' light you heav'n boun' soldier, Hold out yo' light you heav'n boun' soldier, Hold out yo' light you heav'n boun' soldier, Let yo' light shine aroun' de world."

Connected to this image of heaven is the double meaning/hidden code/secret message/ "mask" in many spirituals. When the enslaved desire heaven as a manifestation of hope, it is not just other-worldly but this-worldly. Heaven was in the present not just in the future because in the light of God's future, there was the potential of concrete hope now.

> Steal away, steal away,
>
> Steal away to Jesus,
>
> I ain't got long to stay here.

> My Lord he calls me by the thunder,
>
> The trumpet sounds within-a soul,
>
> I ain't got long to stay here.

This spiritual could refer to going to heaven to be with Jesus but it also refers to escaping to a private place to meet with other slaves or ultimately to "steal away" to a free land. The spirituals then are songs of redemption *and* songs of resistance. Both express the gospel of hope.

Take the example of Harriet Tubman, a key leader in the underground railroad, who "masked" her plan to escape to freedom through a song (in this case, it is not a spiritual). Someone reports this about her.

> The evening before she left, she wished very much to bid her companions farewell, but was afraid of being betrayed, if any one knew of her intentions; so she passed through the street singing,
>
> "Good bye, I'm going to leave you,
> Good bye, I'll meet you in the kingdom"
>
> As she passed on singing, she saw her master, Dr. Thompson, standing at his gate, and her native humor breaking out, she sung yet louder, bowing down to him,
>
> "Good bye, I'm going to leave you."
>
> He stopped and looked after her as she passed on; and he afterwards said, that as her voice came floating back in the evening air it seemed as if—
>
> "A wave of trouble never rolled
> Across her peaceful breast."[25]

Tubman masked her real intentions to escape by talking about leaving for the kingdom, which in this case represented an earthly freedom. Another example of the hidden code is, "Deep River, my home is over Jordan; Deep River, my home is over Jordan. O don't you want to go to that Gospel Feast, that Promised Land where all is Peace? Deep River, I want to cross over into camp ground." This spiritual is not necessarily a longing to go to heaven but a desire to "cross over" into a promised land of the free where there is peace from the pain of bondage. In the biblical narrative, over Jordan was Canaan land, a place of promise and hope.

---

25. Blassingame, *Slave Testimony*, 458–59.

Some scholars think that an "other-worldly hope looms large" in the spirituals.[26] Others say that heaven was a historical category and not a metaphysical one for slaves. I would agree with those that say heaven represents both the land of freedom and the world beyond death.[27] Frederick Douglass himself notes,

> A keen observer might have detected in our repeated singing of 'O Canaan, sweet, I am bound for the land of Canaan,' something more than a hope of reaching heaven. We meant to reach the north—and the north was our Canaan. In the lips of some, it meant the expectation of a speedy summons to a world of spirits; but in the lips of our company, it simply meant a speedy pilgrimage toward a free state, and deliverance from all the evils and dangers of slavery.[28]

"Heaven" in the spirituals is both a transcendent present and a transcendent future. Salvation is both now and later.

But this hope is not individualistic. For the enslaved, heaven symbolizes a space where all forms of alienation and division are ended and people are in community with God and each other. Hope expressed through the motif of heaven is tied up with the presence of others. There is no hope without someone else with whom to share it. "I got a robe, you got a robe, all o' God's chillun got a robe." This communal sense of hope also reveals itself with the equation of home with heaven. Home is with God. Home is with the family. Home is with others. That is heaven. There is no heaven without someone else there. To be lonely is hell. To be with someone in the bond of love is heaven creating a sense of home and acceptance. Here are a few examples of spirituals that speak of "home":

> Swing low, sweet chariot, coming for to carry me home . . .

> Soon-a will be done with the troubles of the world, goin' home to live with God . . .

> Got a crown up in de Kingdom, ain't dat good news? I'm a-goin' to lay down dis world, goin' to shoulder up mah cross, goin' to take it home to Jesus, ain't dat good news?

The good news voiced through the spirituals had strong links to Jesus. This is undeniable even though not every spiritual mentions Jesus. Because of this, one may assert that the gospel story sung by the unknown Black

26. Thurman, *Deep River*, 25.

27. Spencer, *Protest and Praise*, 24.

28. Ibid., 17.

bards was a cruciform hope, yet, nonetheless, hope. As hope, these spirituals were songs in weary throats and the songs were the gospel, a gospel of
suffering, community, and hope. But the phenomenon of singing itself was
vital just as it is for the gospel.

Reasons to Sing the Gospel

The practice of singing may be underestimated but the spirituals reveal that
singing is an *essential* response in situations of suffering. It has been said that
in the cotton field during the time of slavery, the machete was dull without a
song. It has been said that "songs are free" even while in oppressive chains. It
has been said by Bernice Johnson Reagon that "you cannot sing a song and
not change your condition."[29] Singing was a sign of the slave's refusal to be
stopped. Thus, singing is possible and preferable in painful predicaments as
a sign of life, hope, and the presence of God through human voices and bodies. This differs from the commercialization and commodification of musical voices and bodies in a "bling-bling" business. Singing is deeply spiritual,
deeply human, and enfleshed in the face of the proliferation of disembodied
technologies and even congregations that have lost their singing voice. The
spirituals show us that singing is a matter of life and death and is a viable
homiletical strategy. Singing spirituals is not art for art's sake to perpetuate
a consumeristic, capitalistic society. Singing spirituals *is* life in the crucible
of suffering and death. The spirituals sang stories that were not just songs of
the soul, but life itself, essential to survival. Singing was living and life was
a song. The unknown Black bards reveal that if we do not sing as people of
faith, we will die as victims to the sting of suffering. But if we sing, we join
the angelic chorus of eternal life and hope.

In addition, it is important to note that the gospel story throughout
Scripture cannot help but include song. Thus to sing the gospel is to be *biblical* in one sense. Of course the Psalms exhort the reader to sing at numerous
junctures but there are also other portions of scripture that express gospel
by using hymns, suggesting that the gospel should not solely be spoken, but
sung. When Mary learns that she will give birth to Jesus, she responds by
singing the Magnificat, a hymn (Luke 1). When reflecting on God's future
hope for the world, John, the revelator, turns to hymnic material in Revelation (e.g., chapters 4 and 5). Furthermore, the story about the descent and
ascent of Christ for the life of the world is told through a hymn known as
"the Christ hymn" in Philippians 2, implying that the gospel story of Christ
should be sung because flattened prose cannot capture the totality of the

29. Bernice Johnson Reagon with Bill Moyers, "The Songs are Free."

work of Christ. Just like the spirituals, it takes melody and harmony to attempt to fully grasp this holy mystery. The gospel is told through song in the Bible, thus the way is made clear for today's preachers to do the same.

To sing the gospel is also to embody the *incarnational* nature of the gospel story. The spirituals were sung with clapping, dancing, and body movement. As the Spirit moved, the people moved because the gospel is not static or status quo. It moves us because it is an embodied story that took on human flesh in Jesus Christ. To sing is to be human and incarnational. It takes our hearts, hands, bodies, and voices to sing because the gospel requires all of us to express the inexpressible. The gospel is more than a word. It is a word that is expressed through a body just as God's Word became a human body. Thus to sing the gospel is to embrace one's humanity even as a person of faith. It is to be incarnational when certain settings only stress the intellectual. To sing the gospel is to affirm an incarnate God testified to by the proclamation of an incarnate, holistic gospel. This approach is necessary when we are speaking of a God who is "so high you can't get over Him, He's so low, you can't get under Him, He's so wide, you can't get around Him." Singing the gospel is one way of expressing the surplus of God.

Last, singing the gospel is *devotional* in nature as a form of prayer. There is an early church adage that captures this: "He who sings prays twice." This indicates that our musical preaching is always a prayer. An African proverb states, "The gods will not descend without a song." Singing a sermon is an epiclesis. It is a path to receiving the life of God while expressing this same life. It is a way to open oneself to God the Spirit as the writer of Ephesians asserts, "be filled with the Spirit as you sing . . ."(Eph 5:18–19). There is a connection between the Spirit and song even as I mentioned earlier in relation to the spirituals. As prayer, singing the gospel invites God to be present even as God makes the singing possible. This devotional understanding may also be the pathway toward healing and bringing others to voice.

Naomi, a Jewish woman, becomes vulnerable as she sings Christian songs to Gladys, an elderly, fragile African American woman with Alzheimer's who is unable to speak. She does this as a way to reach her because she knew Gladys grew up with these songs in church. Naomi rubs Gladys's right arm up and down, stares into her eyes, and then begins to sing, "Jesus loves me . . . " As Naomi continues to sing, Gladys begins to keep tempo with her right hand. When that song is finished, Naomi rubs both of Gladys's cheeks with her hands as she begins to sing the spiritual, "He's got the whole world in his hands." Something amazing happens when Naomi starts to sing the verse, "He's got the mothers and the fathers in his hands." Naomi sings, "He's got the mothers and the fathers" and Gladys, who could not speak, responds antiphonally, "in his hands." This happens twice. After the singing stops,

Naomi, with her hands on Gladys's cheeks, asks Gladys, "You feel safe? With Jesus?" and Gladys, in a soft whisper responds, "Yeah." Singing the gospel story will lead others to come to voice even when they are at the end of their own words. Words may cease but the gospel song continues into eternity.

We sing the gospel because it is our eternal vocation. In the world without end, there will be a song without end. The unknown Black bards "sang far better than they knew" because their gospel story still echoes truth today. The spirituals are not just their story and song. This is our human story, a human song of running, like the unknown Black bards, a "race from wood and stone to Christ," from suffering to hope. The race is won by singing the gospel story, therefore:

> I'm gonna sing when the Spirit says sing
> I'm gonna sing when the Spirit says sing
> I'm gonna sing when the Spirit says sing
> and obey the Spirit of the Lord.

Bibliography

Blassingame, John W, ed. *Slave Testimony: Two Centuries of Letters, Speeches, Interviews, and Autobiographies.* Baton Rouge: Louisiana State University Press, 1977.

Callahan, Allen Dwight. *The Talking Book: African Americans and the Bible.* New Haven: Yale University Press, 2006.

Cone, James. *The Spirituals and the Blues: An Interpretation.* Maryknoll, NY: Orbis, 1991.

Davis, Gerald L. *I Got the Word in Me and I Can Sing It, You Know: A Study of the Performed African-American Sermon.* Philadelphia: University of Pennsylvania Press, 1985.

Douglass, Frederick. *My Bondage and My Freedom.* New York: Dover, 1969.

Dubois, W. E. B. *The Souls of Black Folk.* 1903. Reprint. New York: Penguin, 1969.

Gilkes, Cheryl Townsend. "Shirley Caesar and the Souls of Black Folk: Gospel Music as Cultural Narrative and Critique." *The African American Pulpit* 6:2 (2003) 12–16.

Holmes, Barbara A. *Joy Unspeakable: Contemplative Practices of the Black Church.* Minneapolis: Fortress, 2004.

Hurston, Zora Neale. *The Sanctified Church.* Berkeley: Turtle Island, 1983.

Johnson, James Weldon. *God's Trombones: Seven Negro Sermons in Verse.* New York: Penguin, 1927.

Johnson, James Weldon, and J. Rosamond Johnson. *The Books of American Negro Spirituals.* 2 Vols. 1969. Reprint. New York: Da Capo, 1977.

Kirk-Duggan, Cheryl A. *Exorcizing Evil: A Womanist Perspective on the Spirituals.* Maryknoll: Orbis, 1997.

Murray, Pauli. "Dark Testament: Verse 8." Personal Blog. Online: http://paulimurrayproject.org/paulimurray/poetry-by-pauli-murray.

Paris, Peter J. "When Feeling Like a Motherless Child." In *Lament: Reclaiming Practices in Pulpit, Pew, and Public Square,* edited by Sally A. Brown and Patrick D. Miller, 111–20. Louisville: Westminster John Knox, 2005.

Pinn, Anthony B. *Terror and Triumph: The Nature of Black Religion.* Minneapolis: Fortress, 2003.

Powery, Luke A. *Dem Dry Bones: Preaching, Death, and Hope.* Minneapolis: Fortress, 2012.

Raboteau, Albert J. "'The Blood of the Martyrs is the Seed of Faith': Suffering in the Christianity of American Slaves." In *The Courage to Hope: From Black Suffering to Human Redemption,* edited Quinton Hosford Dixie and Cornel West, 22–39. Boston: Beacon, 1999.

Reagon, Bernice Johnson. "The Songs are Free." Interview with Bill Moyers. Online: http://billmoyers.com/content/songs-free.

Spencer, Jon Michael. *Protest and Praise: Sacred Music of Black Religion.* Minneapolis: Fortress, 1990.

Thurman, Howard. *Deep River and the Negro Spiritual Speaks of Life and Death.* Richmond: Friends United, 1975.

Speaking Gospel in the Public Arena

Willie James Jennings

> Let the same mind be in you that was in Christ Jesus, who, though he was in the form of God, did not regard equality with God as something to be exploited, but emptied himself, taking the form of a slave, being born in human likeness. And being found in human form . . . — PHIL 2:5–7 NRSV

FREDERIC BANCROFT, IN HIS famous text, *Slave Trading in the Old South*, tells the story of a slave family sold at auction in Savannah, Georgia, in the late 1850s. Primus, a plantation carpenter, his wife Daphney, their daughter Dido, and their newborn baby, all stood in front of would be buyers, being carefully examined by them. Strange to these calculating eyes, Daphney had a large shawl with which she wrapped herself and her newborn baby. To the plantation owners and other buyers this concealing behavior was highly unusual and inappropriate. The bodies of slaves are for public viewing, never hidden from the operations of market and desire. Bancroft reports that these slave consumers pressed their concerns with the following comments:

> What do you keep your n—— . . . covered up for? Pull off her blanket. What's the matter with the gal? Has she got the headache? What's the fault of that gal? Ain't she sound? Pull off her rags and let us see her. Who's going to bid on that n—— . . . , if you keep her covered up. Let's see her face.[1]

Bancroft notes that the auctioneer explained that this cloaked mother and child was not a deception that covered inferior product, but was a simple human indulgence. Since she had just given birth to this baby fifteen days ago, she wanted to protect herself and her child from the cold and driving

---

1. Bancroft, *Slave Trading*, 231–32. I have purposely designated the derogatory word "nigger" with the "n——" rather than write it out.

rain that covered the auction and their bodies.[2] The slave's body occupied public space like no other body. There at the nexus of commodity exchange and market forces, the body of the slave was stretched out across a network of production and consumption that defied compartmentalization. Wherever the market could go, the slave's body could go. Wherever need and desire merged with money you could find a slave in service.

The public nature of slave existence in slaveholding society in the United States is the perfect place from which to begin reflection on speaking gospel in the public arena. The gospel has a unique relationship to the slave. The form of the gospel and the form of the slave are bound together in Jesus Christ. The well known hymn from Philippians captures their joined existence, ". . . [Jesus Christ] . . . emptied himself, taking the form of a slave, being born in human likeness" (Phil 2:7). Of course, there is some slippage between the slave condition and the slave position; the former is a condition of being owned and intensely vulnerable and the latter is a condition of being intensely vulnerable and subject to becoming enslaved. If we take Jesus' body as marking less the actual reality of the slave and much more the position of the slave, then a different kind of vision of the public comes into view.

Theologians, ethicists, and homileticians have struggled in recent decades to define what the public is. David Tracy in his classic text, *The Analogical Imagination*, famously suggested that the theologian engages the three publics of society, academy, and church. One of Tracy's crucial points in this work was that the theologian in her discursive practice internalizes to various degrees these three publics, never just one.[3] I want to suggest a more intense internalization, articulated by the life of Jesus and echoed in the lives and legacy of slaves that should reframe for us what it means to speak gospel in public space. I want to imagine public space from the crucial position of subjugation. This essay explores the contours of speaking gospel in public space from that position, the position of the slave. I am less concerned with what slaves actually saw and more concerned with the meaning of seeing public life from the position of those caught in the most detrimental effects of the operations of the market, the military, and statecraft. The slave position is the position of bodies encircled and penetrated by these very public forces and having one's life made grotesquely vulnerable by them.

The body of the slave always occupies public space. In fact, the slave could be understood as synonymous with public space. The life and ministry of Jesus shows us an intense reality of public existence that resists any

2. Ibid., 232.
3. Tracy, *Analogical Imagination*, 30.

separations of life into walled arenas—religious, political, economic, gendered, etc. The world that flowed through Jesus' life engendered words from him that flowed through all of life, moving through walled existence and joining Jew and Gentile, bond and free, rich and poor. The words he spoke aimed at Israel always hit more than their target, always reached beyond Israel to overhearing goyim and claimed their lives through his life.

This is the power of the slave's position that illumines public spaces, large or small, benign or malignant, dangerous or safe, life affirming or soul killing, and this is the trajectory of the gospel—always toward a public viewed from the position of subjugation. The public nature of the gospel is best seen in the public nature of the slave and the public nature of the slave clarifies the work of giving witness to the gospel in the world. The slave's position has both theological and historical precedent for establishing the nature of public address of gospel truth. There is a sense in which all preaching is public address, aimed at any would-be listeners whether in ecclesial settings or nonreligious spaces. But public address rooted in the slave's position aims at a much more intense public reality—that of addressing the powers that enslave people economically, politically, socially, spiritually, and physically. This kind of public address by its very nature exposes networks of oppression and violence that run through any given society and connects people through the gospel to a shared work of announcing the will of God for human flourishing.

There is a necessary ambiguity of fit and of placement that comes with this kind of public address that echoes a question put to Jesus by the religious leaders of Israel, "By what authority do you speak and do these things?" (Matt 21:23). Yet this ambiguity is inherent in the slave's position. Where is a slave properly to be found—in sacred space or in the street, in someone's home or working in someone's field, in someone's kitchen or in their bedroom, preparing food or caring for children? The answer is yes. That yes undergirds not only the sense of Jesus' authority—wherever creatures are subjugated to the forces of death, there the gospel may and must reach, announcing the claim of God on creation—but it also characterizes a body extended across a vast terrain of need and suffering as when Jesus looked out onto the crowd and had compassion for them (Matt 14:14). Indeed the hermeneutical key to understanding the public reality of Jesus' body is the crowd. One of the most important realities present in the life of Jesus was the crowd. Few theologians or New Testament scholars have ever thought seriously about the crowd in the gospels. The crowd is the quintessential reality of the human creature. In their interaction with Jesus, the crowd showed us the relation of the creature to the creator. That crowd screaming, crying, yielding after Jesus, calling out for help, pushing, and pulling one another in order to get something from him. This is humanity. This is us.

The crowd witnessed in the New Testament presents public life as a state of emergency. This is public life in its truest form, its urgent form, filled with people in desperate need, looking for help and willing to do whatever is necessary for relief. These were people from all social backgrounds, economic levels, and ways of life, some of Israel, some Gentiles, some who believed, others who did not believe anything, some revolutionaries, others supporters of the regime, some marked by temple life, others who lived on the streets. Yet all were joined in chaotic struggle and messianic expectation, hoping to hear and see the beginning of a new possibility of flourishing life for themselves and their loved ones. The crowd according to the gospels is not an occasional scene that dots the Jesus story. It is the subtext of everything. The crowd is the deepest truth of human existence flowing just below the surface of organized living. The reality of the crowd is masked to many, but not to one who understands the position of the slave. Such a person feels the crowd and is one with the crowd. The body of the slave is mapped across the crowd. The crowd screams out to Jesus and he shares in their screams. This gospel is fitted for this public, a crowd public.

Not enough Christian intellectuals imagine this crowd-public. It requires those who have a deep sense of the legacy of slaves and who envisage their speech acts from the position of those seeking to be freed from subjugation. An example of such envisioning can be found in the Black church tradition of public address. Richard Lischer's classic text, *The Preacher King*, gives marvelous examples of this tradition in his trenchant examination of the preaching style, content, and theology of Martin Luther King, Jr.[4] King's public was a crowd public. It was first and foremost the descendants of slaves in urgent need of relief from racial oppression. His crowd public grew to include others from all stations in life who shared in this struggle. King consistently engaged the public from within the reality of the crowd and from the position of the slave. In this regard he stood in a long line of preachers and others who spoke a non-bifurcated gospel that refused ecclesial segregated speech. That is, they spoke in ways that named the plight of black folks within their specific material conditions and deeply connected that plight with the will of the living God for their redemption and their liberation. This way of speaking has always been resisted by some for fear of confusing or diluting gospel speech with political speech. Yet its abiding characteristics remain crucial for speaking gospel in public spaces today. In what follows I will highlight four characteristics.

---

4. Lischer, *Preacher King*.

First, speaking gospel in public is fragmentary speech. This is a form of gospel speech that has been stretched past its breaking point and has shattered into small pieces. Such speech follows the path of Jesus of being broken open in eucharistic form. Just as Jesus took bread, blessed it, broke it, saying, "This is my body, broken for you," so too gospel speech aimed at the crowd must be broken speech, piecemeal speech. A biblical phrase here or there, a Scripture quoted in part or full, an allusion to a biblical story, song, hymn, or psalm, each word echoing the giving of his body and blood. When strung together they aim to reach into the depths of the absurdity of suffering caused by processes created for the public good but that disadvantage people, as for example, people of color: an education system that impedes the growth of young black minds, a health care system that allows black life to drain away, and public protection through policing that is a great threat to black lives. Public speech that captures these kinds of absurdities already leans toward the body of Jesus who claimed his life as the fulfillment of the time of the Lord's favor (Luke 4:18), a time in which the poor hear good news, those incarcerated are set free, and people are released from oppression. Gospel fragments flow from his broken body and find their way into such speech in ways that are not just rhetorical ornamentation, but give shape to a verbal confrontation with powers arrayed to do harm. Martin Luther King Jr.'s 1965 pre-Selma voting rights march address gathers such fragments.

> You can't stop a people like this . . . We will appeal to the conscience of Selma. This is Selma's opportunity to repent! This is Selma's opportunity to say to the nation. "We've gone down the wrong path . . . like the Prodigal of old. We've strayed to the far country of brutality" . . . Monday can be a day when Selma will "come to herself" and move back to the Father's house.[5]

King's words expose an incarnational logic that is the logic of insurgency. The gospel story may confront anything that has become a structure of oppression. This is an example of far more than analogical thinking—Selma's anti-voting rights forces are like the prodigal Son—because it narrates real world resistance inside the real world of the Bible. The fragments of the gospel story target those whose souls had been twisted by hate and fear that would manifest itself in deadly consequences as was to be seen on the Edmund Pettus Bridge on March 7, 1965, best known as Bloody Sunday. We can see a more recent example of this kind of public address in the words of The Reverend William Barber, architect and leader of the Moral Monday movement in North Carolina who in a July 2015 rally in Winston-Salem,

5. Cited in Lischer, *Preacher King*, 260.

North Carolina, spoke out in protest of laws engineered to suppress voter turnout.

> We need to remember that these rights were won by blood. . . . The Blood speaks . . . Blood has been shed—back then and right now. How dare the Tea Party trample on the blood of our martyrs? How dare the Koch brothers, with their money, try to violate our rights that were written in blood? Fifty years after the Voting Rights Act was signed in blood, how dare somebody try to use political power to desecrate the blood of the martyrs? We must resist this sin because too many have died! Too many have suffered! Too many have bled! There's too much power in the blood for us to be silent now! So you want to know why we've come to Winston-Salem? You want to know why this is our Selma? We have come to recommit and reconsecrate ourselves back to the movement. We will not let what was won be taken away. We will restore the dream.[6]

The Reverend Barber's address weaves together past and present, ancient sacrifice and contemporary black deaths binding them all to the blood of Jesus. For some, such public address transgresses sacred space, merging differences that should be held apart or at least in tension. However Barber understands, like King understood, that suffering bridges bodies, joining ancient sacred space to contemporary spaces. All share in a holiness constituted by divine presence at the sites of protest where the crowd cries out for help and longs for justice. The crowd forces connections. To speak gospel in this public space is to make connections.

Second, speaking gospel in public demands we make connections. Making connections is inherent to Christian witness as it seeks to articulate the saving actions of the triune God in the world. We serve a God eagerly claiming the creation, drawing all things to the divine life and inviting us to be messengers of this good news. The body of Jesus is always the basis of making connections, because he offers himself precisely in the space where bodies are taken, stolen, exploited, and destroyed. We must remember the ways in which the body of the African slave was configured in slaveholding societies of the Christian west in order to grasp the importance of making connections. Black slaves were not only chained to the new republic that would become the United States of America, but their bodies were chained to many other nations as well. These slaves and their children were inescapably imbricated in the mechanics and machinations of statecraft, the operations of capital, and the social designs of white imperialism. Their bodies

---

6. Press Release, July 13, 2015, North Carolina NAACP.

were spread over a vast racist and sexist architecture that required a way of speaking that could capture the suffering of black flesh, speaking concretely and precisely of its manifold tortures. That work of capturing suffering, giving accurate witness to its interworking, requires making connections. Connecting, for example, how the decisions of local real estate agencies join with the actions of a school board to create segregated poorly funded schools that are detrimental to a mother's efforts to keep her discouraged child from quitting school. Connections must be made between, for example, zoning policies formed in city halls that shape policing procedures that in turn spiral down into antagonistic interactions of children and teenagers with the police. A gospel word spoken in public that does not show these kinds of connections fails to be a gospel that speaks to the crowd and fails to give witness to bodies at the site of pain and suffering.

The civil rights activist, Fannie Lou Hamer, in a speech delivered at the founding of the National Women's Political Caucus in Washington, DC, July 10, 1971, drew on the story of Esther to speak about the interlocking struggles of white and black women for equality and justice.[7] She ended her speech with a familiar refrain from the book of Esther, prefaced with the words, ". . . when women team up together we can do a whole lot of things." Hamer states, "So, I am saying to you today, 'Who knows but that I have cometh to the kingdom for such a time as this.'"[8] The time of Esther was for Hamer exactly this time, the time of coalition building, of shared struggle against oppression, and of broad based community organizing. Hamer's legendary speeches articulated a remarkable coherence that invited her hearers to see the connections between her personal experience with violence (she was mercilessly beaten in jail), the civil rights and women's liberation movements, anti-poverty work, political activism, and a whole host of other matters.

This work of making connections in gospel address makes no claim to exhibit exhaustive political, social, cultural, or economic analysis. It only claims to see the lines that run from structures to bodies, from macro-processes to the tears and cries of individuals or groups of people. Naming connections requires first and foremost the courage to speak the unspoken and cast light on those using their power and privilege in ways that create and/or sustain abiding disadvantage for people.

Third, speaking gospel in public means uncovering those with power who are being influenced by the principalities and powers. Slaves had masters and the master class, while glad to be seen, rarely wanted their actions examined,

7. Hamer, *Speeches of Fannie Lou Hamer*, 136–37.
8. Ibid., 139.

interrogated, and challenged. Yet, uncovering the actions of the master class has always been fundamental to the gospel voiced in public spaces. Even during American slavery Frederick Douglass in his famous speech entitled "Slaveholding Religion and the Christianity of Christ" engaged in a courageous unmasking of the powers by noting the deep hypocrisy in US Slaveholding Christianity.

> I am filled with unutterable loathing when I contemplate the religious pomp and show, together with the horrible inconsistencies, which every where surround me. We have men-stealers for ministers, women-whippers for missionaries, and cradle-plunderers for church members. The man who wields the blood-clotted cowskin during the week fills the pulpit on Sunday, and claims to be a minister of the meek and lowly Jesus. . . . He who sells my sister, for purposes of prostitution, stands forth as the pious advocate of purity . . . The warm defender of the sacredness of the family relation is the same that scatters whole families. The slave auctioneer's bell and the churchgoing bell chime in with each other, and the bitter cries of the heartbroken slave are drowned in the religious shouts of his pious master. . . . The dealers in the bodies and souls of men erect their stand in the presence of the pulpit, and they mutually help each other. . . . Dark and terrible as is this picture, I hold it to be strictly true of the overwhelming mass of professed Christians in America. They strain at a gnat, and swallow a camel.[9]

His famous words here rehearse gospel cadence that echoes the prophetic sound of Jesus' voice as he unmasked the hypocrisy of the religious caste of Israel. This uncovering of the actions of the powerful has always been a hallmark of gospel speaking in public that runs from people like Frederick Douglass to our present moment. It has always carried the deepest reality of tension, because it raises the most serious question that could ever be asked in public. Who is to blame? Who should be called out? Such questions when answered in public space complicate the theological distinction between sinners and their sin. The issue has not been carefully distinguishing the sin that God hates from the people God loves. The issue is the naming of sin in and with the concrete actions of those with power. Actions named as sinful actions (e.g., voter suppression, the denial of benefits to poor and poor working class people, the failure to expand health care opportunities for the disadvantaged) by particular legislators, or business

9. Douglass, "Slaveholding Religion," 104–6.

people, or judges, expose people in ways that challenge their careful work of crafting and sustaining their image.

Exposing those who wield power and privilege destructively has always run the risk of demonization. Yet for those who speak prophetically, speaking gospel at the sites where truth must be spoken, there is greater risk of substantial harm when we fail to expose the demonic activity at work in the destructive use of power. This decision to speak and name demonic activity at work in and with those with power is in a real sense what fundamentally distinguishes speaking gospel in public space. This is also why so few people actually speak gospel in public: accusations spoken elicit accusations returned. Anyone who names the sinful actions of those with power is subject to be accused of being unfair, a nuisance, or even a threat. The goal, however, is to reach for clarity and precision in articulating the exact actions, policies, and procedures that damage life and turn people toward despair. Here rigorous analysis joins relentless courage.

A marvelous example of someone who showed such a joining through the speeches she made and all the organizing she did was the civil rights activist, community organizer, and political strategist, Ella Baker. Baker was masterful in the ways she helped people identify the specific operations of oppression in their communities, named the constellation of operators and agents, and built specific strategies with concrete actions to move toward liberation.[10] Such specific naming could easily become overwhelming and sometimes it is for speaker and listener alike, as people come to reckon with the layers of oppression that they face, yet the fourth characteristic of speaking gospel in public draws such speech to its proper end, hope.

Fourth, speaking gospel in public makes hope public. Hope in Christian thought is most often articulated as an eschatological reality that turns our attention to its temporal and linear dimensions. We hope for a better day and a future in God. Hope, however, has most decisively a spatial dimension and a communal character which is rooted in the incarnation itself. In Jesus, God lodges hope in the space of the creature and brings hope to the places of suffering, pain, and death. Jesus' words and actions with Martha in view of her brother Lazarus' death testify to hope's spatial density (John 11:21–27). Martin King's last words of his famed final speech illustrate hope's spatial dimension.

> Well, I don't know what will happen now. We've got some difficult days ahead. But it really doesn't matter with me now, because I've been to the mountaintop. And I don't mind. Like anybody, I would like to live a long life. Longevity has its place.

10. Ransby and Baker, *Black Freedom Movement.*

> But I'm not concerned about that now. I just want to do God's
> will. And He's allowed me to go up to the mountain. And I've
> looked over. And I've seen the Promised Land. I may not get
> there with you. But I want you to know tonight, that we, as a
> people, will get to the promised land![11]

The crucial matter here is not how hope is articulated but from where and with whom is hope articulated. Those who speak this gospel word understand that God does not offer hope from heaven but, in Jesus and through the Holy Spirit, God offers hope at the sites of suffering and struggle. The word of hope offered in such spaces binds hearers together inviting them to hold each other in hope and lean on each other in anticipation of God's future. Through such gospel addresses we find Christian faith in its most humanizing form as an always open invitation to those who believe and those who do not believe or who believe differently to share in the creaturely reality of life as a gift. The gift of life is the gift of hope and hope offered in faith gives witness to God's love.

As a participant in the Moral Monday movement in North Carolina where we have marched, picketed, and protested the state legislature on numerous occasions, I have listened to countless speeches that have outlined in marvelous detail the specific challenges facing the people of my adopted state. And with many of those speeches I have also marveled at speakers who have drawn a crowd of people (from all walks of life, believers of many different faiths, people of no faith, people of high and low stations in life, people politically radical and people politically conservative) toward hope, drawing them into a shared project of hoping together—seeing things that be not as though they were. This is hope in its proper home, the crowd.

Speaking gospel in public space is speaking in a unique location through a vista that reaches from the vision of Jesus through the vision of slaves and to the vision of Jesus' disciples who dare to call themselves his slaves. This is, of course, not slavery that glories in physical subjugation but glories in the overcoming of subjugation. Those who speak this gospel word know that public space is holy space, where a God made flesh walks among the crowd.

Bibliography

Bancroft, Frederic. *Slave Trading in the Old South*. Columbia, SC: University of South
    Carolina Press, 1931.

11. King, "I've Been to the Mountaintop."

Douglass, Frederick. "Slaveholding Religion and the Christianity of Christ." In *African American Religious History: A Documentary Witness, 2nd ed.*, edited by Milton C. Sernett, 104–06. Durham, NC: Duke University Press, 1999.

Hamer, Fannie Lou. *The Speeches of Fannie Lou Hamer: To Tell It Like It Is.* Jackson, MS: University of Mississippi Press, 2011.

King, Martin Luther, Jr. "I've Been to the Mountaintop." *American Rhetoric.* Online: http://www.americanrhetoric.com/speeches/mlkivebeentothemountaintop.html.

Lischer, Richard. *The Preacher King: Martin Luther King Jr., and the Word that Moved America.* New York: Oxford University Press, 1995.

North Carolina NAACP. Press Release, July 13, 2015. Video of the march and rally available online: https://www.youtube.com/watch?v=w3YaJd1iG8g.

Ransby, Barbar, and Ella Baker. *The Black Freedom Movement: A Radical Democratic Vision.* Chapel Hill, NC: The University of North Carolina Press, 2003.

Tracy, David. *The Analogical Imagination: Christian Theology and the Culture of Pluralism.* New York: Crossroads, 1981.

Preaching Gospel in a Gendered World

Jennifer E. Copeland

AIR BAGS HAVE BEEN saving lives since they were introduced into the automobile industry in 1973, using technology that was patented in 1953.[1] Yes, 1953. Through a series of lobbying efforts putting cost efficiency ahead of consumer safety, air bags did not become an industry norm until the early 1990s and Congress did not make them mandatory until 1998. There's an essay in that! This essay, however, swirls around test dummies modeled after a human who is 5'9" tall and weighs 172 pounds, the famous "50th percentile male."

In 1953, acetaminophen replaced aspirin as the go-to pain killer in most hospitals and became available for adults over the counter in 1961. By the 1970s it was *the* over-the-counter drug choice for "minor aches and pains." Heralded as a wonder-drug, it was prescribed for every imaginable pain from headaches to flesh wounds, especially flesh wounds produced by surgical incision. When post-surgery pain did not abate according to expectations, the dosage was increased. If the increased dosage failed to reduce pain, the patient was told nothing more could be done. Two decades later tests revealed the pain receptors in women do not respond to the active ingredients of acetaminophen in the same manner as pain receptors in men.[2] In all the years women continued to complain about post-surgery pain after receiving the maximum dose of acetaminophen, no one had run that test.

In 2015, the NCAA made sexual assault on college campuses the focus of their primary advertising campaign during the men's basketball playoffs. Such highlighting is only a re-run of news we have heard for years about the predatory nature of college campuses for women. Statistics indicate a

1. Saporito, "Air Bag Blowout," 23.
2. Moon, "Effects of Preoperative Intravenous Acetaminophen," 1455–60.

college woman has a better chance of being sexually assaulted (one in four) than contracting the flu (one in five).[3] Since this number represents only the reported assaults, most college administrators admit the actual number is much higher.

These examples play well as sermon illustrations in the plethora of sermons we preach about the worth of women, the need for mutual respect, or the cry for gender justice. I have preached those sermons, as have many of my colleagues, male and female. Lately, I have decided those sermons are "the opium of the people." They satisfy us that we have done our part to support women or to point out the injustices perpetrated against women. We highlight the truth that women are more often killed by airbags because they are shorter than the "50th percentile male." We adjure that for decades women suffered needlessly following surgery because their pain receptors differ from those of the people funding and administering drug trials. And we remind our daughters not to leave their drinks unattended at a party.

Modest adjustments have been made. Newer cars come equipped with a seat occupancy detector that activates the airbag based on the weight of the seat occupant. This saves the lives of lightweight people if not short people. Medical trials now take into consideration the differences not only between men and women, but also differences between ethnic groups. Complaints about post-surgery pain are met with an array of pain killers, specific to the body in pain. College parties, however, are not yet safer for women, influenza holding steady in second place behind sexual assault.

The modest adjustments are late coming and, on the whole, culture and society continue to privilege men in crash tests, drug tests, and judicial "tests." A bevy of sermons calling attention to current prejudices are crucial, but they do not expose the root of the privilege problem. The privilege goes back further than last week's sermon. The privilege is hard wired into the tradition Christians have inherited from the nomadic people of ancient Mesopotamia.

Shepherds and "wandering Arameans" favor a different set of characteristics than do farmers and "tillers of the ground." Shepherds move around a lot, sometimes into the territory of other shepherds. Arguments occur over who has the right to occupy certain grassy knolls. Farmers tend to stay put, nurturing the same plot of ground. Bartering becomes an effective way to manage excess produce and procure scarce goods. Arguing and bartering work on different premises and require different aptitudes for success. Over time, in this case millennia, one set of strengths and skills become more valuable than others, and those who possess them become the standard by

3. Wiley, "Universities Struggle."

which all others are measured. Conquest more than cooperation is our inheritance. Confrontation over compromise is our typical response. Without
assigning generic gender stereotypes to these traits, it is not hard to imagine
how inheriting a theological system from shepherds would render a different value system than one inherited from farmers. Still, enough of the minor
story permeates our scriptures for us to know there is a different way that
has always been in tension with the dominant norm.

Until we are willing to look behind and beneath the dominant narrative, we will only stand in the pulpit and deride a bunch of wayward college
boys for a night of rowdy behavior, boys who will become the men piloting
the ships of industry that commission crash tests and drug tests. I no longer
want to teach daughters and granddaughters how to guard their drinks at a
party. I want to change the party. Changing the party requires changing the
story, changing the story about the "wandering Aramean" and the "carpenter from Galilee."

More of the Story

Changing the story means less about rewriting history—how can that ever
be done anyway?—and more about hearing the story through different perceptions and new concepts. One way to hear anew is by paying attention to
the little known parts of the story. By now we are well aware of the injustices
created by privileging only one version of a story. Multiple versions of any
story do not invalidate the previous story, but they will complicate it. For
instance, when I was in elementary school, we celebrated Columbus Day
and lauded the person who "discovered" America. It was a school holiday.
By the time my children reached elementary school, they knew a bit more
about the conquest of the Americas and the colonizing effect on indigenous
populations. They did not have a school holiday. Currently, the cities of
Minneapolis and Seattle mark the second Monday in October as Indigenous
People's Day, no longer recognizing the federal holiday granted on this day
as Columbus Day, even while acknowledging that Christopher Columbus
is still a very large part of the story. Telling more of the story does change
the story we have always been told, but it does not invalidate the old story.

Likewise, biblical interpretation is an evolving narrative, balanced
within the historicity of the events and the interpretive communities receiving the narrative. Historical critical analysis has unraveled some of the
archaic rituals encountered in Scripture, and responsible scholarship has
helped us understand the implications of those interpretations on our lives.
For example, because women, children, and slaves were the property of

their male patrons during the years the biblical narratives originated, the property laws of the ancient near east gave rise to many of our theological perceptions about those relational dynamics. We need that important information about the origin of the dynamic before we start reading the rules in Leviticus, and we definitely need to know about it before we start applying the rules in Leviticus to our own lives.

More important than grasping the historical context for a biblical imperative, however, is recognizing the power of the interpretive community. The tendency when we encounter an enigmatic passage is to fill in the blanks with what we think we know or what we have been conditioned to expect. So, for instance, in the troublesome account of Jephthah's daughter, glaringly absent from the revised common lectionary, we invent ways to compensate for Jephthah's dilemma.[4] Preachers have suggested he must be commended for keeping his word even at great cost to himself. This commendation is offered without a lot of commentary about the cost to his daughter. The other favorite explanation avers he expected a different person, probably a servant, to exit the house first. Again without much thought to the terror for the servant. We have spent millennia feeling sorry for Jephthah even as we make a lesson out of the story, something like, never make rash promises. The truth is, this is a horror story. Jephthah is not brash and hasty, he is unfaithful and disobedient, and his daughter is a blameless victim.[5] That is a different interpretation than we are usually offered, reached only after learning a lot more about the setting of this story and then hearing the story in ways that do not privilege the dominant norm.

Interpretative communities hold the formula for a new hearing, and the sermon should be the stimulus for starting the process. Preachers are responsible for troubling the waters of smug assumptions by introducing a catalyst to the calm. This does not mean we abandon Scripture. It means we interpret Scripture with an eye toward the fissures in the stories. It means we trust our own experiences, especially when our experiences indicate a different conclusion than the standard reading. Make no mistake, it takes practice to approach Scripture this way because preachers have been so well trained on how to read the narrative tradition we often ignore our own experiences when they contradict what we have been taught. Lodged within these familiar accounts are clues to different interpretations. Knowing the historical setting of a biblical narrative is important, but paying attention to the interpretive community where we are located provides the change element to hear anew a Word from the Lord. To demonstrate the possibilities,

4. McCain, *Judges*, 77–90.
5. Trible, *Texts of Terror*, 97.

here are four well-known and oft preached pericopes that generated four atypical sermons.

From Sloth to Steward

In the fall many churches conduct stewardship campaigns. When the church conducts a stewardship campaign, the preacher often turns to the Parable of the Talents. Preachers from a multitude of theological traditions and social settings will find creative ways to remind all of us that we should always use our God-given gifts to the fullest of our ability. The challenge for most of us is to spin these "talents" into an analogy that connects with our current congregation, theologically and socially. Some of us need cash for the capital campaign so we will focus on investment returns, which after all, is exactly what the story is about. Some of us will drill deeper and help folks understand worth is not calculated only in dollars. We can help with Bible School or serve on the Worship Committee or volunteer at the Food Pantry. The important thing is to use that talent and not bury it in the sand. Some of the most creative sermons I have heard on the Parable of the Talents make the simple point: use it or lose it. Those sermons always propel me to leave worship and *do* something.

Asked to preach a sermon in the fall of 2008, Barbara Brown Taylor laid bare this oft used tactic, naming for us the expectations we already had. The pretext for hearing the Parable of the Talents as a call to action has a long and proud history. Our bookshelves are full of commentaries disparaging the single talent servant from lazy or fearful to worthless and guilty. No one wants to be like him. We want to be brave and trustworthy; we want to double our investment; we want to enter into the joy of our master. Hearing a different verdict for this parable requires abandoning the pretext, in so far as possible, and listening one more time for a word from the Lord. Such a hearing was achieved by Taylor in the sermon, "The Parable of the Fearful Investor."[6]

Taylor is among the best at producing sermons that challenge the dominant norms without eroding our faith foundation. She begins this sermon by admitting we have all made up our minds about the meaning of this parable. She cites interpretations from some of the best known New Testament scholars of the twentieth century, implying that to reach a different conclusion would be to challenge the foundation of our faith. And then she reaches a different conclusion.

6. Taylor, "Fearful Invester."

The moves within the sermon are uncomplicated. State the obvious interpretation, raise the possibility of counterpoint, illuminate the context of the parable using something familiar, challenge the dominant interpretation, and compare both interpretations with the gospel message. Taylor's ruling on which interpretation reflects the gospel is captured in these words: "I have been trying to imagine Jesus coming up to one of them and saying, 'I've come for my profit . . .' And you know what? I can't imagine it. *I can't imagine it at all* [emphasis Taylor's]."

The interpretive twist comes in Taylor's ability to stand alongside the single talent servant and consider the situation from his perspective. The story looks different from that angle. From this difference, she crafts a sermon that complicates our preconceived notions without erasing the truth of the story that the first two servants were indeed courageous and trustworthy. For instance, referencing *The Gospel in Solentiname*,[7] she tells the story of Pastor Ernesto Cardenal's conversation with his congregation about the Parable of the Talents. Oppressed by a system that concentrated money and resources in the hands of a few wealthy politicians, Cardenal's congregation immediately identified with the single talent servant. Taylor explains why by discussing the economic realities of first century Palestinian peasants, Jesus' congregation.

> Wealthy householders were happy to help out in circumstances like [making ends meet]. There was nothing to it: if you were strapped for cash, you got the best interest rate you could, you put up your land as collateral, and you got busy bringing in the sheaves. By the time you noticed what 60 percent interest really meant, it was too late. Your land went into foreclosure, and quicker than you could say, "Leviticus," it was not yours anymore.

Since all of us like to believe *we* are members of Jesus' congregation, forcing us to identify positively with the single talent servant moves us off the center of our preconceived notions. From a sense of shame and cowardice we may have believed we have more in common with the single talent servant than with the first two investors; thus, we have always wanted to be more like the first two, courageous and faithful. Taylor is suggesting the single talent servant may have more to offer us than the first two servants given that our own current economic system has gone awry.

With the recitation of a different reality experienced by a different interpretative community, we can hear a different version of the story even while we remain cognizant of the capitalist read that has dominated the

7. Cardenal, *Gospel in Solentiname*, 39–40.

interpretation of this parable for more than a century. Prior to highlighting compound interest as the primary method for evaluating the servants, older commentaries emphasized the single talent servant's sloth.[8] While it may be true that Matthew recorded the story to highlight the need for risk and courage in the face of a world hostile to the claims of the gospel, the hostility facing the gospel today wears a different face. The gospel has not changed; the challenges to it have changed. Taylor's sermon equips us to face that challenge and align ourselves with an interpretation that unmasks the exploitation we unwittingly perpetuate.

From Penitent to Friend

The acclaimed preacher Gardner C. Taylor offered many profound interpretations of Scripture urging listeners to believe in the good gifts of the Lord and to live as the worthy people God believes them to be. Sermon after sermon proclaims God's faithfulness and affirms our value in God's sight. Yet even with this predictable conclusion, Taylor uses unpredictable methods to make his point. His sermon, "A Newfound Friend,"[9] based on Luke 23:40–43, points us to a quality possessed by the thief on the cross that is even more distinctive than his oft lauded confession of faith.

We are accustomed to hearing the story of the thief on the cross through the lens of repentance and forgiveness. His is the classic example of salvation attained even at the point of death. It is never too late, we tell parishioners, commending the thief for his behavior. Wrapped up in his confession of sin is his confession of faith. He witnesses to the truth about Jesus that is ignored by all the other participants in the passion drama. The disciples desert him. The chief priests and scribes accuse him. Pilate orders him flogged. The crowd forsakes him. The soldiers mock him. One thief derides him. The other thief, Taylor's protagonist, believes him.

Rather than focusing on the thief's two confessions, confession of his own misdeeds and confession of his faith in Jesus as the Christ, Taylor names the thief a friend, indeed the only friend Jesus has left at this point in the story.[10] Taylor punctuates the description of Jesus' walk to Calvary with

8. "He is pronounced wicked, because he was a slothful, an unprofitable servant. So mere harmlessness, on which many build their hope of salvation, was the cause of his damnation!" John Wesley, *Explanatory Notes, Vol.* 1. 3rd edn. Bristol, 1760–62, 123.

9. Taylor, *Words of Gardner Taylor*, 2:152–57.

10. I would aver that Jesus did have other friends still on site, namely "the women who had come with him from Galilee," (Luke 23:55). I feel sure Gardner Taylor would concede my point since in other instances he readily praises those women. See especially, "Silence and Sorrow," *Words of Gardner Taylor*, 2:150, in which he writes: "No

words that heighten the intensity of the scene: "emptiness, forsakenness, abandonment, desertion, estrangement." Who else would be so in need of a friend if not the one described by Taylor as consumed by "lostness and loneliness"? He reminds us that even God is silent in the face of Jesus' lament. Once our sensibilities are fully engaged, he announces the thief as a friend.

Before this revelation, however, Taylor invites us to look at our own experiences of loneliness and to remember our own times of aloneness. He wants the interpretive community to identify with Jesus, even while he reminds us that the drama in which Jesus participates has been orchestrated since the dawn of time. Taylor conjures up images of being alone that many people have faced: surgery, travel, final exams. Unlike those of us who are wheeled into surgery, set off on a long journey, or sit for exams, with knowledge of family and friends supporting us through the ordeal, Taylor claims Jesus had no such comforting sentiments.

> He was alone. Make that word *alone* sound with all the emptiness, the forsakenness, the abandonment, the desertion, and the estrangement that you can give to it and you only begin to touch the awesome and numbing experience through which our Lord passed at Calvary.

Once he has established loneliness as something we know about and differentiated the loneliness of Jesus from anything we could know about, Taylor declares the friendship. Yet the thief is hardly a friend in the way we normally define friendship. He has not watched the wondrous healings, heard the great lessons, or endured the endless travels alongside Jesus. To understand the friendship Taylor is assigning to the thief we must expand our ideas about friendship. Friendship is more than going along for the ride. Friendship could mean standing in opposition to the way things are. Taylor points out the divide which occurs between the two thieves who might be considered more natural friends. One thief stays the course, deriding Jesus along with all the other detractors on the scene, and the other defends Jesus' innocence in the face of his own guilt. The befriending thief speaks a word of justice while surrounded by a miscarriage of justice: ". . . we are getting what we deserve for our deeds, but this man has done nothing wrong" (Luke 23:41).

The appeal to justice, Taylor reminds us, is not a profession of faith. In denouncing the injustice around them, the thief becomes Jesus' friend. With

---

woman deserted him! No woman denied him! No woman betrayed him! No woman persecuted him! They followed him, ministered unto him! What a legacy! Can heaven ever forget that? Be sure the Lord Christ will not." For Taylor's purposes in this sermon, however, claiming Jesus friendless allows his point.

the words, "Jesus, remember me when you come into your kingdom," the thief becomes Jesus' follower. The friendship is made greater in the profession of faith. Taylor says:

> The dying thief saw more in the dying Savior than a good man. Through the haze of the heat and through the agony of the pain, as death closed in upon him, the thief, dying, saw not another sufferer sinking into the embrace and arms of death. He saw a King climbing great red stairs of pain toward a coronation. He saw not a victim, but a brave, bloodied warrior striking down the last of his foes and reaching for the laurel wreath of victory. He saw a King with blood marks reaching forth to take the scepter of the world in his nail-pierced hand. He saw the Prince of Glory approaching the moment of his enthronement.[11]

At the moment of his greatest despair, according to Taylor, when Jesus might have believed his entire life had been in vain, here was one person making it worthwhile. This one, at least, saw the point of it all. Placing an emphasis on the friendship of the thief does not reduce the importance of his repentance and reconciliation. It does, however, challenge many of our preconceived interpretations about the story and allow us to consider new ideas. The primary idea suggested by Taylor involves standing up for what is right on behalf of those for whom no one else will stand. Such a view complicates our notion of friendship as a gathering of like-minded people out for a good time. Certainly there is more to friendship than good times, but we do tend to make friends with those who are like-minded. Jesus and the thief are unlikely friends, made more so by the natural allegiances the thief abandons in order to be a friend for Jesus in his greatest hour of need.

From Lost to Hungry

The quality of being lost permeates Scripture and provides an overt pretext for many of the narratives most familiar to us: the Hebrews are lost in the wilderness after fleeing Egypt, the prophets describe God's people as lost when they ignore God's precepts, and of course, Jesus makes regular mention of the lost ones for whom God is searching. Being lost at some point in one's faith journey seems to be a prerequisite for the people of God.

Midway through the Gospel of Luke, we encounter three lost and found stories in a row: the lost sheep, the lost coin, and the lost, or prodigal, son. Because of their proximity to one another we tend to read the stories

11. Taylor, *Words of Gardner Taylor*, 156.

as a unit, drawing the same basic conclusion about all three, even while the third story is longer and more developed.[12] Like the first two, the third story highlights the joy of finding that which was lost, adding details about the family dynamics of the main characters that allow for the exploration of selfishness, jealousy, and repentance. Still, the quality of being lost dominates the story. The younger brother's selfishness in claiming his inheritance and leaving home is constructed as a form of being lost. The older brother's jealousy metaphorically causes him to be lost outside the family having a party for the one who is found. There are any number of ways to use the quality of being lost to relate the story of these two brothers to the stories of our lives in relation to each other and the stories of our lives in relation to God.

In the sermon, "Naming the Famine,"[13] I attempt to shift the antagonist's dilemma from lost to hungry in order to expose a different set of foils through which to read our own modern dilemmas. While the shift from lost son to hungry son is not as shocking as Taylor's suggestion that the single talent servant is actually the "good and faithful servant," my interpretation does require us to expand our pretext for the parable of the prodigal son without giving up the truth that God searches for the lost.

The clue for my interpretation comes straight from the story itself, the younger son's exclamation: "here I am dying of hunger!" Once he admits to himself that his father's servants have more to eat than he, the second heir of his father's fortune, has to eat, he determines to go home. He is not lost. He knows exactly where he is and exactly where he is going. The famine in the land where he resides and the hunger he experiences provide the opening to talk about the many forms of hunger, literal and figurative, that constrain our lives. I start with biblical references about famine's impact on the lives of certain biblical characters: Joseph's brothers, Naomi's husband, Elijah's friend at Zarephath. These ancient descriptions of hunger morph into modern examples of hunger in a city where food insecurity increased nearly ten percent in one year. Famine is not an old problem or a problem only in a land far, far away.

The real essence of the sermon, however, comes by naming the hungers in our lives that have nothing to do with food. Those hungers assume the guise of insatiable desire and inexhaustible consumption. We hunger for more power and more stuff, and this famine compels us to do things far

12. Most scholars agree that the lost sheep and lost coin stories in Luke 15:1–10 are a pair meant to be told together. Scholars differ on whether the lost son in Luke 15:11–32 belongs with the first two stories or is a separate story offered for a different point. See Jeremias, *Parables of Jesus*, 128–36; Hultgren, *Parables of Jesus*, 63–87, 468–71.

13. Copeland, "Naming the Famine."

worse than "filling ourselves with the pods that the pigs were eating." The two sons from the parable mimic the contrast between our famished lives and the abundant feast that could be ours. We identify with first one and then the other.

> The bad boy comes home and in a typical parabolic reversal of
> fortune becomes the good boy, while the good boy who stayed
> home obediently to do what all good boys do becomes a bad boy
> by refusing to join the party. It's feast or famine all over again.

The hunger of the younger brother cannot be assuaged by wealth and adventure, but those are the courses he consumes. The hunger of the older brother cannot be satiated by hard work and obedience, but those are the only meals he will eat. In fact, the older son believes a simple goat would abate his hunger when all along he has been surrounded by everything his heart could desire—"all that is mine is yours" (Luke 15:31). He has always had goats and calves and love and acceptance without even asking. In the end, acceptance and abundance can satisfy both their hungers, and both are gifts of the father who waits anxiously for both of his children to come to the table. The table is set for all of us and filled with gifts of abundance and acceptance. Like these brothers, we more often consume a diet of empty calories and puzzle that we are hungry again so quickly.

Being famished creates a different kind of despair than being lost. Neither is particularly frightening for most of us. Many of us travel all over the world and usually manage to know approximately where we are. If not, in a world full of smart phones with talking direction guides, we can soon find out. Lostness takes on a different hue for us, just as important as being physically lost. Likewise, hunger as a category has to be reclassified so we can see ourselves in the story. While most of us know there are hungry people all around us, we seldom think of ourselves as those without food. We have to catalogue hunger differently in light of the excess all around us. Accustomed to hearing sermons about metaphorical lostness and inured by an increasing sense of self assurance, shifting the conversation to our hungers can allow for a new understanding of the gospel truth. The gospel is the same, whether we are lost or hungry. God searches in order to feed.

From Rules to Redemption

This article would not be complete without examining a sermon by the one in whose honor the article is composed. Among Richard Lischer's many sermons challenging our staid faith interpretations is a sermon he preached at the inauguration of Duke's ninth president.[14] He chose Eph 5:15–20 and used the more archaic rendering for verse 16: "redeeming the time," rather than the now typical translation, "making the most of the time." The sermon focuses on redeeming time, but not before he draws out the seeming impossibility of such a prospect. The sermon is replete with time-bound references that propel the congregation into the understanding Lischer wants to evoke. He leads the congregation through familiar terrain about how we understand time: passing time, time gone by, make the most of time, etc.

Certainly, one delivering an inaugural sermon for a university president would be entitled to follow a more traditional interpretation of Ephesians 5 and focus on ethical behavior. Most college students could stand for some boundaries, and some of them probably expect to hear this kind of pulpit harangue. Many excellent sermons have followed Paul's lead by using the wisdom literature of the Old Testament to encourage congregants to live wise, sober, disciplined lives.[15] Most sermons stay safely within the terrain of faith formation for right living or call for sustained focus on the will of God. Other less laudable sermons rebuke the congregation by providing specific examples about the "days of evil," even while this was likely not Paul's impetus for the letter to the Ephesians.

Lischer's sermon barely pays heed to these typical readings of Ephesians and takes the congregation into the remarkable territory of redemption. This is not novel for a Lischer sermon. On the whole, his sermons consistently mine the depths of reconciliation: with others, with God, and with our own selves.[16] Cataloguing time as that which can be redeemed extends our possibilities for reconciliation. The past is not necessarily the past; instead, the past held in God's good time still holds hope for the future.

With a series of references to academia in general, the former institution of the newly installed president, and the particulars of their now shared institution, Lischer nuances our notions of time. All of this, of course, sets up the sermon for the importance of the time at hand, the specific time in which this particular president will assume leadership of this precise institution. Only after establishing this specificity of time does Lischer tell us, time can be redeemed.

> . . . we [Christians] do claim to know something about redemption. We know what it looks like. We know how it works. We worship a redeemer who was baptized by immersion into time . . .

14. Lischer, "Redeeming the Time."
15. Barth, *Ephesians* 4–6, 585–86.
16. Lischer, *End of Words*, 135–36.

We can do much more, according to Lischer, than "make the most of our time"; we can redeem it because it has already been redeemed by the one who defied death and redefined time. Redeeming time rather than passing time forces us to think differently about a concept we thought we understood. Time can be redeemed in all our moments because we are living toward the end of all time as redeemed by God. Lischer readily admits the paradox of such a claim:

> "Redeeming the time" is a bit trickier. This is why it is so good to have an English professor as president! English professors know an impossible metaphor when they see one.

Redeeming time, according to Lischer, means much more than remembering well. It means living well in the time we have been given, regardless of the circumstances confronting us. The circumstances are not the defining criteria for our lives. When he has focused our attention squarely on the situation before us, Lischer's illustrations become even more precise, honing in on the dynamics of the first month of this particular fall semester. He references two items germane only to this incoming first year class, which also means they are unique to this incoming president. Time is no longer merely a concept, but has become definitive for the intimacies of our own time frames.

God's redeeming love, manifest in the very real and time-immersed Jesus, defines our lives and our time for living them. From this vantage, a behavior check list is unnecessary. All the do's and don'ts we might impose on university students or suggest to university presidents are subsumed under the quality of redemption. The rules for living provided in the letter to the Ephesians do not disappear, but their specificity is absorbed into a larger construct for our lives. We are not trapped by mores incumbent upon Christians living in a Roman-occupied first century country, but are free to employ the appropriate behavior for the time before us. In other words, the specific rules from the letter to the Ephesians are less important than the reason for the rules. The reason—God's redemption of time—remains constant across all time. The rules need not.

Making a Difference

None of these examples showing a different reading from our typical associations contain material specific to gender dynamics or highlight women in any explicit way. Each, however, does offer a catalyst for shifting the ground of the interpretive community. To preach the gospel in a gendered world is to be painfully aware of the ground beneath our feet and mine for interpretations that challenge the norms. This does not mean we twist every sermon into a diatribe against sexism. Sometimes it is enough to preach the gospel and, by doing so, stand for those created in the image of God, including women.

In his preaching courses Richard Lischer often talks about God's "for-ness." By this he means a word from God always brings grace even when it is preceded by the troubling news of judgment. This is not the cheap grace against which Dietrich Bonhoeffer warned us, but a grace that beckons us to let the manner of our lives reflect what God has done for us. We become who we already are by finding ourselves incorporated into the story of God's salvation. By this Lischer does not mean we identify with a particular char-acter or single aspect of the scripture narrative, but rather we identify with the full story of salvation through the particularities of our own lives as reflected in the specific stories from scripture. Most of us, especially preach-ers, Lischer suggests, tend to identify with Jesus over and against the angry authorities or disbelieving crowds. In truth, however, we are more like the folks who get angry and who do not believe Jesus. We more often stand against that which God stands for. When we find ourselves incorporated into the story of God's salvation, we understand this story is for us. God is for us, even us, and because God is for us, we can be for others as well.

Preaching the gospel in a gendered world requires us to be FOR wom-en, but not necessarily against anyone else. We read scripture and interpret tradition with an eye for the gospel message—the for-ness—found in the story. When we mine the depths of scripture with an eye toward the for-ness of salvation, we often arrive at different conclusions than those handed to us by the tradition. Some of the best homiletical material lies in what is NOT said in the recitation of a narrative. Our default as listeners is to fill the lacu-nae with our own assumptions about missing meanings, but such defaults only reinforce our preconditioned dominant interpretations.

One of the ways we can avoid this trap is to begin the exegetical pro-cess from within our present situation. Lischer suggests we ask questions about the historical, social, and cultural setting of the biblical narrative only after we have answered the question: How is it with me? Exegesis starts with where we are now, not where the biblical narrative started thousands of years ago. Starting in the present, we have no need to avoid scripture narratives foreign to our modern sensibilities or explain away scripture sec-tions archaic in the twenty-first century. We simply tell the truth about these passages in light of the gospel we are called to live. The gospel will challenge our traditioned readings and staid interpretations. The gospel will change the story we thought we knew. The gospel will provide the catalyst for new ways of hearing. The gospel will change the party.

Bibliography

Cardenal, Ernesto. *The Gospel in Solentiname.* Translated by Donald D. Walsh. Maryknoll, NY: Orbis, 1976.

Copeland, Jennifer E. "Naming the Famine." March 21, 2004. Online: https://chapel. duke.edu/sites/default/files/Redeem%20the%20Time%209-19-04.pdf.

Barth, Markus. *Ephesians: Translation and Commentary on Chapters 4–6.* New York: Doubleday, 1974.

Hultgren, Arland J. *The Parables of Jesus: A Commentary.* Grand Rapids: Eerdmans, 2000.

Jeremias, Joachim. *The Parables of Jesus.* 2nd edn. New York: Charles Scribner's Sons, 1954.

Lischer, Richard. *The End of Words: The Language of Reconciliation in a Culture of Violence.* Grand Rapids: Eerdmans, 2005.

————. "Redeeming the Time." September 19, 2004. Online: https://chapel.duke.edu/ sites/default/files/Redeem%20the%20Time%209-19-04.pdf.

McCain, J. Clinton. *Judges.* Louisville: John Knox, 2002.

Moon, Young-Eun, et al. "The Effects of Preoperative Intravenous Acetaminophen in Patients Undergoing Abdominal Hysterectomy." *Archives of Gynecology and Obstetrics* 284.6 (2011) 1455–60.

Saporito, Bill. "The Air Bag Blowout." *Time* 184:23 (2014) 50–53.

Taylor, Barbara Brown. "The Parable of the Fearful Investor." November 13, 2011. Online: http://chapel-archives.oit.duke.edu/documents/BBT—FearfulInvestor.pdf.

Taylor, Edward L. *The Words of Gardner Taylor, Volume 2: Sermons from the Middle Years, 1970–1980.* Valley Forge: Judson, 2000.

Trible, Phyllis. *Texts of Terror: Literary-Feminist Readings of Biblical Narratives.* Philadelphia: Fortress, 1984.

Wesley, John. *Explanatory Notes upon the New Testament, Vol. 1.* 3rd edn. Bristol, 1760–62. Eighteenth Century Collections. Online: http://find.galegroup.com.proxy.lib. duke.edu/ecco/infomark.do?&source=gale&prodId=ECCO&userGroupName=d uke_perkins&tabID=T001&docId=CW119257423&type=multipage&contentSet =ECCOArticles&version=1.0&docLevel=FASCIMILE.

Wiley, Sean. "Universities Struggle to Address Sexual Violence on Campus." *Chicago Policy Review* (2015). Online: http://chicagopolicyreview.org/2015/04/16/uni versities-struggle-to-address-sexual-violence-on-campus/.

Memoir and Gospel

THE THEATER OF GOD'S GRACE

Heidi Neumark

Luther would have agreed with William Faulkner's dictum, "The only thing worth writing about is the human heart in conflict with itself." Like Faulkner, he would never have limited himself to so small a canvas, but the gospel always begins by laying claim to the nearest available heart, in this case, that of the preacher. God speaks to *me*. The facts of the Bible record nothing but "dead history" until they are activated in the heart of the believer.[1]

The whole point, [Luther] insisted, is to *use* the gospel in any circumstance for the comfort and renewal of human life. To know Christ, is to know what he can do for you. In the light of the gospel the believer is free to embrace the whole marvel of nature and culture as the theater of God's grace.[2]

THESE TWO QUOTATIONS FROM Richard Lischer's preface to a book of Martin Luther's selected writings provide an apt description of the interplay between gospel and memoir in Lischer's own work: knowing Christ is knowing what he can do for you. The importance of "for you" in Luther's interpretation of the gospel cannot be overestimated. It is found in his theology of Scripture, preaching, worship, and the sacraments. It is at the heart of his understanding of God's grace, the priesthood of all believers, and the theology of the cross. It is also at the heart of Lischer's use of memoir.

1. Lischer, "Preface," xx.
2. Ibid., xxi.

In translating the Bible, Luther sought to liberate God's word for the German people in language that was accessible to the whole community, rather than only to a tiny elite with the education required to understand Latin: ". . . we must inquire about this of the mother in the home, the children on the street, the man in the marketplace. We must be guided by their language, the way they speak, and do our translating accordingly."[3] The Bible is not to be held captive in a tower of ecclesiastical power and privilege. In other words, the Bible is not just "for them" (the elite), it is "for you"—the mother, the child, the common worker, the person struggling with confusion, despair, sin, death, and evil.

In Luther's 1519 Good Friday sermon, "A Meditation on Christ's Passion," he reiterates the importance of the biblical narrative, in this case the passion, coming to engage each person here and now: "Of what help is it to you that God is God, if he is not God to you?"[4] This is how Luther understands the purpose of all preaching. "Christ ought to be preached with this goal in mind—that we might be moved to faith in him so that he is not just a distant historical figure but actually Christ for you and me. In other words, the purpose of preaching is to make what is said about Christ effectual in us."[5]

Christ "for you and me" indicates not only the direction of the Word but the content—that in Christ I see God is not against me, but for me. God's Word, Jesus Christ, has come to enter fully into human experience, including and especially in those places and persons and moments of life considered to be the most degraded. This is Luther's theology of the cross. Faith comes not through right doctrine but in the thick of life, even in the worst of life; "it is living, no rather dying, suffering and facing damnation, not thinking, reading and speculating that makes a theologian," said Luther.[6] Christ is for us when all else is against us.

This "for you" is the basis of Luther's understanding of the church's worship and sacramental life. Like the Bible, the language of worship must reflect the language of the people. It is the setting for preaching and the sacraments where the people can absorb the gospel *pro nobis,* for us. Here is Luther on Holy Communion:

> I remind you again of this small particle: "for you." Remember
> to include yourself in this "for you." . . . You take the sacrament
> on the strength of these words "for you." . . . The benefit is "given

3. Ibid., xxiii.

4. Luther, "A Good Friday Sermon."

5. Luther, *Freedom of a Christian*, 69.

6. Luther, *Sämmliche Schriften*, 4:455.

for you, shed for you" . . . Here you have medicine, not poison.
. . . It is an antidote which means salvation, blessedness, life,
forgiveness of sins.[7]

The preceding is a very brief overview of the "for you" at the heart of Lutheran theology, worship, and preaching. I believe that it is also the key to the intimate relationship between memoir and gospel exemplified in the writing of Richard Lischer. Of course, the memoir form can be used for narcissistic, self-indulgent ends. The anatomy of a memoir can be, as Luther would say, *incurvatus in se*, curved in on itself. But that is not what Lischer is about. Memoir can also be a way to love and serve one's neighbor, offering one's own life as a theater of God's grace for the sake of others. This is where Lischer's offering of self through memoir becomes radiant gospel proclamation. His work demonstrates how memoir is a way to translate the gospel into the present tense of one individual life so that others can recognize the contours of their own experience and discover the presence of the gospel in their own lives.

The gospels themselves convey universal truths though many particular and peculiar encounters. In commenting on Luther's sermons, Lischer writes:

> The realism of his portraits demystifies and at the same time universalizes Christian dogma by giving it social size and psychological scope. In his sermons they (we) are all there: the anxious mother who doesn't understand her precocious son—and then loses him on the way home from the Temple! A foreign woman who endures a racial insult in order to save her child; a prostitute who alone among her respectable critics understands the meaning of love; a rich burgher who distains a beggar's cry but wishes to be known as a benefactor . . .[8]

Memoir can serve to extend these demystifying portraits into the writer's own life for the sake of the reader.

Lischer gives us a superb example of this approach in the memoir of his early years as an inexperienced pastor: *Open Secrets: A Spiritual Journey through a Country Church*. He shares his own struggles, pretentions, disappointments, fears, and worries. He is open with self-remonstrance and regret. He introduces us to the nitty-gritty of congregational life without pat answers and ready resolutions. Through memoir, Lischer exemplifies what he extols in preaching: "We will love our listeners with our words as

7. Luther, *Faith and Freedom*, 139–40.
8. Lischer, "Preface," xxv.

God has loved us in the word made flesh, and in so doing we will discover a surprising new power of expression, one that does not 'win over' but 'joins with' its audience."[9]

Lischer joins with his readers as he uses personal narrative to translate potentially heady concepts like reconciliation into the language of his experience with the community he serves. Instead of an academic treatise on a key theological concept, the reader is schooled in reconciliation by way of a farmer's side of beef. This is biblical translation with one ear to the marketplace in the tradition of Luther. Lischer's church is located in the small, Illinois town of New Cana, and while he never references water turned to wine, each chapter becomes a brimming jar of ordinary, relatable moments, suddenly transformed into something more.

When Lischer describes having to preside over a funeral that went from tasteless to farcical he ends his account with a preteen girl who stuns everyone when she picks up her cornet for what Lischer assumes will be a perfunctory rendition of taps. Instead, she plays a hymn and "the clear voice of her cornet reached us, it seemed, a half second after we saw her breathe, extend her neck, and puff her cheeks. It was as if her music were a time-delayed message coming to us from a saner and more beautiful world. . . . All Lent lay before us, but now, for the first time, I could stand in the lumpy mud of our cemetery and see Easter."[10] Lischer's prose takes hold to move us from farce to glory. His narrative shows us divine love adhering to the lumpy mud of our human condition, bearing the gospel and offering hope. Somehow we know that if it is for him, it can be for us. We are part of the ragtag group around the grave. We stand with the hapless pastor, hardly deserving such an ending to the day, but "here you have medicine, not poison. . . . It is an antidote which means salvation, blessedness, life, forgiveness of sins."

In his book on preaching, *The End of Words: The Language of Reconciliation in the Culture of Violence*, Lischer writes of "narrative chaos," the unfolding of events that resist a narrative arc that comes to rest on solid ground. It is the chaos of suffering, the chaos of Calvary: "It is important to know that God has taken up the 'narrative wreckage' of our lives into God's own history . . ."[11] In *The End of Words* Lischer speaks this truth. In his second memoir, *Stations of the Heart: Parting with a* Son, he shows us what it is to live this truth.

9. Lischer, *End of Words*, 164.
10. Lischer, *Open Secrets*, 196.
11. Lischer, *End of Words*, 117.

Stations of the Heart is a memoir of narrative wreckage, as Lischer describes his son Adam's final months in the wake of the melanoma that took his life at the age of thirty-three. Tom Long writes:

> As he grieved over the loss of his son, Richard Lischer gradually discovered that he had been given a new role—as the interpreter of his own son's death. In this tender and loving book, Lischer does indeed become an interpreter, not only of his son's death but also of the fragile and beautiful relationships that make life both a peril and a gift for us all. Lischer is a faithful witness whose truthful and searing testimony evokes memory, provokes tears, and finally points powerfully toward hope.[12]

In Lischer's "faithful witness" we see a dinner table, a mall, and a hospital room become the theater of God's grace, enabling the reader to imagine how such grace might also meet us, be for us in such familiar places when our own narrative lies in ruins. Here is death and resurrection. In his memoir Lischer has done more than bear witness to his son; he has born witness to the gospel.

Adam finds strength and solace in conversion to Catholicism and in the sacrament of the eucharist. Daily mass with his wife becomes the best part of the day where God's body meets his in cruciform wreckage and transfiguration. *Stations of the Heart* is sacramental in its own way. Lischer offers his readers the brokenness of his own anguish and grief. Because his story is unquestionably real, the reader is led to trust the real presence of Christ. This is prose as sacrament.

Lischer teaches homiletics and treasures the sermonic form, but he also shows us how memoir can serve a homiletical function, bearing the gospel in a way that a sermon cannot. Most sermons come in at under thirty minutes, often less, and in some traditions twice that, but rarely longer. Like pericopes in the gospels themselves, each encounter, each story, each narrative arc is necessarily short. To be sure, Lischer weaves biblical text and story throughout his writing. The gospel message that carries any sermon worthy of the name shines through his memoirs as well, but the format allows for an unhurried immersion. The reader can set the pace for the story to unfold and absorb the material bit by bit. There is ample time to learn or relearn the language of faith and how it speaks to you, for you. I have never heard Lischer preach, but the homiletical power of his memoirs will never leave me.

Lischer's use of memoir defies any condemnation of the form as self-centered. Instead, he bares his soul for the sake of serving and loving his

12. Long, "Review."

neighbor. He sacrifices a significant degree of privacy so that others might be nourished. This is how Luther understood the sacrifice of the mass that so captivated Lischer's son, Adam: "sacrifice is the living out of baptism, the surrender of our bodies as a living sacrifice. 'I give myself for the common good. . . . Thus I am your food, just as you make use of bread when you are hungry that in turn your body may help and give strength to the one who is hungry. Therefore when I help and serve you in need, I am your bread.'"[13] Memoir is just one of the many splendid ways that Richard Lischer has given of himself for the common good, serving us in our need and meeting us in our deepest hungers.

Bibliography

Long, Thomas G. "Review of *Stations of the Heart*." Online: http://www.amazon.com/ Stations-Heart-Parting-Richard-Lischer/dp/110191047X/ref=sr_1_1?s=books&i e=UTF8&qid=1438184287&sr=1-1&keywords=stations+of+the+heart.

Lischer, Richard. *The End of Words: The Language of Reconciliation in a Culture of Violence*. Grand Rapids: Eerdmans, 2005.

———. *Open Secrets: A Spiritual Journey Through a Country Church*. New York: Doubleday, 2001.

———. "Preface." In *Faith and Freedom: An Invitation to the Writings of Martin Luther*, edited by John F. Thornton and Susan B. Varenne, xiii–xxviii. Vintage Spiritual Classics. New York: Vintage, 2002.

Luther, Martin. "'All Become One Cake.' A Sermon on the Lord's Supper," Maundy Thursday, 1523. Translated by Matthew C. Harrison. St. Louis: LCMS World Relief and Human Care, 2005. Online: http://www.lcms.org/Document. fdoc?src=lcm&id=718.

———. *Faith and Freedom: An Invitation to the Writings of Martin Luther*. Edited by John F. Thornton and Susan B. Varenne. Vintage Spiritual Classics. New York: Vintage, 2002.

———. *The Freedom of a Christian*. Translated by Mark V. Tranvik. Minneapolis: Fortress, 2008.

———. "A Good Friday Sermon on How to Contemplate Christ's Holy Sufferings," 1519. Online: http://www.lectionarycentral.com/friday/LutherGospel.html.

———. *Sämmliche Schriften*. 22 vols. St Louis: Concordia, 1957.

---

13. Luther, "All Become One Cake," 3.

Breakfast on the Shore

Gail Godwin

As soon as they were come to land, they saw a fire of coals there, and fish laid thereon, and bread. Jesus saith unto them, bring of the fish which ye have now caught. Simon Peter went up, and drew the net to land full of great fishes, a hundred and fifty and three: and for all there were so many, yet was not the net broken. Jesus saith unto them, come and dine. And none of the disciples durst ask him, Who art thou? Knowing it was the Lord. Jesus then cometh and taketh bread, and giveth them, and fish likewise. This is now the third time that Jesus shewed himself to his disciples, after that he was risen from the dead. —JOHN 21:9–14, KJV

CHAPTER 21 OF THE Gospel of John tells of three events taking place at the sea of Tiberius during a single night and morning.

The first event begins with the return of the fishermen/disciples after catching nothing. Jesus stands on the shore, but they don't know it is Jesus. The man on the shore says cast your net on the right side of the ship. They do this, not far from land, and their net is filled. At this point the disciple whom Jesus loved tells the others on the ship that the man on the shore is the Lord. When naked Peter hears this, he rushes into his fisherman's coat and leaps into the sea. The others follow in their little ship, dragging the net with fishes.

This first and most dramatic event was my introduction to John 21 in Sunday School. The colored illustration on the front of our leaflet for that lesson showed men in a boat wrestling with a net overladen with fish. ("It's one of the miracles," our teacher says. "Does it remind you of any other miracles? That's right. The loaves and fishes that served the multitudes who went to hear the Sermon on the Mount.")

The second event (21:9–14) is not so dramatic, and liable to be skipped right over by early teachers and one's earlier self. The disciples come to land, see fish and bread cooking on a fire of coals. The man who is cooking says, "Come and dine," and none of them dares ask him, "Who are you?" Yet they know it is the Lord. Jesus then gives them bread and fish. The narrator of the gospel tells us this was the third time Jesus showed himself to his disciples after he was risen from the dead.

The third event takes place after they have eaten and consists mostly of dialogue between Jesus and Peter. This was the important event for the nuns who taught us at the Roman Catholic school I attended. The emphasis was less on the miracle of the fish. For them, the protagonist of John 21 was Peter. Impulsive, competitive, headstrong Peter! Larger than life! There he goes again, throwing his coat over his naked body and leaping dramatically out of the boat to get there first. The important part of breakfast is what happens afterwards when Jesus asks Peter three times "Lovest thou me?" Peter is grieved that Jesus has to ask him three times. "But," explains our teacher, "this was the Lord's way of forgiving Peter for having denied him three times. Jesus was preparing Peter to lead his church, to be the rock. But we already know this, don't we, because in Luke 16:18, what did Jesus say? Jesus said, 'Thou art Peter, and upon this rock I shall build my church.'"

●

As I am writing this, our country is in the early throes of the 2016 presidential race. A currently popular candidate says his favorite book is the Bible, he is never without it. Asked by an interviewer to share one or two of his favorite Bible passages, the candidate answers without a beat: "I like all of it."

"Which do you like better?" pursues the interviewer, "the Old or the New Testament?"

This time the candidate pauses to think. His face puckers, then brightens. "I like . . . *both*," he decides with a huge smile.

Nobody has ever put me on this particular spot, but I've had my answer ready for years. "The last chapter of John's gospel. Especially verses nine through fourteen. There is a mystery in it that always re-connects me to the glow of faith."

Here I sit, facing my bookshelves (so many books on God!) and take down a few to help me with this essay. In the 1990s I became obsessed with two new books by the Jesus Seminar: *The Five Gospels: The Search for the*

Authentic Words of Jesus (1993) and *The Acts of Jesus: The Search for the Authentic Deeds of Jesus* (1998). Internationally recognized gospel scholars had inventoried all the surviving ancient texts for words and acts attributed to Jesus. First they produced their own translation of the gospels, known as the Scholar's Version, and then they got together and debated and color-coded their collective votes: red for the words and actions most probably his; pink for "those that may have suffered modifications in transmission"; gray for "did not originate with him but may reflect his ideas; and black for "inauthentic." I looked up the gospel stories that most appealed to me and then checked them against the color code, saving my favorite, John 21, for last.

The centurion of great faith in Matt 8:5 and Luke 7:1–10 ("Verily I say to you, I have not found so great faith, no, not in Israel.") was colored black and assumed to be created by a storyteller.

Jairus's little daughter ("I pray thee come and lay hands on her"; "Get up, little girl.") in Mark 5:23–43, Matt 9:18–20, and Luke 8:40–56, was colored black by common consent. The words of Jesus are not particularly memorable, are not aphorisms or parables, would not have circulated independently during the oral period, and cannot therefore be traced back to Jesus.[1]

The father with the mute boy ("If thou canst believe, all things are possible to him that believeth." "Lord, I believe. Help thou my unbelief.") in Mark 9:24; Matt 17:14–21; and Luke 9:37–43 was colored black. "The incidental dialogue ascribed to Jesus in this story is the creation of the narrator who exercises the storyteller's license."[2]

Now for John 21:1–14 (fishing instructions, breakfast on shore, Jesus' third appearance to the disciples after being risen from the dead). The Jesus Scholars conclude that "The dialogue assigned to Jesus is the result of the storyteller's imagination. Jesus is made to say what the narrator thinks he might have said on such an occasion."[3]

In the second volume, *The Acts of Jesus*, the Jesus Scholars suggest that John 20:30–31 reads like it was meant to be the end of this gospel. Later tradition, they say, assumes chapter 21 was added by the disciple John.[4]

All my favorites coded black! It would take a while to absorb this. Meanwhile I would see what sayings or actions had earned the red. Jesus' provocative parable of the good Samaritan was in red, his enigmatic repartee about paying the emperor was in red. There were far fewer reds than pink,

---

1. Funk, et al., *Five Gospels*, 62.

2. Ibid., 82.

3. Ibid., 468.

4. Funk, *Acts of Jesus*, 440.

gray, or black. I broke down halfway into the pink. Not only was I becoming confused but I was probably committing some form of Bible abuse. So I shelved the Seminar volumes among the rest of my Religion and Psychology books and allowed them some peace.

What has remained with me from that compulsive exercise was the Seminar's conclusion that Jesus' voice was a distinctive one. They went on to say why. His sayings and parables cut against the social and religious grain of the times. They were often characterized by exaggeration, humor, and paradox. They surprised and shocked. They called for a reversal of roles. They frustrated ordinary expectations.[5]

The Scholars reaffirmed for me that this was definitely a teacher and preacher worth a lifetime's pursuit.

⠀⠀⠀⠀⠀⠀⠀⠀⠀⠀⠀⠀⠀⠀⠀⠀⠀⠀⠀-❧-

"But we, who have undertaken God, can never finish," maintains the young narrator of *The Notebooks of Malte Laurids Brigge*.[6]

"She belonged to that class of human beings of whom spiritual activity is demanded," Jung writes about a patient who was subsequently cured when her life took on meaning.[7]

As one of those people who have undertaken God and can never finish, and of whom spiritual activity is demanded, I continue to pursue the mystery of John 21 and the figure at the center of it, cooking the breakfast. When I can't "figure out" something through words, I try drawing it with colored pencils. In 1997, after I had read the Jesus Seminar's *What Did Jesus Really Say?* and a year before *What Did Jesus Really Do?* was published, I began drawing, intermittently, a series of pictures of Jesus doing things. I do these drawings in 5" x 7" sketchbooks made with recycled paper. The paper is brown and has imperfections, which often contribute to the way a drawing wants to go. My first Jesus drawing was a close-up head and shoulders of a stern, aggrieved Jesus dressed in regal garments, holding up his palms to show you the spots where the nails went in. I titled it, "Guest Preacher." The next time I was moved to draw Jesus doing something, he was sitting by the shore surrounded by little kids. His expression is relaxed and absorbed. An imperious little girl in a red dress (meant to be me) has possessive hold of his right wrist. A shy older girl leans against his right shoulder and seems to be stroking him. A little boy on his left side is so excited he has left the

5. Funk, et al., *Five Gospels*, 30–31.

6. Rilke, *Notebooks of Malte Laurids Brigge*, 199.

7. Jung, *Memories, Dreams, Reflections*, 138.

ground and is floating away holding on to the tail of the big fish leaping over Jesus's head. Nuzzling against Jesus's left knee and cradled by Jesus' left hand is the smallest boy, hardly out of infancy. The toes of his little right foot are stepping on the toes of Jesus' big left foot. This one was titled "Visit to the Sunday School." Then came a series of turbulent drawings on other subjects, and then back to Jesus: a full body close-up, kneeling in the sand and cooking purple fish on a grill with his left hand. His right hand is raised in greeting toward whomever is approaching by boat. Two playful little purple fish sport in the shallows. "Posthumous Jesus Cooking an Early Breakfast for his Fishermen by the Shore," is the title of this one. There are more in the Jesus series; they still continue, but we'll stop with Jesus grilling the purple fish and waving out to sea.

In 1997, I was writing a sequel to *Father Melancholy's Daughter*. It was called *Evensong*. Margaret, the daughter of the late melancholy priest in the previous novel, is now studying for the priesthood herself.

In the first chapter of *Evensong*, Margaret and Adrian, the man she will marry, are visiting Dr. Stroup, a professor at General Theological Seminary. The professor shows them a new painting he has just acquired, created by a Staten Island artist. The painting is an acrylic rendering of John 21:9–14, done in the iconic style.

"The single area of brightness comes from the glow of the charcoal fire on shore where Jesus, returned from the dead, is cooking their breakfast. All three of us were drawn to the painting and continued to talk about it over lunch, along with the mysterious final chapter of the Fourth Gospel on which it was based."[8]

The professor tells them there is a Greek word, *kalchaino*, which means literally "to search for the purple fish." Adrian, a psychotherapist as well as a priest, is intrigued by the phrase.

"Well, of course you are, dear boy," Stroup tells him, "It's your favorite element, those waters where the purple fish swim." The professor goes on to explain that the purple fish was a fish so highly prized by the Greeks for its rich purple dye that divers went to the bottom of the sea in search of it and that was how "searching for the purple fish" came to be a Greek expression for plumbing the depths of one's mind. The artist, of Greek descent, had told Stroup this was why he had made his sea predominantly purple and why the fish Jesus is cooking are the purplest of all.

8. Godwin, *Evensong*, 27–28.

That makes sense, Adrian says, because in the language of the unconscious, when the dreamer is about to eat something it is often a signal that there is submerged content ready to be assimilated by the dreamer.

Margaret says she is most moved by someone returning from the dead to give sustenance to loved ones when they are most in need of it.

"My dear," Stroup tells Margaret, "you provide the crucial third element of this luncheon triad. I'm the old academic, Adrian's the deep sea diver, but you remind us what it's all about in the first place."

"And what's that?" Adrian asks the professor.

"Love, old fellow, love. He's out there cooking their breakfast because he *loved* them and they knew it."

⚫

My writing life takes me further than I can go by myself. Characters say things I need to hear. They think things I might not think by myself and go to places I haven't gone or haven't dared to go. I wasn't aware of it as I was writing that scene in *Evensong,* but later I saw how the purple fish conversation—sparked by the earlier picture I drew of Jesus cooking the purple fish—had offered me a relaxed way to sneak up on the mystery of John 21. I could explore in fictional safety its lifelong allurement for me. First there was the fictional painting—I wish it did exist; I wish I could paint it.

Bringing their interpretations to the painting were three characters: the professor, the psychologist, and the young woman priest in love. Imagining their points of view gave me new insights into the power of that scene and story that has intrigued me for so much of my life. It's not about dead people, it's not about ghosts, nor is it about history or about storytelling. A teacher kneels on the shore to cook breakfast for his hungry disciples because he loved them. They don't dare say it's their teacher, who was crucified, but nevertheless they know it's him.

The mystery is that the glow from that fire is still burning bright and we still recognize the teacher in our midst.

Bibliography

Funk, Robert. *The Acts of Jesus: The Search for the Authentic Deeds of Jesus.* San Francisco: HarperSanFrancisco, 1998.

———, et al. *The Five Gospels: The Search for the Authentic Words of Jesus.* New York: Macmillan, 1993.

Godwin, Gail. *Evensong.* New York: Ballantine, 1999.

Jung, C. G., and Aniela Jaffe. *Memories, Dreams, Reflections.* Translated by Richard and Clara Winston. London: Routledge and Kegan Paul, 1963.

Rilke, Ranier Maria. *The Notebooks of Malte Laurids Brigge.* Translated by M. D. Herter Norton. New York: Norton, 1949.

Gospel Performance and the Mind of Christ

Charles L. Bartow

THE CONCERN OF THIS essay is not with just any sort of gospel, any sort of good news. Instead, the concern is with "the good news of God," the coming near of "the kingdom of God" that Jesus himself proclaimed and effected (Mark 1:14–15). Further, if it is in any sense fitting to regard such good news as performance, then the performance spoken of must be *actio divina*,[1] God's self-performance and not simply *homo performans*,[2] that is, human self-performance. *Actio*, in rhetorical theory, is the Latin term for delivery, thought of as embodied voice, communicative *action*, also word and *deed* as distinct from mere *pronunciatio*, vocal utterance. In it, for good or ill, the communicating self is revealed to and through audition, listening and acting.[3] *Actio divina* is divine self-revealing, self-disclosure. *Homo performans*, then, is human self-revealing, human self-disclosure. It is rhetorical *action*, speech delivery and related action, a matter going to the very heart of rhetorical practice.[4]

Contemporary scholarship in performance studies puts the human self in its being and becoming at the center of its disciplinary concern.[5] Also, there has been a so-called "performance turn" in rhetorical studies, biblical hermeneutics, and homiletic theory and practice. Rightly, too, some of the concern has been with performance skill, developing ever increasing

1. Bartow, *God's Human Speech*, 3, 27, 35, 44, 48.

2. Ibid., 60, 95, 122.

3. Thonssen and Baird, *Speech Criticism*, 81–89. Compare *actio* defined in Simpson, *Cassell's Latin Dictionary*, 10.

4. McKenzie, "At the Intersection," 60–61.

5. Langellier, "Storytelling, Turning Points," 214–19. Also, Gilbert, "Standing Up to Combat Trauma," 144–63. Also Alexander et al., "Identifying Key Intercultural Urgencies," esp. 58ff.

competence in verbal, vocal, and physical gesture.[6] Those matters, however, will not be dealt with here. Here the focus will be on *actio divina* and *homo performans* biblically attested as divine self-disclosure and human personal and corporate response. In addition, with the help of the Authorized or King James Version of the Bible, our first move will be to attempt a definition of performance nuanced according to the KJV use of the term "performance" to translate a number of words from Hebrew and New Testament Greek usage.

Hebrew words frequently translated by the term "performance" are: *batsa* (to cut off), *gamar* (to complete, perfect), *nathan* (to give), *asah* (to do), *pala* (to separate), *tsaba* (to war, serve, perform), *qum* (to raise up, confirm), and *shalam* (to finish, complete). New Testament Greek terms translated as performance are: *apodidōmi* (to give away), *epiteleō* (to make an end of, complete), *katergazomai* (to work out thoroughly), *poieō* (to do, make), *teleō* (to end, complete), *teleisōsis* (an ending, completion), and *ginomai* (to become, happen, come to pass). In the King James Version of the Bible, the English word perform (or performance, or performed) occurs sixty-six times. Twenty-eight times the reference is to the communicative action of God. Thirty-eight times the reference is to the faithful or unfaithful action (or failure to act) of human beings in response to God's word and act.

Divine Action

The performance, the word and act of God in self-revelation and in the making known of God's will and intention, clearly reveals God's character in establishing and carrying through on covenantal promises. For example, in Gen 26:3, in a time of famine, God instructs Isaac not to flee to Egypt for relief, but to stay in Canaan and trust in God for daily bread. The text reads: "Sojourn in this land, and I will be with thee, and will bless; for unto thee, and unto thy seed, I will give all these countries, and I will *perform* the oath which I sware unto Abraham thy father."[7]

Similarly, in Deut 9:5, God gives instruction to the Israelites as they are about to cross the Jordan to take possession of the promised land. God says: "Not for thy righteousness, or for the uprightness of thine heart, dost thou go to possess their land: but for the wickedness of these nations the Lord thy God doth drive them out before thee, and that he may *perform* the word which the Lord sware unto thy fathers, Abraham, Isaac, and Jacob." Then,

6. Bacon, *Art of Interpretation*, 3.

7. All biblical quotations are from the King James Version unless otherwise indicated.

too, in 1 Kings 6:12, divine covenantal guidance is provided for Solomon with regard to his building of the temple wherein God's name might dwell: "Concerning this house which thou art building, if thou wilt walk in my statutes, and execute my judgments, and keep all my commandments to walk in them; then I will *perform* my word with thee, which I spake unto David thy father."

Grippingly, in prophetic literature (for the most part poetic utterance), God performs the divine word of judgment, mercy, and messianic promise. In what we call First Isaiah, for example, God punishes wayward Jerusalem. Yet, in the same breath, God likewise makes known what is to befall Jerusalem's despoilers in due course. In Isa 10:12, the prophet speaks on God's behalf: "Wherefore it shall come to pass, that when the Lord hath *performed* his whole work upon mount Zion and on Jerusalem, I will punish the fruit of the stout heart of the king of Assyria, and the glory of his high looks."

The prophecy of Ezekiel, a literary achievement[8] and a work of historical interest, speaks of the imminent fall of Judah and Jerusalem to Babylonian conquest: "I am the Lord: I will speak, and the word that I shall speak shall come to pass; it shall be no more prolonged: for in your days, O rebellious house, will I say the word and *perform* it, saith the Lord" (Ezek 12:25).

Still, the word of judgment spoken in Chapter 12 is held in creative tension with God's word of mercy, hope, restoration, and—we might so designate it—communal or national resurrection in Chapter 37.[9] The people are in Exile in Babylon and very well may remain there yet forty more years. But the prophet's vision of the valley of dry bones (part of which has been famously rendered in the joyous African American spiritual) looks to the reestablishment of the house of Israel in its own homeland. God addresses the prophet, and the prophet tells of it thus:

> Then he said unto me, Son of man, these bones are the whole house of Israel: behold, they say, Our bones are dried, and our hope is lost: we are cut off for our parts. Therefore prophesy and say unto them, Thus saith the Lord God; Behold, O my people, I will open your graves, and cause you to come up out of your graves, and bring you into the land of Israel. And ye shall know that I am the Lord, when I have opened your graves, O my people, and brought you up out of your graves, And shall put my spirit in you, and ye shall live, and I shall place you in your own land: then shall ye know that I the Lord have spoken it, and performed it, saith the Lord. (Ezek 37:11–14)

8. Davis, *Swallowing the Scroll*.
9. Lapsley, *Can These Bones Live*, 169–71.

As for a word of messianic promise and accomplishment, there is none more rousing than that word found in Isa 9:6–7. One can hardly read it without a performance of Handel's *Messiah* ringing in one's mind and heart:

> For unto us a child is born, unto us a son is given: and the government shall be upon his shoulder: and his name shall be called Wonderful, Counsellor, The mighty God, The everlasting Father, The Prince of Peace. Of the increase of his government and peace there shall be no end, upon the throne of David, and upon his kingdom, to order it, and to establish it with judgment and with justice from henceforth even forever. The zeal of the Lord of hosts will perform this.

Human Performance

The Call

From *actio divina*, the self-performance of God, we turn to *homo performans*, the self-performance of human beings particularly in response to God. From the start, the people of God, those called upon to enter into covenant with God, were expected to obey God's commandments, to follow God's instructions, and to heed with heart, mind, soul, and strength what God had to say to them by the mouth of prophets divinely appointed faithfully to speak God's word in ever changing times and circumstances. And God's timely word was of judgment and mercy, the two sides, so to speak, of the single coin of divine grace.[10] Regarding the orderly worship of God in the time of Moses, Gershonites were called upon to perform specific tasks of divine service in the tabernacle: "And the Lord spake unto Moses, saying, Take also the sum of the sons of Gershon, throughout the houses of their fathers, by their families; From thirty years old and upward until fifty years old shalt thou number them; all that enter in to *perform* the service, to do the work in the tabernacle of the congregation" (Num 4:21–23).

Kings also at last came to be appointed to particular service in the governance of God's people, and they were to be exemplars of covenantal fidelity in life and in worship. To understate the case, their performance, publicly and privately, did not always measure up to God's expectation. First Samuel 15:11 indicates God's bitter disappointment with King Saul in a dramatically poignant phrase: "It repenteth me that I have set up Saul to be

---

10. Farmer, *Servant of the Word*, 46–47.

king: for he is turned back from following me and hath not *performed* my commandments."

Much later, in 638 BC, in Judah, there came to the throne of God's people a king of apparently more personal integrity and commitment to covenant fidelity than many of his predecessors. With the repair of the temple in Jerusalem, the book of the law was found. And the reading of Deuteronomy to King Josiah seems to have sparked a salutary response.[11] "And the king stood in his place, and made a covenant before the Lord, to walk after the Lord, and to keep his commandments, and his testimonies, and his statutes, and with all his soul, to *perform* the words of the covenant which were written in this book" (2 Chron 34:31).

In the literature of the Psalms there is a beautiful echo of this same intention of the heart: "Thy testimonies have I taken as an heritage forever: for they are the rejoicing of my heart. I have inclined mine heart to *perform* thy statutes always, even unto the end" (Ps 119:112).

The Reality

There is evidence, however, that the human heart can choose to do not only what is contrary to covenant fidelity, but also what is brazenly contemptuous of it. So at the time of Babylon's conquering of Judah and Jerusalem, the prophet Jeremiah spoke to Judaean elites who had fled to Egypt in hope of finding there safe refuge from Nebuchadnezzar. The prophet proffered a sarcastic indictment of the refugees' redoubled commitment to apostasy and idolatry[12]:

> Thus says the Lord of hosts, the God of Israel, saying, Ye and your wives have both spoken with your mouths, and fulfilled with your hand, saying, We will surely *perform* our vows that we have vowed, to burn incense to the queen of heaven, and to pour drink offerings unto her: Ye will surely accomplish your vows, and surely *perform* your vows (Jer 44:25).

It is worth noting that Ezekiel's word of return to Judah and Jerusalem—and resurrection of national identity and purpose to Israel—came to exiles in Babylon, not to those who had fled to Egypt for security from Babylonian domination.

The Authorized or King James Version's use of the term *perform* to translate a variety of Hebrew words, taken in their contexts, reveals ranges

11. Davis and Gehman, *Westminster Dictionary*, 331–32.

12. Note on Jer 44:15–28, *Oxford Annotated Bible*, 1027–28.

of signification well beyond simply getting something done. Over and again the something to be done—or ordered to be done—implies covenantal accountability, a relationship of faithful trust in God on the part of human beings. This trust is to be placed in the Lord God of Israel who is faithful in keeping promises, faithful in carrying out to completion the divine word of judgment and mercy, faithful in restoring once "dried up," "cut off" peoples and nations to new life, faithful in keeping messianic hope alive even in circumstances seemingly unfavorable to deliverance from affliction. *Actio divina*, God's self-performance, reveals God's character in word and deed. It reveals God's "claim and succor,"[13] as theologian H. H. Farmer expressed it. Despite the equivocation, dissembling, and willful disobedience of *homo performans* (human self-disclosure and action in relation to God) there is a steadfast love, a loving kindness (*chesed*), a relentless "blessed disturbance"[14]—from beyond history, but in history—out to get back what belongs to it.[15] Where *actio divina* and *homo performans* meet, there is a "conflagration of love"[16]: ". . . a fallen flare / Through the hollow of an ear."[17]

Gospel Performance in the New Testament

So W. B. Yeats evoked Gabriel's announcement to Mary that she would bear into the world (as a prophet bears the word of God) "a love that makes [her] heart's blood stop,"[18] eternal love, "love divine all loves excelling,"[19] her womb compassing (Jer 31:22) what John Donne called "immensity."[20] But before that announcement to Mary there was the disclosure to Zacharias (NRSV Zachariah) that his longtime "barren" wife, Elisabeth, would bear a son to be named John. John was "to make ready a people prepared for the Lord" (Luke 1:17). Zacharias expressed his doubts: "Whereby shall I know this? For I am an old man, and my wife well stricken in years" (Luke 1:18).

"And the angel answering said unto him, I am Gabriel, that stand in the presence of God; and am sent to speak unto thee, and to show thee these glad tidings. And, behold, thou shalt be dumb, and not able to speak,

---

13. Farmer, *Servant of the Word*, 46.

14. Unpublished comment of Paul E. Scherer in a lecture at Princeton Seminary, 1963.

15. Taylor, "Sweet Torture of Sunday Morning," 20.

16. Bartow, *God's Human Speech*, 95–123.

17. Yeats, "Mother of God," 249.

18. Loc. cit.

19. C. Wesley, "Love Divine, All Loves Excelling," in Jones, *Hymnbook*, Hymn 399.

20 Donne, "Nativitie," 41.

until the day these things shall be *performed*, because thou believest not my words, which shall be fulfilled in their season" (Luke 1:19–20).

Eight days after John's birth, Elisabeth and Zacharias brought their child to the temple to be circumcised. He was about to be named Zacharias after his father. But Elisabeth said no, his name is John. In writing on a tablet Zacharias agreed. He wrote, "His name is John . . . . And his mouth was opened immediately, and his tongue loosed, and he spake, and praised God. . . . Blessed be the Lord God of Israel; for he has visited and redeemed his people . . . as he spoke by the mouth of his holy prophets, which have been since the world began: That we should be saved from our enemies and from the hand of all that hate us; To *perform* the mercy promised to our fathers to remember his holy covenant" (Luke 1:63–64, 68, 70–72).

Homo performans, human self-performance (self-revealing in deed and word) in relation to God's self-disclosure, continues to be of great significance (for good or ill) in gospel attestation just as it was attested to be in the matter of Israel's covenant responsibility to God. Further, it remains significant at both the level of individual life and corporate life. Mary and Joseph's presentation of the infant Jesus to the Lord following his circumcision, for instance, is a personal act undertaken in response to divine and corporate expectation: "As it is written in the law of the Lord, Every male that openeth the womb shall be called holy to the Lord" (Luke 2:23).

Then, following Simeon's song and the thanksgiving of the prophetess, Anna, the narrator concludes his rehearsal of these events thus: "And when they [that is, Mary and Joseph] had *performed* all things according to the law of the Lord, they returned into Galilee, to their own city Nazareth" (Luke 2:39). In other words, Mary and Joseph completed their obligation to God and community. Performance denotes such follow through and completion just as it implies those other denotations and connotations previously discussed. One cannot help but conclude, then, that the King James Version translators used it because of its efficiency of denotation and connotation in a wide range of circumstances.

Gospel Performance Embodied in the Community

We move then to its use in depicting corporate embodiment of response to God, corporate gospel attestation. St. Paul adjured the Corinthian Church not only to *will* charity, for instance, but to *enact* that charity. He entreated the Corinthian congregation to give substantially to the relief of the Jerusalem Church which had great need. In doing so, he mentioned the generosity that the Macedonian Churches (Philippi and Thessalonica) had already enacted. The apostle Paul said: "And herein I give my advice: for this is expedient for you, who have begun before, not only to do, but also to be forward [that is, desirous to give] a year ago. Now therefore *perform* [*epitelesate*, complete] the doing of it; that as there was a readiness to will, so there may be a performance also out of that which ye have" (2 Cor 8:10–11). In writing to Rome, Paul indicated that he himself would deliver to the Jerusalem Church the gifts from Macedonia and Achaia (the province wherein Corinth was located). He wrote, "When therefore I have *performed* this, and sealed to them this fruit, I will come by you into Spain" (Rom 15:28).

Of course, fulfilling obligations to God and neighbor, ecclesial community to ecclesial community, is seldom so easy as it may at first appear. Thus, with regard to oath-taking and truth telling, for example, would oaths be necessary if telling the truth, and following through (giving away, *apodidōmi*), all in fulfillment of vows or oaths, were a sure thing? So, seeking to preserve the integrity of the truth, Jesus warned his followers against oath-taking, especially frivolous oath-taking: "Again, ye have heard that it hath been said by them of old time, Thou shalt not forswear [perjure] thyself, but shalt *perform* unto the Lord thine oaths: But I say unto you, Swear not at all; neither by heaven; for it is God's throne: Nor by the earth; for it is his footstool: neither by Jerusalem; for it is the city of the great King. Neither shalt thou swear by thy head, because thou canst not make one hair white or black. But let your communication be, Yea, yea; Nay, nay: for whatsoever is more than these cometh of evil" (Matt 5:33–37).

With brutal forthrightness, the apostle Paul noted in himself an inability to perform, to work out thoroughly (*katergazomai*), the best intentions of his inward self. In fact, he said, as often as not, he did what he hated (Rom 7:15). He wrote: "I know that in me (that is, in my flesh) dwelleth no good thing: for to will is present with me; but how to *perform* that which is good I find not. . . . O wretched man that I am! Who shall deliver me from the body of this death? I thank God through Jesus Christ our Lord" (Rom 7:18, 24–25a).

In Philippians, Paul expressed his gratitude for the Philippians' support and participation with him in gospel proclamation. He wrote: "I thank my God upon every remembrance of you, Always in every prayer of mine for you all making request with joy, for your fellowship in the gospel from the first day until now; Being confident of this very thing, that he which hath begun a good work in you will *perform* it until the day of Jesus Christ" (Phil 1:3–6).

Gospel performance, it seems clear, finally is not strictly or even primarily a human work. It is a divine work in and among us. It is God, in Christ, in the power of the Spirit bringing the form of divine truth through to clarity of articulation.[21] It is God bearing witness that what is to be accomplished, perfected, performed in personal and ecclesial life—and in the life of the world—"to the praise of the glory of his grace" (Eph 1:6) is God's own accomplishment in and for us. It is divine promise and divine promise fulfilled. Its end is a new heaven, and a new earth, a new human being, and a new kingdom come. It is *actio divina* insinuating itself thoroughly into *homo performans*, taking ourselves and our communities as they are and pressing them into the service of what God would have them be.[22] "For," says the apostle Paul, to persons in community charged to exhibit the kingdom of God,[23] "ye are dead, and your life is hid with Christ in God. When Christ, who is our life, shall appear, then shall ye also appear with him in glory" (Col 3:3–4). Gospel performance thus is carried out always under the sign of the cross. Until the kingdom of this world at last shall have become the kingdom of our Lord and of his Christ (Rev 11:15), ecclesial life in proclamation and exhibition of the kingdom of heaven is cruciform.

Gospel Performance in Practice:
A Sermon on Philippians 2:1–11

We turn, then, from gospel performance in theory to gospel performance in practice. We turn from exposition to proclamation. Specifically we turn to a homily treating gospel performance and the mind of Christ. Our text is Phil 2:1–11, an "arrested performance"[24] (which is what any text to be read and preached from is) concerning the mind of Christ in song. Hear the word of God:

> If there is any encouragement in Christ, any consolation from love, any sharing in the Spirit, any compassion and sympathy, make my joy complete: be of the *same mind*, having the same love, being in full accord and of *one mind*. Do nothing from selfish ambition or conceit, but in humility regard others as better than yourselves. Let each of you look not to your own interests, but to the interest of others. Let the *same mind* be in you that was in Christ Jesus,
>
> who, though he was in the form of God,
> did not regard equality with God

21. Ward, *Speaking from the Heart*, 77.
22. Bartow, *God's Human Speech*, 49.
23. *Book of Order*, Presbyterian Church (USA), G.1.0200.
24. Long and Hopkins, *Performing Literature*, 2.

as something to be exploited,

but emptied himself,

taking the form of a slave,

being born in human likeness.

And being found in human form,

he humbled himself

and became obedient to the point of death—

even death on a cross.

Therefore God also highly exalted him

and gave him the name

that is above every name,

so that at the name of Jesus

every knee should bend,

in heaven and on earth and under the earth,

and every tongue should confess

that Jesus Christ is Lord,

to the glory of God the Father (Phil 2:1–11).[25]

The apostle Paul's letters are laced throughout with thanksgivings, dox-ologies, benedictions, and songs—hymnic poems as readily sung as spoken. And his letter to the Philippians is no exception. As Lutheran theologian, Joseph Sitter, pointed out, "When the church emerges out of the shadows of antiquity, we hear her with a song in her mouth."[26] Saint Paul sings of the mind of Christ, a song (virtually all scholars agree) that is the heartbeat of his letter to the church at Philippi. The song, quoted by the apostle, or perhaps even composed by him,[27] is a hymn of *kenosis* or self-emptying. Yet it is a self-emptying from glory unto glory. According to this hymn, the Son of God, from all eternity, had a mind to join us "in this vulnerable flesh/to place his Father's kiss upon our faces."[28] In his flesh, according to the book of Hebrews, Jesus suffered with an inexplicable, solemn joy the enslavements and degradations of our human story (cf. Heb 12:2). But he did this not as some unwitting victim, but as the divine champion of a better destiny for human beings than the best and brightest, the most accomplished and for-tunate among us can dream up for themselves. In fact, even at their finest, all our philosophical systems, all our systematic theologies, all our cunningly

25. This, and the remaining biblical quotations, are from the NRSV.

26. Childs and Lischer, eds. *Eloquence of Grace*, 197.

27. Scott, "Philippians," 11:46–47.

28. Brower, "Advent" in Bartow, *God's Human Speech*, dedication page.

or compassionately devised forms of common life and governance have but a day. As Tennyson's hymn, "Strong Son of God, Immortal Love," sings: "They have their day and cease to be: / They are but broken lights of Thee / And Thou, O Lord, art more than they."[29]

Nevertheless, so sings the apostle Paul, this "Strong Son of God," this "Immortal Love," did not regard his status as divinity "something to be exploited, but emptied himself, taking the form of a slave, being born in human likeness. And being found in human form he humbled himself and became obedient [to his calling, to his vocation, to his chosen destiny] to the point of death—even death on a cross" (Phil 2:7–8). "Therefore," the apostle sings, "Therefore, God also highly exalted him" (Phil 2:9a). This is not the way to exaltation of ancient pagan divinities. It is not the way of classical theism. It is not the way of seventeenth- and eighteenth-century deism advocated by some—though certainly not all—of the founders of our country. Nor is it the way divinity is thought of in popular religion today. Here is no "prosperity gospel." Here is the Holy Trinity of Christian faith, Father, Son, and Holy Spirit, overflowing in love, divesting itself of self-regard, eternally, eternally, eternally pouring out its beauty, holiness, and favor upon peoples, many of whom couldn't care less about the gift. But the mind of Christ, Christ's self-emptying from glory unto glory, is to be the mind of the church at Philippi. So sings Saint Paul. Such a mind was not—and never could be—the mind of the empire of which Philippi remained something of a strategic city.[30]

The caesars of Jesus' day, beginning with Octavian Augustus Caesar (grandnephew and heir of Julius) who ruled the Roman Empire at the time of Jesus' birth, waded through blood to dominance. Through political intrigue, victory in war, and no little achievement in governance, Octavian made a name for himself. We must also acknowledge in his favor his promotion of literature—he was himself something of a writer—and the arts, architecture, and projects to facilitate commerce. Octavian made a name for himself, a two hundred year long legacy of renown and public gratitude. His successors, on the whole less compelling, attempted to do the same. The intimidating symbol of empire all along, however, was the Roman cross upon which, for the sake of political expediency, Jesus was hung. The same fate awaited hundreds upon hundreds of non-compliant Jews—eventually many hundreds in a single day—upon the walls of Jerusalem. So the attempted revolt was put down. Despite their periodic brutalities, Rome's caesars were voted their honors by an obliging senate, with a chorus of adoration from an on the whole appreciative citizenry. The title Augustus means consecrated,

29. Tennyson, "In Memoriam," 163.

30. Lightfoot, *Saint Paul's Epistle*, 47–55.

holy, majestic, dignified. By such a standard our most celebrated contemporary politicians, statespersons, and ecclesial dignitaries are pikers.

Human vaunt can have no higher goal than to look into a mirror and see not merely a woman or a man, but a person consecrated, holy, majestic, dignified, a veritable goddess or god, or, as a current academic euphemism identifies it, an "autonomous moral agent" subject to no authority except the self.

At the end of the nineteenth century, the cusp of the twentieth, the unmitigated disaster of the Civil War (and what brought it about) seemingly ended, the promise of science, technology, and industry alerted humankind to its happier prospects, and an American poet of lasting distinction and influence, Walt Whitman, sang a transcendental anthem still resonant in the lives of many today. Here is a sound bite! "I say to mankind, Be not curious about God. . . . In the faces of men and women I see God, and in my own face in the glass. . . ."[31] This is not human self-divinization in the way the caesars aspired to it. It is more generous, democratic, even egalitarian. Nevertheless, grab a mirror, face up to the looking glass. What do you see?

Of course all this celebration of human spiritual, intellectual, and material advancement was before our two world wars, before the ensuing—ongoing—"wars and rumors of wars" (Matt 24:6a), before the ginning up of medieval religious hatreds in our twenty-first century, before the ethnic cleansing still happening, now here, now there. Think of the threats by ISIS aimed at Christians in Iraq whose presence there predates by hundreds of years the coming into existence of the Muslim faith—not itself to be equated with or blamed for its self-proclaimed, largely inappropriately titled,[32] jihadist perversions: "Convert! Pay a tax! Get out! Or die!" In our own land—God forgive it!—back in the 1960s and 1970s there was a chant, not quite as appalling, but nevertheless nasty, "America! Love it or leave it!" A minister friend of mine once got at the root of it in a sermon: "What will we do when we've nobody left to hate?"[33]

Despite the caveats just mentioned, there is something to all this celebration of human giftedness and potential. There is the *imago dei*, the image of God, in human nature as Genesis refers to it, sings of it (Gen 1:26–29). Surely it is poetry trembling on the brink of song. That image has been mocked by our false pride, and by our barbarisms and inanities. But it has not been erased, even by the self-promotion and clamoring for privileged

31. Whitman, *Leaves of Grass*, 16.

32. Denny, *Introduction to Islam*, 136.

33. Comment in an unpublished sermon by the Rev. Blair Moffett in Wellsboro, PA, early 1970s.

status in relation to God evident in Christian communities from the very start. Remember James and John, prominent among the twelve, who in the beginning were entrusted with the gospel, the good news of God's kingdom (God's just rule) that Christ Jesus taught, and lived, inaugurated? Remember how they inquired after positions of privilege in the kingdom of God? Jesus, with them following, was on his way to Jerusalem and to the cross. Think of the irony! Grant us to sit, one at your right hand and one at your left, in your glory" (Mark 10:37). Remarkable audacity! Jesus let them know that they didn't have the slightest idea of what they were asking. He said, "Are you able to drink the cup that I drink, or be baptized with the baptism that I am baptized with" (Mark 10:38)? James and John replied, "We are able" (Mark 10:39). They did not yet understand that Jesus' baptism was his upcoming passion, and that the cup was the cup of his humiliation and suffering. Eventually James and John, with the rest of the twelve, would drink from that cup at Jesus' institution of the Lord's Supper, Holy Communion, the Eucharist. "Drink of it all of you," Jesus said to James, John, Peter, and the rest (Matt 26:27). And, according to apostolic testimony, Jesus says it in our own time and place and in our ecclesial communities (cf. 1 Cor 11:25).

In Philippi there apparently was some bickering and pursuit of self-interest among persons who had labored with Paul in the work, the performance of the gospel. In particular, Paul urged the Philippians to help two congregants, Euodia and Syntyche, to set aside their differences and agree in the Lord. He urged them, as he urged all the congregants in the Church at Philippi, to be of *the same mind*, that is, the *mind of Christ*, who humbled himself at a cost to himself we cannot calculate. In other words, if I might risk expressing it in the language of our moment, Saint Paul was asking: Could there not be a little fence mending in the church, some making up of hurt feelings? Could there not be some putting each other ahead in line as my former pastor, Earl Palmer, urged in his commentary on our text.[34] And what shall we say of ourselves here, now, in our respective congregations and in the academies of the church, the church's seminaries and divinity schools?

John Calvin thought such humility the very essence of our life in Christ.[35] Christ's humiliation, though, was more prototype than model,[36] was not the basis for mere moral earnestness in imitation of Christ, was not congregations "thrown back upon [their] own powers of imitation,

---

34. Palmer, "Second Lesson," 354.

35. Calvin, *Institutes*, II.2.11.

36. Lischer, *Theology of Preaching*, 63.

but fueled by a gospel which creates of its own truth faithful sons and daughters."[37] This particular humility, this *possessing the mind of Christ*, has nothing to do with self-abnegation, with thinking of ourselves or others less highly than we ought. Instead, it has to do with our dignity as citizens of the commonwealth of heaven, that alternative *polis* (with its own unique call to comportment) spoken of in Phil 1:27. This humility is evidence, as the apostle Paul put it, of "God at work in [us] both to will and to work for his good pleasure" (Phil 2:13). And God's good pleasure, let it be said, is human flourishing, not human diminishment. However, there can be no flourishing for any of us apart from the flourishing of our brothers and sisters in Christ. Christ humbled himself, Paul's Philippians hymn attests. Yet therefore, *therefore*, "God highly exalted him and gave him the name that is above every name, so that at the name of Jesus every knee shall bend . . . and every tongue . . . confess that Jesus Christ is Lord to the glory of God the Father" (Phil 2:7–11).

    In the liturgy of the Orthodox Church—so I am reminded by Marija DiViaio, my much esteemed and beloved secretary, a devout lay woman of the Russian Orthodox Church—there are profound moments of embodied gospel performance when the choir (on behalf of the congregation) sings in descending scale and decrescendo, then in ascending scale and crescendo: "Господи помилуй!" (*Gospodi pomiluy*)! At the time of the final blessing, while the choir sings, the priest lowers the cross and then raises the cross, a liturgical enactment of Christ's humiliation and exaltation as attested in Phil 2:6–11. *Gospodi pomiluy* means, "Lord have mercy." By the mercy of the Lord, the church today and hereafter may embody the gospel of our Lord Jesus Christ who evermore lives and reigns, "for the glory and praise of God" (Phil 1:11b).

Bibliography

Alexander, Bryant Keith, et al. "Identifying Key Intercultural Urgencies, Issues and Challenges in Today's World: Connecting our Scholarship to Dynamic Contexts and Historical Moments?" *Journal of International and Intercultural Communication* 7 (2014) 38–67.

Bacon, Wallace A. *The Art of Interpretation*. New York: Holt, Rinehart and Winston, 1972.

Bartow, Charles L. *God's Human Speech: A Practical Theology of Proclamation*. Grand Rapids: Eerdmans, 1997.

Book of Order, 1999–2000: The Constitution of the Presbyterian Church (U.S.A.) Part II. G.1.0200. Louisville, KY: The Office of the General Assembly, 1999.

---

37. Ibid.

Brower, William. "Adven." In *God's Human Speech*, by Charles L. Bartow, dedication page. Grand Rapids: Eerdmans, 1997.

Calvin, John. *Institutes of the Christian Religion*. Edited by John T. McNeill Jr. Translated by Ford Lewis Battles. Philadelphia: Westminster, 1960.

Childs, James M. and Richard Lischer, eds. *The Eloquence of Grace: Joseph Sitter and the Preaching Life*. Eugene, OR: Cascade, 2012.

Davis, Ellen F. *Swallowing the Scroll: Textuality and the Dynamics of Discourse in Ezekiel's Prophecy*. Sheffield: Almond, 1989.

Davis, John D., and Henry Snyder Gehman. *The Westminster Dictionary of the Bible*. Philadelphia: Westminster, 1944.

Denny, Frederick Mathewson. *An Introduction to Islam*. New York: Macmillan, 1994.

Donne, John. "Nativitie." In *Garlands for Christmas*, edited by Chad Walsh, 41. New York: Macmillan, 1965.

Farmer, H. H. *The Servant of the Word*. Philadelphia: Westminster, 1944.

Finnerman, Richard J., ed. *The Collected Poems of W. B. Yeats*. New York: Simon & Shuster, 1989.

Gilbert, Christopher J. "Standing Up to Combat Trauma." *Text and Performance Quarterly* 34 (2014) 144–63.

Jones, David Hugh, ed. *The Hymnbook*. Philadelphia: John Ribble, 1955.

Langellier, Kristin M. "Storytelling, Turning Points and Wicked Problems in Performance Studies." *Text and Performance Quarterly* 33 (2013) 214–19.

Lapsley, Jacqueline E. *Can These Bones Live? The Problem of the Moral Self in the Book of Ezekiel*. Berlin: Walter de Gruyter, 2000.

Lightfoot, J. B. *Saint Paul's Epistle to the Philippians*. Grand Rapids: Zondervan, 1953.

Lischer, Richard. *A Theology of Preaching: The Dynamics of the Gospel*. Nashville: Abingdon, 1981.

Long, Beverly Whitaker, and Mary Frances Hopkins. *Performing Literature: An Introduction to Oral Interpretation*. Englewood Cliffs: Prentice-Hall, 1982.

McKenzie, Alyce M. "At the Intersection of *Actio Divina* and *Homo Performan*." In *Performance in Preaching: Bringing the Sermon to Life*, edited by Jana Childers and Clayton J. Schmit, 53–66. Grand Rapids: Baker Academic, 2008.

Metzger, Bruce M. and Roland E. Murphy, eds. *The New Oxford Annotated Bible with the Apocryphal/Deuterocanonical Books*. New York: Oxford University Press, 1994.

Palmer, Earl F. "Second Lesson: Philippians 2:1–13." In *The Lectionary Commentary: Theological Exegesis for Sunday's Texts: The Second Readings: Acts and the Epistles*, edited by Roger E. Van Harn, 350–54. Grand Rapids: Eerdmans, 2001.

Scott, Ernest F. "The Epistle to the Philippians: Introduction and Exegesis." In *The Interpreters Bible*, edited by George Arthur Buttrick, 11:14–129. Nashville: Abingdon, 1955.

Taylor, Gardner. "The Sweet Torture of Sunday Morning." *Leadership* 3 (1991) 20.

Tennyson, Alfred Lord. *The Poetic and Dramatic Works of Alfred Lord Tennyson*. Boston: Houghton Mifflin, 1898.

Thonssen, Lester, and A. Craig Baird. *Speech Criticism*. New York: Ronald, 1948.

Ward, Richard F. *Speaking from the Heart: Preaching with Passion*. Nashville: Abingdon, 1992.

Whitman, Walt. *Leaves of Grass: Selected Poetry and Prose*. Edited by C. Merton Babcock. Kansas City: Hallmark Cards, 1969.

A Final Word on Richard Lischer as Preacher of the Gospel

Richard B. Hays

It is my task, and my great honor, to write a final word—a kind of benediction—for this rich collection of essays offered to a consummate preacher of the gospel, our friend and colleague Richard Lischer. The authors of these essays have come at the theme of "gospel" in many different ways; each one attempts to shine light on some facet of the luminous stone of Lischer's lifelong work of preaching and teaching the craft of preaching.

What makes Lischer a consummate preacher of the gospel? What is it about his proclamation that makes it ring true and touch the heart?

First, Richard Lischer is a lover of words. We serve a God who has chosen to speak through the Word made flesh, and through the words of prophecy and testimony recorded in the scriptures. Therefore, the medium of language matters deeply. The art of speech is at the heart of conveying the good news. Lischer has mastered the art of listening carefully to the words of scripture and re-proclaiming their message in new words that are beautifully crafted—honed to become a two-edged sword that pierces our hearts. Reflections on the social and political impact of Martin Luther King's leadership are many, but it was Lischer who wrote the definitive study of King's *words*, focusing on the rhetoric and poetry of *The Preacher King*. Words matter. For many years Lischer has taught a course on the parables of Jesus, beckoning his students to ponder the words of these concise masterpieces of literary and theological art. And now he has distilled his reflections on the parables into a wonderfully illuminating book, *Reading the Parables*. From the Apostle Paul, Lischer has learned that we cannot believe in one of whom we have never heard, and that we cannot hear without someone to proclaim him. And he also knows what Paul practices but does not explain: that we cannot proclaim him with power unless our words are exact and gracefully

241

shaped. Books and sermons by Richard Lischer are beautifully written because he knows that it is an act of discipleship to choose our words well.

Second, Richard Lischer is a consummate preacher of the gospel because his Lutheran tradition has taught him, deep in his bones, that the gospel of Jesus Christ is the gospel of the cross. Lischer's preaching embodies the paradox that the cross is the wisdom and the power of God. Neither in the first century nor in the twenty-first is the cross a welcome message. Much preaching today goes to some lengths to avoid the uncomfortable word of the cross, but Lischer's preaching has returned to it again and again. In April of 2015, in the final week of classes, Lischer was the preacher for the service at which graduating seniors in Duke Divinity School were presented with a stained-glass cross. He opened the sermon by recalling a recent celebration in Cameron Indoor Stadium in honor of Duke's national championship basketball team. He noted that students had cheered the players and managers, and that the senior members of the cheerleading squad were each given a bouquet of roses. And then he said this:

> And today, graduates, it is your day, and in recognition of your
> achievements, we will give you each a cross—the universal sym-
> bol of shame, suffering, death, and redemption. Congrats.

The rest of the sermon was a masterful exposition of the meaning of the cross as the place where "the pain of the world and the love of God meet and all our histories become one."

Third, Richard Lischer is a consummate preacher of the gospel because he is a teller of truth. He names our human condition in unsparingly honest terms. In his memoir *Open Secrets* he tells the truth about his early years in parish ministry, telling the story with precise observation and self-deprecating humor. His later memoir *Stations of the Heart* tells the truth about the death of his thirty-three year old son Adam with searing honesty. His characteristic sense of wry humor is still there in the midst of pain, but Lischer's account discloses complex depths of the suffering of a family grappling with a life cut short by cancer. There is no dissembling here, only a truthful grappling with death and loss. Another memorable sermon that Lischer preached in Goodson Chapel at the Divinity School came in his first return to the pulpit about a year after Adam's death. He spoke rivetingly about Mother Teresa's account of her experience of the absence of God. We trust Lischer as a proclaimer of good news because, like Job, he does not sugar-coat the bad news. He is therefore able to name truthfully the ways in which the grace of God can reach down into the depths of our despair. He tells the truth about pain and grace alike.

The mention of grace points to the fourth reason why Richard Lischer is a consummate preacher of the gospel: all of his artful words, all his proclamation of the cross, and all of his truth-telling finally point to the unfathomable love of God made known to us in Jesus Christ our Lord. Lischer never loses sight of that mystery, that love that fires the stars, and on which the world is founded. Lischer's writing and preaching embodies an indelible *gravitas* because it is never diverted by trivialities or by shallow moralism; his preaching focuses finally on the grace and love of God. That, too, is something he learned from his Lutheran heritage, but in Lischer, the message of God's love is refracted through his particular artistic gifts and theological sophistication in such a way that we can see it with new eyes.

For the past twenty-five years, I have been privileged to count Lischer as a colleague and friend. Whether we were trading deep theological thoughts, sharing the struggles of our families, pondering the political intrigues of the university, or discussing the fate of Lischer's beloved St. Louis Cardinals, I have found our *koinōnia* in the gospel to be deep and satisfying. The collection of these essays represents an attempt by many of his friends to honor him. However, I know that Richard Lischer, the consummate preacher of the gospel, will in the end be most gratified if these essays serve not so much to honor him as to point readers to the love of God declared in the gospel of Jesus Christ.